Studies in German Literature, Linguistics, and Culture

Virtual Walls?

Political Unification and Cultural Difference in Contemporary Germany

Edited by
Franziska Lys and Michael Dreyer

CAMDEN HOUSE
Rochester, New York

First published 2017
by Camden House

Camden House is an imprint of Boydell & Brewer Inc.
668 Mt. Hope Avenue, Rochester, NY 14620, USA
www.camden-house.com
and of Boydell & Brewer Limited
PO Box 9, Woodbridge, Suffolk IP12 3DF, UK
www.boydellandbrewer.com

ISBN-13: 978-1-57113-980-1
ISBN-10: 1-57113-980-X

Library of Congress Cataloging-in-Publication Data

Names: Lys, Franziska, 1955– editor. | Dreyer, Michael, 1959– editor.
Title: Virtual walls? : political unification and cultural difference in contemporary
  Germany / edited by Franziska Lys and Michael Dreyer.
Description: Rochester, New York : Camden House, 2017. | Series: Studies in German
  literature, linguistics, and culture | Includes bibliographical references and index.
Identifiers: LCCN 2017037966| ISBN 9781571139801 (hardcover : alk. paper) |
  ISBN 157113980X (hardcover : alk. paper)
Subjects: LCSH: Germany—History—Unification, 1990. | Germany—History—
  Unification, 1990—Social aspects. | Germany—Civilization—21st century.
Classification: LCC DD290.25 .V57 2017 | DDC 943.088—dc23 LC record
  available at https://lccn.loc.gov/2017037966

This publication is printed on acid-free paper.
Printed in Great Britain by
TJ International Ltd, Padstow, Cornwall

"Strebe nach Einheit, aber suche sie nicht in der Einförmigkeit."
[Strive for unity, but do not look for it in uniformity.]

—Friedrich Schiller

Contents

Part I. What Remains:
History and the Constitution

Part II. What and How Do We Remember?
Literature, Film, and Exhibitions

Part III. A Changing Reception:
Painting, Orchestras, and Theaters

Part IV. A Virtual Wall?
Education and Society

Acknowledgments

THE IDEA OF THIS VOLUME was conceived at an international conference at Northwestern University in Evanston, Illinois, entitled "The Fall of the Wall Reconsidered: Progress and Perspectives." It was jointly organized by Northwestern University and Friedrich Schiller University in Jena, Germany. The conference was financed completely by the gracious cooperation of several departments at Northwestern University, namely, the Alice Kaplan Institute for the Humanities and the Departments of French, German, History, Philosophy, and Political Science. The Goethe Institute Chicago organized the exhibit ORTSZEIT*LOCALTIME* by Stefan Koppelkamm, which was a valuable addition to the conference. We would like to thank the Consulate General of Germany Chicago for its support and our friends and colleagues at Northwestern—from the History Department, Peter Hayes; and from the German Department, Peter Fenves, Jörg Kreienbrock, Denise Meuser, John Paluch, Rainer Rumold, Kristine Thorsen, Katrin Völkner, and Ingrid Zeller. We would also like to thank Kristine Ogilvie, our departmental assistant, for her organizational skills.

The various contributions in this volume, most of them presented at the conference, are interdisciplinary in nature and approach the topic of German unification from different thematic perspectives focusing on history, politics, society, and education, on the one hand, and art, literature, film, and music, on the other. The contributions have been extensively revised, and we would like to express our deep gratitude to our contributors, who have unfailingly and with good humor responded to our many suggestions and requests for editorial changes. We also thank Jim Wagner (New York University) and Jonathan Gibbs (Geneva, Switzerland), both graduates from the German Department at Northwestern, who were instrumental in editing the contributions by nonnative speakers. The volume has also benefited from two anonymous readers who have provided us with detailed and constructive reports. We are especially grateful to Camden House and its editorial director, Jim Walker, for including this collection of essays in its program: we could not have done it without his invaluable comments and his supportive and encouraging words—thank you. Thomas Lys, Franziska's husband, also deserves a special mention for his patience and understanding, which were much appreciated. And finally, it was enlightening and personally enriching to collaborate with such a dedicated group of people from many disciplines who all worked together with patience and enthusiasm. The editors hope that the readers will feel this enthusiasm as well.

Introduction: United Politics— Divided Culture?

Franziska Lys and Michael Dreyer

From a Divided to a Unified Germany

On October 30, 1990, precisely at midnight, the flag of a reunited Germany was raised over the Reichstag in Berlin, accompanied by celebratory fireworks across the city. This act signaled the end of one state, the German Democratic Republic (GDR), and the continuation of another, the Federal Republic of Germany (FRG), albeit slightly enlarged: the five new federal states comprising the former GDR were united with the Federal Republic and adopted its legal, political, and economic structures. Hence, the GDR had officially ceased to exist.

There is no doubt that the events leading up to the collapse of the GDR and the subsequent process of unification were challenging: East and West Germany were socialized in quite different ways, and especially for the people in the East, life as they knew it changed completely: economically, politically, ideologically, socially, and culturally. Wolfgang Thierse, an East German citizen before unification and later the president of the German Bundestag, described it in the following way during a speech on the occasion of the twenty-fifth anniversary of the fall of the Wall: "When a strong, successful community and a failed, collapsed, rejected system come together, then the weights are clearly distributed: One is the norm which the others have to take over; one is the teacher, the other the apprentice; in the case of the one, everything can stay as is; in the case of the other, everything has to change; German unity is for some the confirmation of the status quo, for the others it causes a radical upheaval."[1] It is clear that the process of growing together was experienced differently by East and West Germans: While many East Germans initially felt heightened optimism for freedom and a less complicated life than the GDR offered, the process of unification was overshadowed by uncertainty, doubt, vulnerability, mourning, and a sense of loss that brought about a yearning (especially among the older GDR generation) for the small, familiar country in which they had grown up and a sense of nostalgia for the former GDR that became known as *Ostalgie*. But it was also difficult for West Germans: many felt that they were carrying a disproportionate share of the cost for integrating the two former states.

Nowadays, on the surface, there is little to distinguish life in the East and West in many ways, yet there are subtle reminders of life during the GDR: the East German pedestrian crossing lights with the little green and red *Ampelmännchen*, for example, more than anything else symbolize a yearning for the GDR. Designed by Karl Peglau as part of a proposal for new pedestrian crossing lights in the GDR, they became a contested symbol when a newly unified Germany took steps to eradicate reminders of the GDR. A group called "Rescue the Ampelmännchen!" asked the government to preserve this GDR symbol. Since then, they have been installed on traffic lights in former West Berlin, as well as in various other west German cities. "The Ampelmännchen . . . are an example of Berliners' ability to recognize the good parts of their past—amid all of the atrocities—and to preserve them" (Khazan 2013).

Of course, for some it is hard to comprehend how one can feel nostalgic for a regime that for forty years spied on its citizens and kept secret files on them. These files, known as the *Stasi Akten* (secret-police files) and left behind by the past bureaucratic state, are a stark reminder of the shocking operations of the GDR's secret police, the Stasi, and the abuses of power and authority perpetrated by the East German regime. None of these files were ever meant to be seen by the public. In November 1989, when the Berlin Wall opened, Stasi agents were given the order to destroy them. Their plans were thwarted, however, by ordinary East German citizens who were intent on saving these documents for posterity. Today, every citizen has the right to request access to these files at the Stasi Records Agency (Bundesbeauftragte für die Stasi-Unterlagen, BStU) so that they can confront the past. For many, such a confrontation is vital for their future in order to come to grips with a repressive regime, or with, as Joachim Gauck (1991) called it, "The eerie legacy of the GDR" (Das unheimliche Erbe der DDR).

The most famous symbol today of oppression and lack of individual freedom and self-determination, however, is the Berlin Wall. For almost thirty years it stood as a bulwark between East Germany and West Berlin, designed not only to keep East German citizens from fleeing the Communist regime but also as an antifascist barrier (*antifaschistischer Schutzwall*) to protect them from the ruination of the West. The construction of the Wall, first only a barbed-wire fence enhanced with concrete blocks intended to separate and seal off the two parts of the city from one another, began in the early morning of Sunday, August 13, 1961, which came to be known as the *Stacheldrahtsonntag* (barbedwire Sunday). In the following days, panic ensued: iconic photographs, from that of an East German woman jumping from the upper story of a building that formed a part of the newly erected wall along Bernauer

Street to that of the East German soldier who leaped over the barbed wire to freedom, are indelibly burned into our minds. In its final form, the Berlin Wall stretched over a hundred miles, snaking through the center of Berlin and around the western part of the city, encapsulating it to keep East Germans from leaving for West Berlin. Today, only a few sections of the actual physical Wall remain as a reminder of the German division. The central memorial site is the Gedenkstätte Berliner Mauer (Berlin Wall Memorial) along an old section of the Wall on Bernauer Street. The memorial landscape presents to its visitors relics of the concrete section of the Wall, the border strip, and a watchtower. Where the original concrete wall is missing, there is a virtual wall—reddish-brown steel bars, signifying a visible trace not only of the physical division that once existed but also of the struggle to unify.[2] The image on the cover of this volume shows a concrete section of the Wall still standing and the reddish-brown steel bars.

For many, Ampelmännchen, Ostalgie, Stasi-Akten, and the memorialized remnants of the Wall are obvious and strong reminders of the GDR. What else, however, remains after more than twenty-five years of trying to shape a collective sense of German identity? What was the GDR and how do we remember it? Are there any suitable monuments to commemorate a regime that brought neither unity nor justice nor freedom to its citizens? In what way does the residue of the two separate nations speak to the process of unification and the struggle to make sense of the GDR legacy? And why does a virtual wall, a barrier in terms of the outlook and socialization of the citizens of the former East and those of the former West, still seem to exist in Germany today despite its peaceful unification?

Economic, Political, and Cultural Changes

There are no serious museums or memorials to the former East Germany, and there are certainly no counties (*Landkreise*) named after Erich Honecker or Walter Ulbricht, the two dictators of East Germany. While Ostalgie has been a constant cultural reminder of the historical division, the political unification of 1989/90 has never been challenged in any serious way. There is widespread discontent in the former East, but there is no narrative of a "lost cause," as there was in the American South after the Civil War.

Arguably, some differences between the former East and former West in terms of culture and economics are to be expected. The political system is but one subsystem of society, as Niklas Luhmann (1984, 2000) has pointed out in numerous publications, and societies also have economic, social, and cultural subsystems. While political, economic, and social changes are perhaps easier to grasp, culture tends to be most resistant to change: real and imagined cultural differences between East and West are expressed with conviction even long after unity has been achieved in other areas.

The political aspects of German unification have been much more visible than their cultural counterparts. On November 22, 2005, Angela Merkel assumed the office of Germany's federal chancellor. She made history not only because she was the first female chancellor and the youngest but also because she was Germany's first leader from former East Germany. Merkel was born in Hamburg on July 17, 1954. Her father was a Protestant minister who moved to East Germany when Merkel was three months old to look after a small church in Brandenburg. Merkel has a biography that is rather typical for those who found their niche in East German society: she neither actively defied the regime nor enthusiastically embraced it. She served as a minor functionary in the socialist Free German Youth, studied physics in Leipzig, and became a research physicist with a PhD and standing in her field. After the fall of the Wall, she entered politics and headed toward a stellar career in the conservative Christian Democratic Party (Christlich-Demokratische Union, CDU). Today, Angela Merkel is not only the leader of Europe's strongest economy; she is often referred to as "the world's most powerful woman" ("Angela Merkel" 2011) and was *Time Magazine*'s "Person of the Year" in 2015—the magazine dubbed her "Chancellor of the Free World." Angela Merkel is, however, not the only former East German who has assumed high office in the new Federal Republic.

On March 18, 2012, Joachim Gauck was elected president of Germany. Although the position of president is largely ceremonial, it is formally the highest position in the German political system—the head of state. After a stint as an unsuccessful left-of-center candidate for president in 2010, Gauck finally became the consensus candidate for a broad coalition after his predecessor had to leave office after less than two years under a cloud of suspicion regarding his financial dealings. Gauck, a Lutheran pastor by profession, was born on January 24, 1940, in Rostock. As a pastor in an officially atheist state, he was by definition a dissident, even though he did not play a major role in opposition groups until 1989/90, when he was swept into electoral politics. After unification (also called the "Change" or *Wende*), he became the federal commissioner for the Stasi archives, a new office that was, colloquially, simply called the "Gauck Agency." As federal commissioner, Gauck was in close quarters with the professional politicians without being formally part of partisan politics. Gauck's particular contribution was already recognized right after he took office. The *Wall Street Journal* ("Gauck File" 2012) described him as "the last of a breed: the leaders of protest movements behind the Iron Curtain who went on to lead their countries after 1989."[3]

These biographies indicate that the journey Germany embarked on roughly twenty-five years ago has been a remarkable one. Moreover, it is even more extraordinary because virtually no one seems to dwell on the idea that it is extraordinary in any way. Twenty-five years. For some, a long time; for others, but a brief interlude: what we see and how we interpret it depends on where we are standing. The British politician Harold Wilson (prime minister of the United Kingdom from 1964 to 1970 and 1974 to 1976) once said that "a week is a long time in politics," meaning that political affairs can change extremely rapidly. The changes in Germany since the emotional days of the Wende have indeed been substantial; not just in the realm of politics but also in a variety of cultural manifestations. Although it is difficult to argue that political equality has not been achieved when the two most visible political positions are held by former East Germans, plenty of Germans do still attempt to make precisely that argument. As a matter of fact, in a study published in 2009 in *Welt online*, Germans in the east and the west perceived their mentalities and worldviews as diverging instead of growing closer together (Solms-Laubach 2009).

The question of the extent and progress of integration of the two Germanys and the accompanying issues have been discussed in numerous studies, mostly but not exclusively published in Germany. The HOLLIS catalog of Harvard's Widener Library lists almost 1,200 studies on German unification and its aftermath since 1990. There are general surveys that closely monitor the social aspects of the post-Wende developments, both for Germany as a whole (Bohr and Krause 2011; Gerstenberger and Braziel 2011; Besier 2012; Sabrow 2016; Thieme 2016; Apelt, Jesse, and Reimers 2016) and for the provinces (Cliver and Smith-Prei 2014). There are studies on the party system and how it changed after 1990 (Patton 2011; Decker 2015; Niedermayer 2015). There are works examining how the social sciences have looked at unification (Lorenz 2011; Matthäus and Kubiak 2016), or even how political cartoonists have weighed in (Martens 2016). "Ostalgia" and the "cultures of memory" debates have been analyzed as well (Saunders and Pinfold 2013; Apelt, Grünbaum, and Schöne 2016). As to the economic disparity between the two parts of Germany, it has decreased, but only slowly, as confirmed by a considerable amount of socioeconomic data. Already in May 2012, Germany as a whole saw its unemployment rate fall below 6 percent: the best figures in many years, and an excellent rate compared to other OECD countries (Bundesagentur für Arbeit 2012a, 19). But unemployment in eastern Germany (10.6 percent) was still much higher than in the west (5.7 percent) when looking at the aggregate data for the two regions (Bundesagentur für Arbeit 2012b). By November 2015, these rates had decreased to 8.5 percent (east) and 5.4 percent (west)— even lower than before, with the east-west gap closing, yet still significant (Bundesanstalt für Arbeit 2015a). The picture gets more complex when examined more closely. There are successful regions in eastern Germany (e.g., the technology centers of Jena and Potsdam) that easily outperform the cities of the old rust belt in the Ruhr region, Germany's former industrial heartland (*Wirtschaftswoche* 2012). Jena had an unemployment rate of 6.4 percent in November 2015 (vs. 6.9 percent in 2012), while former West German steel industry powerhouses like Duisburg (12.9 percent in both 2012 and 2015), Dortmund (11.9 percent, vs. 13.1 percent in 2012), or Gelsenkirchen (15.0 percent, vs. 14.4 percent in 2012) were (and are) much worse off (Bundesagentur für Arbeit 2012b; Bundesanstalt für Arbeit 2015b, 2015c). Still, there is a persistent, even widening income gap between east and west; while the average east German household had only 75 percent of the income typical for west German households in 2008 ("Einkommensunterschiede" 2010), that number had slightly declined to 74 percent by 2013 (Statistisches Bundesamt 2015).

Cultural and civic integration (not to be confused with the realm of high culture) of east and west is just as important as political and economic integration; in some sense, this cultural integration may be even more important, since cultural traits form identities beyond the mere realm of culture (Fuchs, James-Chakraborty, and Shortt 2011). The proper space and place for *Heimat* and identity have been topics throughout German cultural history, from the question of regional identity (e.g., Leeder 2015) to the intricacies of regional German cuisine—there is nothing too trivial to become problematic during the process of unification or lack thereof. Even the topic of growing different kinds of apples in the eastern and western parts of Germany, for most a rather trivial thing, can morph into an east-west debate about differences and can "turn out to be deeply connected to shared understandings of the past and future and to collective memory and identity" (Jordan 2011, 48), thereby becoming part of the discourse about German unity and identity.[4]

At first glance, integration has met with success in culture as well. One example would be the Deutscher Buchpreis (German Book Prize), a highly regarded literary prize comparable to the Man Booker Prize. It has been awarded annually to the best German novel since its initiation in 2005. It was won by authors with a western background in 2005 and 2006. In seven of the ten years from 2007 to 2016, however, the winning author has had an eastern biography.[5] Some of the winning books, especially Uwe Tellkamp's *Der Turm* (2008), Eugen Ruge's *In Zeiten des abnehmenden Lichts* (2011), and Lutz Seiler's *Kruso* (2014), did not just enjoy critical acclaim but became runaway bestsellers and were translated into English.[6] The first two books offer sensitive autobiographical narratives about growing up in privileged and politically well-connected East German families—and they sold and still sell in huge numbers, not just in the former East but in the former West as well. *Kruso* looks at the opposite milieu, namely the fate of outsiders during the collapse of East Germany, and it was just as successful as its predecessors.

There have been similar developments in contemporary German art: Neo Rauch and the other protagonists of the *Neue Leipziger Schule* (New Leipzig School) are among Germany's most prominent contemporary artists (Lubow 2006). Among the great orchestras and opera houses in Germany, the Leipzig Gewandhaus, the Dresden Semperoper and State Orchestra, and the State Opera in the former East Berlin easily hold their own in Germany's musical landscape. There are, measured by population, more opera houses, orchestras, and theaters in the former East than in the former West, and the former Eastern state of Thuringia has become one of the foremost destinations for tourists who want to immerse themselves in German culture. Does this mean that unification has run its course and led to equal standing for east and west at least in the cultural arena, even though deficits may remain in other areas? Upon further examination, as this volume shows, such hasty conclusions prove less than solid.

The Essays

Taking culture as broadly defined, this volume examines unification and the results of unification along two theoretical perspectives: on the one hand, German unification can be seen as a process of fusion, as expressed in the passage from Wolfgang Thierse quoted above, according to which a strong established community absorbs a failed, discredited, and collapsed system, "a confirmation of the status quo" for the one and "a radical upheaval" for the other (11). A similar idea is expressed by Paul Cooke (2005, 11), who discusses cultural unification in terms of colonialization, claiming that the view that East Germany was colonized by the Federal Republic has shaped both east and west German culture. On the other hand, unification can also be seen as the process of molding historical narratives and memories. In their volume *Remembering and Rethinking the GDR: Multiple Perspectives and Plural Authenticities*, Anna Saunders and Debbie Pinfold contend that memories of the GDR are ever changing "partly in response to shifting political, social, and cultural agendas, but also as a result of the passing of time, the coming of new generations and the exploration of new media" (2013, 4). It is the changing nature of memories that define the complex process of unification and its public discourse in which post-Wende identities and attitudes are negotiated.[7]

The various contributions in this volume approach the topic of unification from different theoretical perspectives representing the multiple narratives that have accompanied unification. The contributions are grouped together into four parts: the topics of history and politics serve as vehicles to discuss the question "What remains of the GDR?"; the topics of literature, film, and exhibitions present examples that touch on the question "What was the GDR and how do we remember it?"; the topics of music and art illustrate how the reception of East Germany changed over the course of unification; and the topics of education and society are used to suggest that there still might be a Virtual Wall.

What Remains: Historical and Political Considerations

A first sequence of essays traces political and legal aspects of the Wende under the aspect of what remains: what remains of a state that simply vanished is considered first; the adoption of a (slightly) amended formerly West German Basic Law as the constitution for both Germanys (the proposal for a revised GDR constitution was dropped) is discussed thereafter.

The historian Charles Maier (Harvard University) provokes the reader with the rhetorical question whether or not the GDR was ever real, followed by an equally rhetorical question whether or not it is still real, in an effort to address the ghostly quality of the former East German regime: "ghostly" because today nothing remains; it only exists in our memories. Maier contends that vanishing states living in our memory are not new in Germany's history, and he compares the GDR, the most recent German state to vanish, to Germany's other ghostly regimes such as Prussia and Weimar. He describes the former GDR as a state of contradictions or paradoxes: a regime that believed itself to be autonomous even though it was created by the Soviet Union and could not survive without the latter; a regime in which at least some of its citizens felt indisputable loyalty to the state even though the government spied on and imprisoned those who criticized it. But paradoxes or contradictions were ultimately most visible in the economic arena, Maier continues: as the GDR was no longer considered to be the source of economic strength by its citizens, it could not satisfy the growing consumer longings for the products of the Western world, and "highly individualized yearnings" were more important than "collective needs." Maier concludes that memory needs to be transformed into history if we want to arrive at a more nuanced assessment of the GDR.

In his essay on constitutional law and politics since 1989, Andreas Niederberger (University of Duisburg-Essen) examines the development of the German Basic Law (Grundgesetz, or constitution) and of constitutional politics in general over the last twenty-five years. He reconstructs the debate during the unification process on alternatives and options for the development of the Basic Law. He first concludes that the fact that the unification of the FRG and the GDR did not produce a new constitution does not mean that they simply perpetuated the pre-1989 West German constitutional order. He believes that the consequence of the discussions and the process itself was that the Basic Law became "newly" constituted. Second, Niederberger contends that what he characterizes as the transition from constitution to constitutionalism increased the visibility of the Basic Law and its importance for politics, bringing the importance of "constitutional politics," as distinct from normal or everyday politics, to the foreground.

What and How We Remember: Film, Literature, and Exhibitions

The next set of essays explores the demise of the GDR under the focus of what and how we remember, stressing the centrality of these memories and the debates surrounding them to the success of German unification. Film, literature, and exhibitions, through their creation of memories, imagery, and thought, are particularly important vehicles to reflect on the process of memory culture and how it shapes our present view of the former GDR.

Stephen Brockmann (Carnegie Mellon University) explores the question of how to remember the GDR through a discussion of East German literature. Specifically, he ponders the question whether we can still use the terms "East German literature" or "East German writers" when discussing works that appeared after the Wende. He claims that the use of those terms was problematic even before the Wende but that it has become even more complicated since the GDR ceased to exist. He raises the issue of how we are to classify authors, for example, who did not publish before 1989 but "who were socialized and came of age in the GDR, and whose topic, to a large extent, is the GDR." In the end, he maintains that these writers are indeed East German authors, their literature East German literature, and claims that their writings preserve elements of East German culture worth preserving, as they enrich German literature as a whole.

Mary-Elizabeth O'Brien (Skidmore College) believes that the German Democratic Republic lives on in the social imaginary in contemporary German film, which tells "much about the German nation's past and present, shared communal values, and ongoing disputes over what historical legacies are worth preserving, reproaching, and commemorating." She begins her essay with a survey of DEFA films made from 1989 to 1992 and continues with an overview of films produced in the east and the west that present themes associated with unification: comedies about east-west encounters, films offering critical perspectives on the historical legacy of GDR society, and films representing the growing Ostalgie for an era that is over, yet certainly not forgotten. What all of the films make clear, O'Brien concludes, is that the "past is anything but over, mastered, and departed."

The article by Kerstin Barndt (University of Michigan) discusses how post-1989 museum and open-air exhibitions have become crucial spaces to resolve the separate histories and memory cultures of the former Germanys in pursuit of common ground. Barndt focuses on three unusual exhibitions as examples: an open-air exhibition on Berlin's

Alexanderplatz, the German pavilion at Hannover's 2000 world's fair, and postindustrial landscape-art projects in Lusatia. Barndt purposefully focuses on rather unorthodox temporary exhibitions in an attempt to move away from "official architecture and exhibition culture" to exhibitions that involve "historical actors and their feelings" such as the exhibition on the Alexanderplatz or the art projects in Lusatia, which include local mining towns as examples of industrialization. She contends that such exhibitions, witnesses to history, "have marked time and heightened the role of affect in peculiar ways, offering provocative configurations of emotion and temporality quite different from the hegemonic narratives that have begun to emerge in the nation's larger museums and their permanent exhibits." How such exhibitions shape memory and affect and what feelings are carried forward into a possible future are questions Barndt is trying to answer.

A Changing Reception: Painting, Orchestras, and Theaters

This section explores how perception, the way we regard, understand, or interpret our world, has been shaped by Germany's unification. April Eisman (Iowa State University) discusses considerations surrounding the post-Wall reception of East German paintings, using Bernhard Heisig as an example. At the time of the fall of the Wall, Heisig was already well represented in museums in the West, including a major East-West collaborative retrospective in the Martin Gropius Bau in West Berlin. Once perceived as intellectually engaged, political artists both in East and West Germany, Heisig and other artists suddenly saw their fortunes reversed during unification: instead of praising their commitment to the modernist tradition and excellence in the visual arts, the former West German press now condemned them as Communist Party hacks. Eisman's chapter delves into the ensuing debates, known as the *Bilderstreit*, in which the question arose as to what role, if any, East German art and artists should be allowed to play in the new Germany.

Daniel Ortuno-Stühring (Rostock University) turns our attention to music with his essay on the transformation of orchestras and theaters in Germany. As was the case in Eisman's essay, the underlying question here is the nature of art and the role of the artist in pre- and postunification Germany. In addition to private institutions, Germany always had a plethora of publicly funded theater and opera companies. Unification, however, threatened the very existence of this publicly financed system, not only because of insufficient financing but also because it was believed that artistic quality would be harder to achieve with too many orchestras and theater companies vying for public and private support. In tracing the present debate on the cultural role of theaters and orchestras, Ortuno-Stühring discusses possible directions for the future of orchestras and theaters in Germany: the changes in personnel, a potential move from a traditional German ensemble and repertoire company model to a model that employs temporary guest artists, and the closing or merging of smaller theaters and the reallocation of financial resources.

A Virtual Wall? Education and Society

More than twenty-five years after unification, it appears that there is little to distinguish everyday life in the east and west. But are east and west really united? Are the perspectives of eastern and western Germans the same? And if they differ, how? Does generational change influence the recollection of the GDR? Does the Wall still exist in the minds of Germans? And what are the implications (and limitations) of this "Wall" for politics and society? As we have seen in this introduction, there certainly are tangible differences between the east and the west (for example, there is more unemployment in the east, and more disposable income in the west), but there are also psychological ones: while 75 percent of Germans who live in the new states said in a recent survey that they considered their country's unification a success, only half of former West Germans agreed (Noack 2014). It appears that the emotional legacy of the division clearly remains and that the transformation process to bridge a formerly divided country is not quite complete.

The problem of how to teach the events of the Wende and its impact on Germany to young people for whom this period is truly ancient history is challenging. How much do they need to know about the GDR to be able to gain insight into the politics and culture of today's Germany? Andreas Eis of Kassel University discusses how historical facts about the former GDR and the unification process are being taught to young Germans. Empirical studies have shown that east German students in particular have very limited knowledge of the social and political reality of the former GDR and the peaceful revolution. How "concerning" or "frightening" are the results of surveys that state that a significant number of students and adults overestimate the "welfare state achievements" of the GDR and do not classify the communist SED (*Sozialistische Einheitspartei Deutschlands*, Socialist Unity Party of Germany) regime as a dictatorship as opposed to a social utopia? Eis describes the development of a new history curriculum prepared by the Association of German History Teachers (*Verband der Geschichtslehrer Deutschlands*) and based on an integrative approach to recent German history. He shows examples of a multidimensional model of teaching politics and of comparing political systems that neither minimize oppression nor argue that the FRG was the better state.

Michael Dreyer (Friedrich Schiller University Jena) believes that there is a lack of a balanced public discourse about the transformation process and its impact on life in unified Germany. Dreyer argues that even twenty-five years after unification, differences between east and west persist (beyond cultural differences ascribed to various regions) and that it is challenging to find a united Wende narrative reflecting thought processes in and on unified Germany. He proposes four different discourses that point to the limits of unification, which he calls the "evil empire" discourse, the *Ampelmännchen* discourse (referring to a distinct and beloved East German design of pedestrian signal), the "Who cares?" discourse, and the "Rodney King" discourse (a discourse that centers around mutual recognition and getting along with each other). Dreyer examines these narratives from a broader perspective of long-term trends and divisions in German history, politics, and society and concludes that indifference is what characterizes west Germany's and the west German's attitude toward the east, arguing that a better approach is needed to recognize and acknowledge the east German experience.

Peter Hayes (Northwestern University) closes the volume with an epilogue entitled "The Wende and the End of 'the German Problem,'" arguing that the Wende helped bring about a profound transformation in Germany's international role after 1989 and that this transformation is likely to prove both lasting and beneficial. He defines "the German Problem" in various periods of German history, each of which led to a war, and asks: What was the likelihood of war following unification, as fears about a dominating "Fourth Reich" were quite common in several neighboring countries, including France and the UK? Hayes explains that the reasons it did not happen were centrality, disproportionality, and scarcity, which were the key factors that led to "the German Problem." He believes that changes after 1945 that set Germany on a different path from the one it had followed since 1871 are the main reasons why Germany "has become a pillar of the European political system rather than a menace to it." In this regard, Hayes takes a broader approach than the previous essays and interprets the changes after 1989 in light of the changes occurring between 1945 and 1989. He maintains that in order to explain why, after 1989, a united Germany was not going to be a threat to Europe or the world, as many feared, one cannot begin in 1989 but must include a summary of historical events in postwar Germany, events that ultimately helped shape unification.

The volume *Virtual Walls?* covers an unusually broad range of topics that allows for a particularly comprehensive view of German culture twenty-five years after unification. The volume will appeal to experts in the field but also to scholars beyond German Studies: readers interested in the process and results of unification in a multitude of areas. The topics in which readers are less expert are intended to broaden their understanding of postunification changes and to allow for interesting cross-examinations and meaningful points of departure for further discussions. As such, the volume is a reassessment retracing a journey that Germans in east and west have taken during the past two and a half decades (or perhaps longer, as Hayes asserts). Yet, it is a journey that, in Thierse's words, is not complete: "After all, we did not bring down the Wall in the East to remain among ourselves (as East or West Germans), on the contrary. . . . Much has been achieved, much remains to be done. No reason to complain, but a call for further work!"[8]

Notes

[1] "Wenn nämlich ein starkes, erfolgreiches Gemeinwesen und ein gescheitertes, zusammengebrochenes, abgelehntes System zusammenkommen, dann sind die Gewichte klar verteilt: Das Eine ist die Norm, die die Anderen zu übernehmen haben; die Einen sind die Lehrmeister, die Anderen die Lehrlinge; bei den Einen kann alles so bleiben, bei den Anderen muss sich alles ändern; die deutsche Einheit wirkt bei den Einen als Bestätigung des Status quo, bei den Anderen bewirkt sie einen radikalen Umbruch (Thierse 2014, 11)."

[2] For a description of the development and meaning of this new type of memorial site, see Schlusche (2011).

[3] This assertion is only somewhat correct, given that Gauck did not have any political position between 1990 and 2012, if you define "political position" narrowly as an elected office.

[4] Jennifer Jordan, a sociologist at the University of Wisconsin, goes so far as to claim that "through apples, people can eat the past" and "consume these edible landscapes of memory" (2011, 59).

[5] The first two winners, Arno Geiger (2005) and Katharina Hacker (2006), were from the former West Germany. For the next ten years, seven winners had an East German or Eastern European background, namely Julia Franck (2007), Uwe Tellkamp (2008), Kathrin Schmidt (2009), Melinda Nadj Abondji (2010; with a Yugoslav background and Hungarian ethnicity), Eugen Ruge (2011), Feézia Mora (2013; a migrant from Hungary), and Lutz Seiler (2014). The three winners with a West German background in that ten-year period were Ursula Krechel in 2012, Franz Witzel in 2015, and Bodo Kirchhoff in 2016.

[6] Tellkamp's and Ruge's novels appeared under the titles *The Tower* and *In Times of Fading Light*, respectively, while Seiler's book is titled identically in German and in English, "Kruso" being the name of the protagonist.

[7] See, for example, Mary Fulbrook's essay "Living through the GDR: History, Life Stories, and Generations in East Germany" (2011, 201–20) and Wolfgang Emmerich's essay "Autobiographical Writing in Three Generations of a GDR Family: Christa Wolf—Annette Simon—Jana Simon" (2011, 141–57).

[8] "Schließlich haben wir nicht die Mauer vom Osten aus zu Fall gebracht, um unter uns zu bleiben (als Ost- oder Westdeutsche), im Gegenteil. . . . Es ist viel erreicht, es bleibt noch viel zu tun. Kein Grund zur Klage, aber eine Aufforderung zur Weiterarbeit!" (Thierse 2014, 10).

Works Cited

"Abschied von der homogenen Republik." 2012. *Wirtschaftswoche*, March 23. http://www.wiwo.de/politik/deutschland/ost-west-debatte-abschied-von-der-homogen-republik/6360540.html.

"Angela Merkel 'World's Most Powerful Woman.'" 2011. *Daily Telegraph* (London), August 24. http://www.telegraph.co.uk/news/worldnews/europe/germany/8720698/Angela-Merkel-worlds-most-powerful-woman.html.

Apelt, Andreas H., Robert Grünbaum, and Jens Schöne, eds. 2016. *Erinnerungsort DDR: Alltag, Herrschaft, Gesellschaft*. Berlin: Metropol.

Apelt, Andreas H., Eckhard Jesse, and Dirk Reimers, eds. 2016. *Ist zusammengewachsen, was zusammengehört? 25 Jahre Deutsche Einheit*. Halle (Saale): Mitteldeutscher Verlag.

Berg, Stefan. 2013. "The Demise of Eastern German Identity." *Spiegel online*, August 30. http://www.spiegel.de/international/germany/the-eastern-german-identity-has-disappeared-a-919110.html.

Besier, Gerald, ed. 2012. *20 Jahre neue Bundesrepublik: Kontinuitäten und Diskontinuitäten*. Berlin: LIT.

Bohr, Kurt, and Arno Krause, eds. 2011. *20 Jahre Deutsche Einheit: Bilanz und Perspektiven*. 2nd ed. Baden-Baden: Nomos.

Bundesagentur für Arbeit. 2012a. *Der Arbeits- und Ausbildungsmarkt in Deutschland: Monatsbericht Mai 2012*. Nuremberg: Bundesagentur für Arbeit.

———. 2012b. *Statistik*. http://statistik.arbeitsagentur.de/Navigation/Statistik/Statistik-nach-Regionen/Politische-Gebietsstruktur/Ost-West/Ost-Nav.html?year_month=201204.

Bundesanstalt für Arbeit. 2015a. *Statistik*. https://statistik.arbeitsagentur.de/Navigation/Statistik/Statistik-nach-Regionen/Politische-Gebietsstruktur/Ost-West-Nav.html.

———. 2015b. *Statistik*. https://statistik.arbeitsagentur.de/Navigation/Statistik/Statistik-nach-Regionen/Politische-Gebietsstruktur/Thueringen-Nav.html?year_month=201511.

———. 2015c. *Statistik*. https://statistik.arbeitsagentur.de/Navigation/Statistik/Statistik-nach-Regionen/Politische-Gebietsstruktur/Nordrhein-Westfalen-Nav.html?year_month=201511.

Cliver, Gwyneth, and Carrie Smith-Prei, eds. 2014. *Bloom and Bust: Urban Landscapes in the East since German Reunification*. New York: Berghahn.

Cooke, Paul. 2005. *Representing East Germany since Unification: From Colonization to Nostalgia*. New York: Berg Publishers.

Decker, Frank. 2015. *Parteiendemokratie im Wandel: Beiträge zur Theorie und Empirie*. Baden-Baden: Nomos.

"Die Einkommensunterschiede wachsen." 2010. *Zeit Online*, December 8. http://www.zeit.de/wirtschaft/2010-12/einkommen-schere-ostdeutschland.

Emmerich, Wolfgang. 2011. "Autobiographical Writing in Three Generations of a GDR Family: Christa Wolf—Annette Simon—Jana Simon."

In *Twenty Years On: Competing Memories of the GDR in Postunification German Culture*, edited by Renate Rechtien and Dennis Tate, 141–57. Rochester, NY: Camden House.

Fulbrook, Mary. 2011. "Living through the GDR: History, Life Stories, and Generations in East Germany." In *The GDR Remembered: Representations of the East German State since 1989*, edited by Nick Hodgin and Caroline Pearce, 201–20. Rochester, NY: Camden House.

Fuchs, Anne, Kathleen James-Chakraborty, and Linda Shortt, eds. 2011. *Debating German Cultural Identity since 1989*. Rochester, NY: Camden House.

"The Gauck File." 2012. *Wall Street Journal*, February 22. http://online.wsj.com/article/SB10001424052970203358704577237123740391712.html?KEYWORDS=the+gauck+file.

Gauck, Joachim. 1991. *Die Stasi-Akten: Das unheimliche Erbe der DDR*. Reinbek bei Hamburg: Rowohlt.

Gerstenberger, Katharina, and Jana Evans Braziel, eds. 2011. *After the Berlin Wall: Germany and Beyond*. New York: Palgrave Macmillan.

Gerster, Petra, ed. 2010. *Es wächst zusammen . . .: Wir Deutschen und die Einheit*. Cologne: Lingen.

Harrison, Hope M. 2014. "Five Myths about the Berlin Wall." *Washington Post*, October 30. https://www.washingtonpost.com/opinions/five-myths-about-the-berlin-wall/2014/10/30/f6cf1bc4-5df7-11e4-9f3a-7e28799e0549_story.html?utm_term=.58ceb799646c.

Jordan, Jennifer A. 2011. "Apples, Identity, and Memory in Post-1989 Germany." In Fuchs, James-Chakraborty, and Shortt 2011, 46–64.

Khazan, Olga. 2013. "The 'Little Traffic Man Light' That Could." *Atlantic*, September 25. https://www.theatlantic.com/international/archive/2013/09/the-little-traffic-light-man-that-could/279968/.

Leeder, Karen, ed. 2015. *Rereading East Germany: The Literature and Film of the GDR*. Cambridge: Cambridge University Press.

Lorenz, Astrid, ed. 2011. *Ostdeutschland und die Sozialwissenschaften: Bilanz und Perspektiven 20 Jahre nach der Wiedervereinigung*. Opladen: Barbara Budrich.

Lubow, Arthur. 2006. "The New Leipzig School." *New York Times*, January 8. http://www.nytimes.com/2006/01/08/magazine/the-new-leipzig-school.html.

Luhmann, Niklas. 1984. *Soziale Systeme: Grundriss einer allgemeinen Theorie*. Frankfurt am Main: Suhrkamp.

———. 2000. *Die Politik der Gesellschaft*. Frankfurt am Main: Suhrkamp.

Martens, Ulrike. 2016. *Deutsche Karikaturisten über die Teilung Deutschlands, die Friedliche Revolution und die Wiedervereinigung*. Berlin: Frank & Timme.

Matthäus, Sandra, and Daniel Kubiak, eds. 2016. *Der Osten: Neue sozialwissenschaftliche Perspektiven auf einen komplexen Gegenstand jenseits von Verurteilung und Verklärung*. Wiesbaden: Springer.

Niedermayer, Oskar, ed. 2015. *Die Parteien nach der Bundestagswahl 2013.* Wiesbaden: VS Verlag.

Noack, Rick. 2013. "The Berlin Wall Fell 25 Years Ago but Germany Is Still Divided." *Washington Post,* October 31. https://www.washington post.com/news/worldviews/wp/2014/10/31/the-berlin-wall-fell-25-years-ago-but-germany-is-still-divided/?utm_term=.f6c4421d318a.

Patton, David F. 2011. *Out of the East: From PDS to Left Party in Unified Germany.* Albany: State University of New York Press.

Ruge, Eugen. 2011. *In Zeiten des abnehmenden Lichts: Roman einer Familie.* Reinbek bei Hamburg: Rowohlt.

Sabrow, Martin, ed. 2016. *Die schwierige Einheit.* Leipzig: Akademische Verlagsanstalt.

Saunders, Anna, and Debbie Pinfold, eds. 2013. *Remembering and Rethinking the GDR: Multiple Perspectives and Plural Authenticities.* Houndsmills, Basingstoke, Hampshire, UK: Palgrave Macmillan.

Schlusche, Günter. 2011. "Remapping the Wall: The Wall Memorial in Bernauer Strasse—From an Unloved Cold War Monument to a New Type of Memorial Site." In *The GDR Remembered: Representations of the East German State since 1989,* edited by Nick Hodgin and Caroline Pearce, 112–32. Rochester, NY: Camden House.

Schröder, Klaus. 2010. *Das neue Deutschland: Warum nicht zusammenwächst, was zusammengehört.* Berlin: WJS.

Seiler, Lutz. 2014. *Kruso.* Berlin: Suhrkamp.

Solms-Laubach, Franz. 2009. "Ost- und Westdeutsche entfernen sich voneinander." *Welt Online,* May 20. http://www.welt.de/politik/article3775359/Ost-und-Westdeutsche-entfernen-sich-voneinander.html.

Statistisches Bundesamt. 2015. *Einkommen, Konsum, Lebensbedingungen.* https://www.destatis.de/DE/ZahlenFakten/GesellschaftStaat/Ein kommenKonsumLebensbedingungen/EinkommenEinnahmenAus gaben/Tabellen/Gebietsstaende.html.

Tellkamp, Uwe. 2008. *Der Turm.* Frankfurt: Suhrkamp.

Thieme, Tom, ed. 2016. *25 Jahre deutsche Einheit: Kontinuität und Wandel in Ost- und Westdeutschland.* Chemnitz: Universitätsverlag.

Thierse, Wolfgang. 2014. "Rede zum 25. Jahrestag des Mauerfalls. November 21." http://www.thierse.de/reden-und-texte/reden/rede-zum-25-jahrestag-des-mauerfalls/.

Part I.

What Remains: History and the Constitution

1: Lost in Transition: Reflections on the Spectral History of the GDR

Charles S. Maier

Did the GDR Ever Exist?

TWENTY-FIVE YEARS AFTER THE FALL of the Wall, German watchers might be tempted to pose two totally opposing questions about the GDR. The first question is: Did the German Democratic Republic ever really exist? Of course, it did exist, but it seems to have faded such that its historical presence appears pale and unreal—as if a dream that had once been vivid disappeared upon awakening. The second question is the opposite: Doesn't the German Democratic Republic really still exist? Of course, it doesn't, but it seems to have left sufficient habits, traces, and memories that haven't quite faded. This essay is an effort to grasp the ungraspable; that is, to reflect on why and how this forty-year experience retains such a ghostly quality.

Memories are strong; cinematic reconstructions are vigorous. The successor to the GDR's once-ruling party is and has been part of several state-level governing coalitions, and it deeply influences the German "Left." Most significant, a residual awareness of being a separate half of the country persists, whether in terms of income differentials, habits, regional cityscapes—a bit as if one had traveled into the Italian South or the American South fifty years after unification had brought those regions into their respective national governments. Thus, on the one hand, we recall a state that seems to have been ghostly even when it was real; on the other hand, we confront a spectral presence that still persists. This essay is prompted by that apparent paradox—it is an effort to puzzle through the semisovereign country that never really fully existed and the mental state that never totally disappeared. The history of East Germany encompasses other paradoxes as well. The GDR would never have endured had it not been for Soviet troops who arrived in 1945, who then put down workers' protests in 1953 and finally allowed the hermetic sealing of the border in 1961. Nonetheless, although it was guaranteed ultimately by an implicit recourse to force, it still generated real loyalties. It governed, on the one hand, through surveillance, but surveillance that was accepted and even shared by a significant fraction of the country's educated classes. And even while surveillance was elevated into a governing principle, it was simultaneously mobilized for civic efforts, peace campaigns, and competitive sports. The GDR hovered between repression and enthusiasm. It nurtured children who became the bearers of its collective memories, officially inculcated, and bearers of its collective consciousness, so carefully shaped. It lasted four decades: long enough to outgrow the circumstances of its birth; long enough to allow two generations to come of age within its limited possibilities; long enough to create a feeling of security for many of its citizens (as well as oppression for others); long enough to let Western as well as Eastern intellectuals forget that it would just blow away were Soviet soldiers to retreat from its territory; and long enough so that it still tugs at our historical consciousness.

Leaving Tracks: Regimes and Memory

Memories more than history can provide an initial access to this vanished regime. There are Christa Wolf's memoirs of violated political innocence, *Was bleibt* (What remains, 1990). The title has stuck, not only to describe Christa Wolf's concern, which was really what remained of the hopes and aspirations of the GDR after she discovered a regime built on secrecy and surveillance, but also to ask the question that motivated so many after unification in 1990: What remains of the GDR *überhaupt*, after its disappearance?

So-called collective memories have become a major theme for historians. Etienne François, the long-serving director of the Marc Bloch center for French historians working in Germany, and Hagen Schulze have produced a massive three-volume German echo of the French collection of *lieux de mémoire* with the title *Deutsche Erinnerungsorte* (François and Schulze, 2003). Its graceful and imaginative essays focus on places, but more generally on associative nexuses: people, including Napoleon, Bismarck, and Rosa Luxemburg; events, such as 1848 and 1968; institutions, such as the Bürgerliches Gesetzbuch (civil law); battlefields, such as Stalingrad and the Leipzig Völkerschlacht of 1813; and musical associations, such as Der Schlager or Hausmusik—all in all an imaginative approach to a cultural history with resonance. For the GDR, entries include the Stasi, "Wir sind das Volk," the Mauer, and the Palast der Republik, which really was an Erinnerungsort and as such had to be torn down. As the editors say in their preface, quoting Pierre Nora, "Germany has entered the Age of Memory," or perhaps we can say more accurately, the Age of Memory Work.

The editors claim that they are on the critical side of memory work: they intend no *Sinnstiftung* or mystical evocations but rather distancing and deconstruction. They want to offer an inventory of German memory cultures and, ultimately, an act of liberation from the past. I am sympathetic—I have pleaded for similar ends (Maier 1988)—but I am also skeptical now about the consistency of the project. The sites of memory and the memories themselves retain radically different valences. Deutsche Erinnerungsorte presuppose an overarching German national collective memory, and their moral starting point—as it is for many thoughtful Germans and was for me, too, in the 1980s—is Auschwitz, used as a paradigm for the Holocaust. But was there one national memory? The melancholy and trauma and sense of guilt that West German intellectuals reconstructed was not really a constitutive element of GDR moral conscience outside of increasingly alienated intellectuals. The regime defined itself as an antifascist institution; its young people were not instructed to acknowledge guilt for the Nazi interlude (Herf 1997). Just as important, the spectral persistence of the GDR has been in good measure the product of nostalgia, a sense of loss that many of its former citizens could confess to and indulge in. Other bygone German regimes left no equivalent longing, and we can differentiate the collective memory that was traumatic and is past from that for a status quo that in retrospect seems warm and comforting. Europe is littered with states that have been terminated. There is Prussia, ended by the command of the victorious Allies after the defeat of the Third Reich; or the Habsburg Empire, more specifically Austria-Hungary, that wonderful repository of sentimentality and nostalgia.

Let us look at some of the earlier specters in this landscape of ghostly regimes, starting with Prussia. It was recently revivified through Christopher Clark's impressive history of the Iron Kingdom and again in 2012 through the three hundredth birthday of Frederick the Great. An early high point of Prussian nostalgia came with the exhibit *Preußen: Versuch einer Bilanz* from August to November 1981 in the Martin-Gropius-Bau in Berlin (*Preußen* 1981), but in fact, Erich Honecker had reinstalled the equestrian statue of Frederick the Great in the middle of Unter den Linden the previous year. The legacy, therefore, served both the GDR as well as the Federal Republic of Germany (FRG) as both states prepared for the five hundredth anniversary of Luther's birth and Chancellor Kohl planned construction of a new Museum of German History. Prussia was a good example because its geography stretched across the north of both East and West and territorially might be claimed by both. Not really a nation, its legacy might legitimate two states, neither of which was quite a nation, either.

Prussia is a rich enough cluster of memories to resonate in many different ways. Conservatives can admire its alleged *Schlichtheit* and sobriety, the old families evoked by Theodor Fontane; and this is probably what has appealed to well-educated intellectuals. Prussia evokes Schinkel's architectural fantasies and, for those with enough artistic background, the "classical modern" of Lovis Corinth. A slightly more populist resonance echoes through Adolf Menzel's paintings, especially those now in the Deutsches Museum, whether the unfinished one of Frederick the Great with his generals or the melancholy of the endlessly reproduced tableau of Frederick playing his flute. Intellectuals of a leftist persuasion could cite Social Democratic Prussia: the stronghold of the SPD between the wars, which was so ingloriously decapitated in the *Staatsstreich* of 1932. And, of course, Marion Gräfin Dönhoff could remember the agrarian landscape of East Prussia with its horse farms and wide fields—the lands from which millions of Germans had to flee in the winter of 1944/45 (Clark 2006; Gräfin Dönhoff 1988, 1989).

Of the *Kaiserreich* there is little resonance. William II, an intelligent but mercurial and unreliable ruler, may not be demonized under the new conditions, but he can hardly be redeemed. For a few years, however, the resonances of Wilhelminian Germany suffused the displays of the new Germany: the curator Christof Stölzel's exhibition of the great historical canvases of Anton Werner to mark the reopening of the old German Historical Museum under new German management; the bizarre project to rebuild the shell of the Berlin royal palace, the Stadtschloss, a project championed by its supporters with a yellow canvas faux façade; and the general mania for restoration of nineteenth-century showpiece buildings in Berlin, making the turn of the twentieth century come again. These years represented the effort to think through the Berlin Republic—the promise of being a unified Germany, the effort to bury as much as possible of the East German interlude, to reorganize its universities, to sell off its productive remnants, in effect to dismantle the intervening institutions as hopelessly permeated by the Stasi or obsolescent industries. No one wanted a restoration of the Wilhelminian regime—but for a decade its aesthetics and *Protzigkeit* (pomposity) threatened to creep in by default. The Second Reich, after all, posed the question what should one do with a united Germany. Chancellor Kohl—a nonPrussian Catholic—had a good answer: work toward a united Europe; and despite his failures to envisage the economic difficulties in store for the East, he resisted what might otherwise have been a Wilhelminian pretension.

Which brings us to the ghosts or resonances of the Weimar Republic. It lingers in two respects. This pertains to the general newspaper-reading public, not historians who have taken to stressing its open possibilities, as Eric Weitz has in his recent survey. "Weimar still speaks to us," Weitz has written. "Its sparkling creativity and emancipatory experiments, politically and culturally, are still capable of inspiring thoughts that a better, more humane, more interesting condition of life is possible" (2007, 367). But is this the way Weimar really speaks to most contemporary Germans? Journalists and talking heads usually describe Weimar as the forlorn predecessor to the Third Reich, the dysfunctional state wedged between a lost war and the breakdown of democracy. It was afflicted with hyperinflation and then mass unemployment. It was burdened with reparations. It suffered from a proportional electoral system that led to a multiparty system and ultimately parliamentary paralysis. What commentators forget, of course, is that as of the late 1920s, it appeared as a model democracy. Proportional representation then appeared as a more democratic way of assuring representation. Moreover, the constitution built in social democratic guarantees. Josef Schumpeter analyzed the situation in 1929 and decided that no matter whether one looked to the Left or the Right, there was no threat of political extremism. The state or *Land* electoral returns across today's Lower Saxony might have suggested otherwise, for the signs of peasant alienation were already present even before the 107 Reichstag seats won by the NSDAP in September 1930 sent a frisson through European observers.

For the historians of the 1950s, such as Karl Dietrich Bracher, it was political failures that had been crucial. For my generation, learning its history in the 1960s and 1970s, class analyses provided powerful explanations. They suggested that Weimar had courted political paralysis and reaction by pressing a naked confrontation of interests—whether for the late Gerald Feldman, Tim Mason, or others of us researching in the 1960s, the politics of class stalemate seemed to decipher the secrets of democratic collapse. But perhaps the culture wars of Weimar were just as potent in undermining republican loyalties. Weimar, of course, left the legacy of a brilliant and brittle culture, always pushing the limits of tradition—whether expressed in the grotesques depicted by George Grosz or the theater of Brecht and the realism of *Neue Sachlichkeit*. Detlev Peukert became the major historian of the 1970s and 1980s to press this interpretation.

It is paradoxical that Weimar, a notable democracy, has been interpreted as a disaster for democracy, whereas the Third Reich, which has defined the public taboos on politics for the last sixty years, could for many decades still be privately taken up as quite a satisfactory time. But private experience and public civic legacy are divergent experiences. Indeed, it is as a set of taboos—taboos, for instance, against seeking to reproportion Holocaust memory, or taboos inhibiting current military intervention—that reveal that the Third Reich still plays a role in German politics. Some significant intellectuals in the 1980s and 1990s resisted the moral pressure exerted by the National Socialist experience. Public scandal erupted periodically over such issues as the *Historikerstreit* or Martin Walser's lament in 1998 that united Germany continued a policy of self-abasement. But these views did not really prevail among political and cultural leaders so attuned to their role in the West and shaped, too, by the generational battles of 1968.

This brings us to the shades of the two last German regimes: the East German Democratic Republic and the West German Federal Republic.

Many Germans would protest calling West Germany a vanished state, for the Bonn Republic segued easily into today's united Germany. Unification proceeded by means of applying Article 23 of the Grundgesetz or Basic Law, which provided for *Beitritt* of the five East German Länder and East Berlin, as it had provided for accession of the Saarland in 1955; it did not take place by means of Article 146, which would have entailed a new constituent assembly. Today's Federal Republic is the Federal Republic from before 1990, with a new eastern boundary and some constitutional reforms. And yet the preunification FRG had characteristics that also clearly belong to the past. Certainly, the regime of the 1950s—the West Germany at the front lines of the Cold War—was a different Germany. It was a state with incomplete sovereignty and unrecovered territory. It was a much more tentative country, a republic of narrow political choices, confronted by Konrad Adenauer and Walter Hallstein, a culture that could produce modernist figures such as Joseph Beuys or Hollywood-like stars such as Romy Schneider, and a culture that was both nervously experimental and hopelessly nostalgic.

The ambiguities of being a state for two thirds of the Germans cast a shadow over the Federal Republic; not so somber as the shadow cast on the GDR by serving as a state for one third of a German nation but with an impact nonetheless. The Bonn Republic built its civic profile on conspicuous renunciation as it could not unilaterally take up the issue of unification. Its identity, as Harold James noted, was built on its economic vocation, which represented a sort of sublimation for earlier nationalism. It accepted its status as a petted junior partner of the United States and decisively rejected what Americans still feared in the 1950s: a sort of Rapallo deal with the Russians. Insofar as politicians spoke for a more ambitious national agenda by the 1960s—for example, Franz Josef Strauß—they aroused mistrust and suspicion. Nonetheless, the Federal Republic survived a major generational upheaval and a sustained assault by terrorists with only relatively minor infringements of the liberal politics it was seeking to build. It also made a fairly fundamental transition from the chastened paternalist Christian Democracy to a more open and daring social-liberal orientation in the late 1960s; a genuine transition but one whose impact was constrained by the Cold War.

Early Bonn was a regime still in a bit of shell shock with the good fortune to have a wise and conservative refounder. American observers kept on waiting for ugly politics to reemerge, but the neo-Nazi right never really achieved more than a tenth of the electorate as sympathizers. Bonn made a deal with the Western world it was joining—allow us to avoid looking too closely at our enthusiasms of the 1930s, and we will assure you that we'll run a decent and modest politics, contribute to the defense of the West without clamoring for nuclear weapons, and pay compensation to the Jewish communities inside and outside Israel.

Indeed, early Bonn was a regime dedicated to keeping ghosts at bay—and it succeeded. It was also an unproblematic state for Americans; in fact, it was *our* state, we godfathered it to a large measure. Even in the 1970s and 1980s as it grew into an economic superpower and its currency doubled in value with respect to the dollar, it played a cooperative role. By the end of the 1960s and the early 1970s it accepted the Berlin settlement, the treaties with East Germany, Poland, and the Soviet Union that seemed to seal the status quo. The architectural representative structure it erected in the 1970s and 1980s in Bonn—the glass-house parliament and the corporate Bundeskanzleramt—testified to its aspirations for integration and cooperation.

After unification, there was a lot of rumination about the Berlin Republic's stepping into a new and more dramatic role. It is unclear what was to be expected. The Cold War was over, and the Germans no longer stood at the edge of the West but were in the middle of Brussels-oriented Europe. Bonn had not become Weimar, and Berlin in the period since 1989 did not become the Berlin of 1929, much less the Berlin of 1939. Despite some new corporate architecture and a vast new Chancellery, Berlin did not become a Paris, London, or Tokyo: it did not suck up all the energies scattered elsewhere. It has become a capital of embassies and front offices: banks and corporations have representational offices in Berlin but make their money elsewhere. It has not developed a first-class newspaper; its public transport has a pleasant down-at-heels amateur quality to it despite a glitzy new rail station. The rather disjointed assemblage at Potsdamer Platz doesn't really make a coherent statement. Flying into Berlin from the west, planes often make a long loop around Marzahn and then double back toward Tegel over the compact central area—and they will continue to do so for a while as Berlin waits for its new airport. What lies below is far less dense than London, New York, Paris, or the great metropolises of Asia. Its intelligentsia and political classes meet modestly enough in common locales: it is totally *übersehbar*. In this sense, the Bonn Republic lives on in its modesty and its nontroublesome cooperation with America (an exception made, perhaps, for Gerhard Schröder's ostentatious disavowal of Washington's policies—but policies that deserved to be disavowed).

We confront finally the spectral presence of the regime that we are trying to assay on the anniversary of 1989: that of the GDR. It would be hard to add much to all that has been written and said about Ostalgie, the continuing economic gradients, the electoral returns that seem to show disaffection or else a sentimental leftism. I remember meeting Bärbel Bohley[1] in the year of unification, and she said West Germans expected that their society would cleanse and rehabilitate East Germany but that in fact, East Germany would infect and help rot the West. Of course, Bohley was a disenchanted participant in the reconstruction of the nation, to be contrasted with such enthusiasts as Richard Schröder or

Wolfgang Thierse. But looking at the basis for a Left party that the Partei des Demokratischen Sozialismus (PDS, Party of Democratic Socialism) has provided, I start to understand Bohley. With the PDS we look at a politics of ressentiment but also at an effort for many East Germans to validate a lifetime of political maturation within the East. Its older voters include those who had achieved a level of prestige or comfort within the old GDR and were then dismissed, and its younger voters include those for whom unification seems to have opened no new pathways.

There was clearly ample room for East German ressentiment. Westerners came as carpetbaggers; they took over staff positions in Land and city governments, they took over university positions and closed faculties. They wanted to erase this unfortunate forty-year interlude in their national history. The former East Germany was the terrain where the West was able to behave as other "ordinary" imperial countries had behaved in their colonies in earlier years. Looking back on these last twenty-five years, it is hard to recall how quickly the picture of the heroic marchers in Leipzig changed to that of querulous complainants. This was part of a whole series of contradictory developments.

Indeed, we do most historical justice to the old GDR by thinking of it as a state of contradictions or paradoxes. Consider two overarching ones: *First*, it was a regime that claimed autonomy but was installed by the Soviet Union and would not have survived were it not for the continued threat until 1989 that Soviet soldiers would intervene to prevent its being overthrown—as they did in Berlin in June 1953, and again in Hungary in October and November 1956, and in Prague in August 1968. *Second*, it had a government that could spy on and imprison its critics and controlled what might or might not be written in its papers and indeed its novels but could still evoke some genuine loyalties among at least some of its citizens and intellectual classes. Conflicting interpretations have emphasized the one or the other of these qualities. For Klaus Schröder (1998), the GDR was totalitarian, characterized by its political repressiveness and subsisting as an *Unrechtsstaat*. From Mary Fulbrook's (2005) point of view, what counted was the warm social fabric of the GDR; and while she admits that politically it was an oppressive regime, she insists that politics played only a small role in the experience of GDR citizens.

Both these views are unsatisfactory. The quality of repression was arbitrary and harsh. Any foreigner (and any West German citizen) could sense the lack of limits on police power every time he or she crossed the GDR frontier. But the regime was not terroristic. It was manipulative, and it functioned by extending privileges and rewards or by denying them. As Andrew Port (2009) has shown in his study of the industrial town of Saalfeld, the very application of incentives and norms at the local level tended to fragment the working classes whose unity supposedly lay at the basis of the state. Instead, their petty discontents and grumbling forestalled any collective challenges. But this meant that the party was setting the conditions for society. *Gesellschaft* could not be separated from *Herrschaft* in the Marxist state. To focus on the political apparatus in isolation, or to presuppose an autonomous societal or cultural domain (even a consumer culture) will miss the artfulness of the Communist project. Contrast again Mary Fulbrook's *The People's State: East German Society from Hitler to Honecker*—whose very title takes us seamlessly from state to society, although she intends to keep them separate spheres—with Stephan Wolle (1998), who insists that "the society of the GDR was corrupted to its core."[2] For Fulbrook, as for earlier commentators before 1989, such as Günter Gaus, the society served as a sort of sanctuary that provided "a wide range of lived experiences" and insulated citizens from "the underlying structures of which contemporaries may well have been unaware . . ." (Fulbrook 2005, xii).

These structures, of course, hardly provided the conditions for a vital and autonomous social development. Attractive as the idea is, we cannot base history on lived experience alone. There were, alas, many Germans who felt that life in the Third Reich was fulfilling and believed that they were creating a vibrant communal social life. Raw social experience requires analytical or interpretive categories to be evaluated. A social history of the regime that cordons off the political dimension (even when it concedes a lot of bad politics) must be incomplete. It is, as mentioned above, impossible to study Gesellschaft without studying Herrschaft under conditions of dictatorship. Indeed, the central claim of theorists of totalitarianism, preeminently Hannah Arendt, is that it is a regime type powerful enough to disaggregate and atomize society primarily through the tools of terror. My own view is that both of these views oversimplify.

Recent discussions of Martin Broszat's work on Nazi rule, for example, emphasize that his effort to "historicize" National Socialism was an effort to critique the claim of atomization. In Broszat's cumulative historical production, the National Socialist regime clearly possessed uniquely terroristic capacities—but individuals in society might still escape relatively unscathed, that is, not bear responsibility for the crimes.[3] As a historian, Broszat was wrestling with personal issues of responsibility. Fulbrook faces no such problem. Both authors, however, raise the general issue of whether people's memories or their belief that their lives were hardly circumscribed under dictatorship can really serve as historical evidence about the nature of the system under which they lived.

The problem with everyday history, or *Alltagsgeschichte*, is precisely that most people can go through life without feeling subjectively impinged on by politics if they make no effort to engage politically. Under such powerful state projects as communism or fascism, to write a history of society as autonomous—or present a view of society as in Edgar Reitz's skillful television series, *Heimat*—must lead to a partial account of the past.[4]

True enough, although the two domains of Herrschaft and Gesellschaft overlapped and powerfully shaped each other, they were not fused. Enough of people's family and personal lives—indeed, enough of their organizational lives—remained distinct to merit analysis. This does not mean that they could always protect them. Not all niches, to use Günter Gaus's (1983, 157) famous image, were sanctuaries: the coercive state could intrude if it had reason to—which is the truth on which Florian von Donnersmarck has built his film *The Lives of Others*. Nonetheless, there was enough differentiation that each domain—political and social—will convey a different total reality. Describe the Communist state, and the historian conjures up an image of illiberal surveillance and the manipulation of fear and privilege. Describe the Communist society, and one can end up with a trivialization of coercive mechanisms.

What was essential and ironic was the fact that this state really wanted the participation of this society. Enlistment of the society in its project was the test of legitimization. Hence, too, the importance of overwhelming election approval even when there was only a single party slate to vote for. But the state project was not, despite its rhetoric, a utopian search for an egalitarian society. Rather, it became merely approval and acclamation in its own right.

Facing the fall of the Wall after more than two decades, the challenge remains (as it always should have been) to write what might be called a "moral history," that is, one about choices. A moral history cannot be one just of late Communist "experience," for an experiential history will tend to document either subjectively perceived autonomy, and implicitly serve apologia, or repeated acts of coercion, menace, or privilege. But neither can a moral history just be an account of the regime, for a regime history will find little but corruption, secrecy, and surveillance. A *Black Book of Communism* (Courtois et al. 1999) can supply an indictment but allows for little discussion of how people might in fact survive terror and coercion. A moral history of late communism must be an account of the continuing negotiation between collective or private action and party control and abuse. Citizens could choose to live private lives and pay the cost of outward obedience, like Vaclav Havel's greengrocer with the party slogan in his window. In this case, the word *citizenship* may be inappropriate. Or inhabitants could become sincerely enthusiastic about the conspicuous campaigns of civic mobilization based on claims of antifascism or involving peace demonstrations. Inhabitants could also withdraw into an oppositional silence. They could become cynical, as in the case of the Stasi informer and intellectual Sascha Anderson; or bemused observers of the foibles of the rulers, as did the novelist Günter de Bruyn or the bleaker young author Christoph Hein. Such stances provided alternatives for negotiation, not of the boundary between private and public, for a firm boundary did not exist, but of a political "trading zone," a jointly occupied frontier at the spiritual and legal edge of the state. A moral history need not condemn citizens for making one or another of these choices (at least as long as compliance did not injure others) but will illuminate the choices faced and the costs of each.

Relinquishing Power

The rulers had choices to make, too, and at the end, the choice they made was to give up power peaceably. When we write about the demise of the East German regime (and not about the appeals of communism more generally), the question that remains so challenging is why power was surrendered so peacefully. Of course, the largely peaceful transition was partially a question of luck and prudence. It would not have taken much for violence to have intervened—a few rocks thrown by demonstrators, panic on the part of young soldiers, and thereafter the unintended escalation of force. Indeed, in Dresden there had been serious clashes with police just a few days before the major demonstration of October 9 in Leipzig that took place without violence. Moreover, some of the leaders were prepared to use coercion or arrests. Consider Erich Mielke, head of the Ministry for State Security: his troops did counter demonstrations in early October with mass arrests up to a certain point, but only to a certain point. And if we argue that Mielke's intentions were delayed and debated by Politburo colleagues or even just undermined by foot-dragging at the local level, we have to explain why the colleagues effectively refused to ratify simple violence.

The reason often cited is that the Soviets—who were instrumental in enforcing Communist rule at several key postwar junctures—made it clear that they were no longer going to provide that support. Under Mikhail Gorbachev they were no longer going to rely on their potential monopoly of violence whether in Eastern Europe, the Baltic regions seeking to recover independence, or at home. But given Soviet warnings that they would not support such an intervention, and the doubts of Honecker's internal party critics, the SED proved unwilling to shut down the process of popular protest, and then agreed to negotiate power sharing. Why the willingness to give way to public protests?[5]

Publication of Stasi memoranda provided some insight into this issue early on. They suggest that by 1989 many of the leaders of the Eastern European nations understood that they had arrived at a dead end in terms of their own aspirations and policies. In part this was a recognition of relative economic failure; in part a generational issue; in part a confrontation with the culture of expressive personal values (call it postmodernity) whose corrosive dissolution of Communist public virtues they could not withstand.

Historians have perhaps paid too little systematic attention to the dialectic of private and public in 1989. For if—as Eastern European intellectuals have often claimed—the private seemed more poignant, and literature, for instance, more significant in a world of repression (just as religious ceremonies are more meaningful when they have to be held in secret or at least defiance), nonetheless, it was the very constraints on the "private" sphere that made the arguments for public transformation so compelling. Private longings and aspirations could be emancipated only by rejecting the ideological straitjacket of a system that did not want to grant their legitimacy. To construct a free interior life, one had to reconstruct the public sphere. But doing so undercut and trivialized the struggle of intellectuals and poets whose writing lost its urgency. Anna Akhmatova in Russia, Wisława Szymborska and Zbigniew Herbert in Poland, and Christa Wolf in the GDR created their art by insisting on the values of interiority and subjectivity—precisely those values that Leninism and later communism could not tolerate since they testified to life spheres more fundamental than building socialism. Instead, Communist censors (including the writers' unions who served as self-censors) condemned subjectivity, indeed any nonaffirmative stance as a seduction of an outmoded and decadent bourgeois culture. For the nomenklatura of 1989, what was taking place was the return of the repressed, not only inexplicable because it had survived so strongly but demoralizing because their own values had apparently taken such shallow root.

Still, the rulers of 1989 faced more than just the irrepressible claims of the private sphere. It was simultaneously a looming failure in the public sphere that they had claimed must be the site of progress. As Stefan Wolle puts it (Mitter and Wolle 1990, 1993; Wolle 1998), many in the security apparatus believed they should be loved and thus were shocked to find that the benevolence of their mission was so repudiated. The more insightful Communist leaders throughout East Central Europe understood, although they might continue to hold on to power by coercion, that they could not manage complex societies that were obviously no longer structured according to the binary principles the leadership had earlier presupposed. How did one maintain a state of workers and peasants when modern societies required teachers, managers, therapists, travel agents, clothing designers, computer programmers, Olympic coaches, restaurateurs, television programmers, fast-food suppliers, and the providers of what the state called "the thousand little things"?

Economic Disorientation

As became evident after unification, it was in the economic sphere that the paradoxes or contradictions of the German Communist regime became most surprisingly visible. The GDR had supposedly become the tenth or eleventh largest industrial economy of the world (following those in today's G-8 and the Soviet Union), and it was the major producer of machine tools for the Soviet bloc. Industrial prowess, however, valued by an earlier generation of planners, no longer sufficed to assure prosperity, nor could it satisfy the consumer longings for the products of "postmodernity." Consumers wanted goods that satisfied highly individualized yearnings and not just collective needs, such as jeans, Walkmen, and cars.

The legacy of state socialism in general was to retard the processes of post-Fordist challenges that afflicted the East German state before its collapse in 1989–90. Like the other economies of the Eastern Bloc, the GDR had experimented with a partial introduction of market criteria for firms (profit incentives) at the end of the 1960s. As was the case with Czech reforms associated with Otto Sik or so-called Libermanism in the Soviet Union, the GDR experiment revealed that a partial dismantling of central planning was very difficult. It led to unanticipated shortages and bottlenecks and often disappointing results. It also seemed to stimulate unacceptable demands for political liberalization, such as characterized the Prague Spring, and thus was further discredited. In place of the New Economic System, the GDR leadership thus introduced at the VIIth Party Congress of the SED in 1971 the supposed "Unity of Economy and Society," a policy mix associated with the growing influence of Günter Mittag. The Unity of Economy and Society meant an effort to combine economic growth with a relatively high degree of social-welfare spending and satisfaction of consumer needs. It was in line with the policies Edward Gierek adopted in Poland after the explosion of worker dissatisfaction in 1970 and the tendencies toward "Goulash Communism," associated with the later phases of János Kádár's administration in Hungary.

Such policies, however, were unsustainable without subsidies or credits from abroad, that is, from either the Soviet Union or more plausibly from the nonsocialist Western economies. The Soviet Union's per capita income was no higher than those of its satellites, but it could provide oil and other raw materials at a price below world-market levels. Oil price subsidies made a difference after the OPEC countries tripled the price of oil they charged Western countries in early 1974. East Germany could buy Soviet oil, refine it further, and sell it at a mark-up to the West. Inexpensive oil also provided the basis for a major chemical industry, as did the earlier development of synthetic oil that had been expanded preparing for and fighting World War II. But in general, the cost of consumer socialism would be covered by the credits Western governments extended especially to Poland and to the GDR. Since the new *Ostpolitik* of the SPD-FDP governments in the Federal Republic specifically sought to moderate East German communist policies by conciliation (*Wandel durch Annäherung*), economic assistance and credits formed part of the package. This would lead to substantial indebtedness on the part of the

East German economy, especially since the Christian Democratic governments after 1982 essentially continued the policies—indeed, with Franz
Josef Strauß's efforts at personal diplomacy extended even greater assistance in the late 1980s.

Essentially the East Germans became the industrial machine-tool producer for the socialist world and depended on credits and outright subsidies and personal remittances from West German relatives for Western
consumer goods. These they distributed through *Intershops* for Western
currency, a system that created a network of privilege that naturally
undermined the socialist ideology that the regime propagated even further (Zatlin 2007; Landsman 2005).

The country had woefully neglected infrastructure in housing and
buildings. The Unity of Economy and Society meant that consumer goods
might be sought alongside the production of exports to the Comecon or
the West, if possible. Investment in the physical plant of cities was sac-
rificed. What is more, during the 1980s the regime devoted much of its
scarce resources for urban planning to projects for the capital. As a stake
in the Cold War, *Berlin—Hauptstadt der DDR* received the lion's share
of urban development funds. The competitive preening for the fifth cen-
tennial of Luther's birth in 1983 provided only a final episode.

Still, within the overall structure set by these political constraints, the
East German economy satisfied a modicum of welfare. Consumers had to
wait for many years and pay a far larger price in terms of their work time
for an inferior automobile; housing was dilapidated and rundown, but
within their little Republic they made do with a certain shabby coziness.
With the fall of the Wall on November 9, however, a new perspective
opened up: the possibility of individual entry into a far richer state. In retrospect one can see a basic inconsistency developing in the East German
population—the vision of a higher standard of living and the preservation
of all the social guarantees they associated with their own socialist state.
But the concept of a currency and economic union seemed to guarantee that both these results might be obtained together. Politically, it was
not yet clear what form closer association might take. Kohl's Ten Point
Program to the Bundestag was a masterly stroke that spoke of progress
toward confederative structures without foreclosing what these might
be or openly disturbing French and British concerns about rapid political unification. On the other hand, the Economic and Currency Union
awakened tremendous anticipation that East Germans would be lifted up
overnight to West German living standards.

Unfortunately, this did not happen. The East Germans awoke on the
Eastern edge of a Western postindustrial world that had no need for what
they produced and once had valued. The six months between the replace-
ment of Erich Honecker in October 1989 and the East German parliamentary (Volkskammer) elections of March 18, 1990, which returned

a working majority for the CDU, was a period of dissipating illusions. The Modrow government's hesitation about dissolving the Ministry for State Security (Stasi) led to public demonstrations that made clear the political fragility of the GDR government and undercut any possibility that it might confront the West German negotiators as an equal partner. During the year after the fall of the Wall, the governments of the transition learned that the national patrimony they thought to base their future wealth on had little value.

Still, in this period several economic-reform proposals emerged that shared the notion that somehow there was a middle or "third way" between the old planned economy and what was feared to be a ruthless competitive capitalism. Among the concepts, most of which remained rather nebulous, the idea that Wolfgang Ullman's Freie Forschungsgemeinschaft (later Kollegium) within the movement Demokratie Jetzt advanced had the most success. It envisaged a Trusteeship Institution or holding company (*Treuhandanstalt*) that would take over the state property of the GDR and provide a substantial asset with which to confront the West (Seibel 2005; Kemmler 1994; Fischer and Schröter 1993). For a brief while, the Treuhand was one of the largest property owners in the world and employed four million workers. It took over 8,000 companies, reorganized them for sale into 12,350 units, sold about 8,400, liquidated 3,700, and transferred the remaining hard-to-dispose companies into a successor agency (Nativel 2004, 50–51). But what its properties were worth and how they might be utilized were the key issues. Early estimates of the socialist patrimony's value were based on assessments of physical property and took little account that the whole demand structure was transformed with unification.

The elections of March 18 to the Volkskammer changed the unification situation with the dramatic victory of the East German CDU led by lawyer (and violist) Lothar de Maizière. Essentially, the new government saw its task as preparing the most rapid and frictionless union possible. Although the committee to ponder a new East German constitution hoped for creating the basis of a state that would be democratized but retain its autonomy for negotiations, the new Volkskammer rejected these projects and pushed through instead an administrative restructuring that recreated five new (or renewed) German Länder that would be able to merge into the federal structure of the West German Basic Law. Overarching the entire settlement was the promise that the Deutschmark was to become the new currency of united Germany and that ongoing obligations in the East such as wages and pensions and interest rates would be valued at a parity of 1:1. Personal savings accounts or company balances in GDR Marks would also be converted at par up to a total of 2,000 DM and at 1:2 for amounts higher than 2,000 (or up to 4,000 for senior citizens). In terms of the monetary claims the Federal

Republic was adding to its money supply, and the reserves required to cover them, the Federal government did not pose an exceptional strain on currency stability. But where the "Mark equals Mark" conversion would have graver consequences was in the continuing burden of pay scales. The West German unions insisted that wages in the East converge on Western levels, although output was far lower. There was a good argument for this policy. Aside from concerns about massive population transfers, the ideology of unification assumed that the new Germany was to share social burdens and provide equal opportunities. Nonetheless, such a hike in real wage costs put new firms under tremendous pressure.

East Germans faced a dual transition: one to capitalism, the second to the postindustrial economy that had taken hold in the nonsocialist world while they remained in their collectivist Comecon cocoon. Ultimately, however, the East Germans had to undergo the transition from an old industrial society to a postindustrial society in a far more compressed time period than other similar regions. The Ruhr was deindustrialized over a generation or more, and Wallonia, the American "rust belt," and the North of Britain revealed similar difficulties: job losses, shutting down of industry, and out-migration to different national regions where it was culturally and linguistically easy, as it was in Britain, the United States, and Germany.

What is more, East Germans always compared themselves invidiously with the prosperous West, not with their former companions in the Bloc. As of 2007, former East German workers, now citizens of united Germany, had far higher incomes than the Czechs who in Communist days had been their rough equals. But they still lagged by a third or so behind workers in the western half of the united country (Pacqué 2009, 201–5). Moreover, the Eastern European societies could enjoy the sensation of being autonomous actors determining their own future. The former East Germans often felt demoralized by the rapidity of the changes and the fact that their living standards depended on subsidies and transfers.

The legacy of state socialism in general was to retard the processes of postindustrial development that took root in the West between the 1960s and the 1980s. Did this have to be the case? The Soviet Union, after all, had developed an aerospace sector that rivaled that of the West. Why could it not have forged an informatics and electronic sector that kept pace? It had the mathematicians. Certainly, the closed economic zone of the socialist bloc limited innovation, and without market-price signals the costs of persisting in aging industrial sectors could not really be measured. I believe, however, that the answer is ultimately a political one: The heroic images of socialism derived from industrial society. In George Orwell's book on the coal miners of Wigan Pier (Orwell [1937] 2001) one can see the industrial romanticism that motivated even a noncommunist English left intellectual. Communism remained wedded to this image of the heroic proletarian, and in the case of the Soviet party, or the Italian Resistance tradition, the heroic idea of labor was augmented by the military heroism of the Second World War. The ideology of the future became frozen in a vision of the past.

The 1960s and 1970s revealed the forces that would corrode this worldview, whether manifested by the Beatles or later by the Xerox machine and by the 1980s by the Walkman. The goods that the Eastern bloc celebrated, and the strengths it sought to perpetuate, whether in Eisenhüttenstadt or Nowa Huta, would be increasingly provided by producers in Asia, who would also turn out the jeans and the shoes, the T-shirts, and the consumer electronics that East Germans craved. Where there were exceptions—highly specialized construction material or optics—there was a future. But it is a painful process to arrive at the future. It was painful in the West for afflicted regions for a generation, and it would be proportionally even more painful packed into a decade.

A Place in History?

What should we conclude about this forty-year experience and its denouement? Could a reformed East German state have been preserved in a confederation of the two Germanys in 1990? Ultimately, the Russians who created the GDR were not willing to sustain it, and the Americans viewed it with mistrust. Gorbachev had decided on a partnership with the West German state, and as the election of March 18, 1990, revealed, the people of the GDR were not willing to choose this alternative. Why should they? The GDR was not an ancient structure like Austria or Bavaria but an artifact of the Second World War, a piece of Soviet booty. East Germans would gain economically in 1990; but what they could not do was to liquidate their economy and also preserve their state as a component of the future FRG.

But consider the counterfactual for a moment. In theory, no insuperable barrier would have precluded a confederation: such a step-by-step process had paved the way for the first German unification of 1871. How might such an outcome have changed our sense of the GDR up to 1989? Such a process would have at least given the old GDR the historical character of one historical source for a unified Germany, and the ghostly fading of its history would have proceeded far less quickly. Instead, the forty-year socialist republic came quickly to appear, as was cruelly noted, as a footnote in history. How states disappear helps determine what is recalled of their history—not necessarily by historians, who have a professional interest in documenting it, but by the general public. Indeed, we can say that vanishing without institutional aftermath leaves only memory unsupported by history.

East Germany is no longer a collective community, but it formed the basis—and will for a bit longer—of a common memory. Citizens of the former East Germany above a certain age could say, "We were in this together." East Germans sometimes developed a contradictory view of what they went through. On the one hand, they suggested that their former state had exerted a degree of totalitarian surveillance through the Stasi that was as evil as the Third Reich. On the other hand, they spoke warmly way into the 1990s of the cozy collective mentality that they had enjoyed, their associative life, and the absence of an "elbow" society, and they threw a warm veil of sentiment over the old days. Their more ambitious young people, however, understood that they enjoyed opportunities and freedoms their parents had never had during the two generations of state socialism. Young Americans liked to say a while back, "That's history," when they meant something was simply past and irrelevant. But East Germany faded into a domain where even "That's history" might seem too existentially definitive. For its former inhabitants now it is just memory. But as memory fades, perhaps it can reemerge as history—historians' history.

Notes

[1] Bärbel Bohley (May 24, 1945–September 11, 2010) was an East German artist. She was the founder of the organization Women for Peace (Frauen für den Frieden) and cofounder in 1989 of the New Forum (Neues Forum). She was arrested in 1983 and again in 1988 because she was a vocal supporter of disarmament, peace, and especially freedom of expression and civil rights.

[2] Wolle (1998, 152–53): "Die Gesellschaft der DDR war bis ins Innerste vergiftet" (The GDR society was poisoned to the core). The relationship of state and society is different from the important issue of the relationship between party and state. For that question see Meuschel (1992).

[3] See the recent conference devoted to the work of Martin Broszat: Frei (2007).

[4] Indeed, a theorist such as Tocqueville suggests in *Democracy in America* that this is true for democratic societies as well, but in a democracy, as he presented it, the causal line runs from society to the state, not from state to society. For a useful effort to capture the interaction of state and society under totalitarianism, see Fitzpatrick (1999).

[5] On this process see Kramer (2009), Williams (2009), Smolar (2009), and Maier (2009); also Henke (2009).

Works Cited

Clark, Christopher. 2006. *Iron Kingdom: The Rise and Downfall of Prussia, 1600–1947*. Cambridge, MA: Harvard University Press.

Courtois, Stéphane, Nicolas Werth, Jean-Louis Panné, Andrzej Paczkowski, Karel Bartošek, and Jean-Louis Margolin. 1999. *The Black Book of Communism: Crimes, Terror, Repression*. Consulting Editor Mark Kramer. Cambridge, MA: Harvard University Press.

Dönhoff, Marion Gräfin. 1988. *Kindheit in Ostpreußen*. Berlin: Siedler.

Fischer, Wolfram, and Harm Schröter. 1993. "Die Entstehung der Treuhandanstalt." In *Treuhandanstalt: Das Unmögliche wagen. Forschungsberichte*, edited by Wolfram Fischer, Herbert Hax, and Hans Karl Schneider. Berlin: Akademie Verlag.

Fitzpatrick, Sheila. 1999. *Everyday Stalinism: Ordinary Lives in Extraordinary Times. Soviet Russia in the 1930s*. New York: Oxford University Press.

François, Étienne, and Hagen Schulze, eds. 2003. *Deutsche Erinnerungsorte*. 3 vols. Munich: C. H. Beck.

Frei, Norbert, ed. 2007. *Martin Broszat, der "Staat Hitlers" und die Historisierung des Nationalsozialismus*. Göttingen: Wallstein.

Fulbrook, Mary. 2005. *The People's State: East German Society from Hitler to Honecker*. New Haven, CT: Yale University Press.

Gaus, Günter. 1983. *Wo Deutschland liegt*. Hamburg: Hoffmann & Campe.

———. 1989. *Bilder die langsam verblassen: Ostpreußische Erinnerungen*. Berlin: Siedler.

Henke, Klaus-Dietmar, ed. 2009. *Revolution und Vereinigung 1989/90: Als in Deutschland die Realität die Phantasie überholte*. Munich: Deutscher Taschenbuch Verlag.

Herf, Jeffrey. 1997. *Divided Memory: The National Socialist Past in the Two Germanies*. Cambridge, MA: Harvard University Press.

Kemmler, Marc. 1994. *Die Entstehung der Treuhandanstalt: Von der Wahrung zur Privatisierung des DDR-Volkseigentums*. Frankfurt am Main: Campus.

Kramer, Mark. 2009. "The Dialectics of Empire: Soviet Leaders and the Challenge of Civil Resistance in East-Central Europe, 1968–91." In Roberts and Ash 2009, 91–109.

Landsman, Mark. 2005. *Dictatorship and Demand: The Politics of Consumerism in East Germany*. Cambridge, MA: Harvard University Press.

Maier, Charles S. 2009. "Civil Resistance and Civil Society: Lessons from the Collapse of the German Democratic Republic in 1989." In Roberts and Ash 2009, 260–76.

Meuschel, Sigrid. 1992. *Legitimation und Parteiherrschaft: Zum Paradox von Stabilität und Revolution in der DDR 1945–1989*. Frankfurt am Main: Suhrkamp Verlag.

Mitter, Armin, and Stefan Wolle. 1993. *Untergang auf Raten: Unbekannte Kapitel der DDR-Geschichte*. Munich: Bertelsmann.

————, eds. 1990. *Ich liebe euch doch alle! Befehle und Lageberichte des MfS, Januar–November 1989*. Berlin: BasisDruck Verlag.

Nativel, Corinne. 2004. *Economic Transition, Unemployment and Active Labour Market Policy: Lessons and Perspectives from the East German Bundesländer*. Birmingham: University of Birmingham Press.

Orwell, George. (1937) 2001. *The Road to Wigan Pier*. London: Penguin Books.

Pacqué, Karl-Heinz. 2009. *Die Bilanz: Eine wirtschaftliche Analyse der Deutschen Einheit*. Munich: Hanser.

Port, Andrew. 2009. *Conflict and Stability in the German Democratic Republic*. Cambridge: Cambridge University Press.

Preußen, Versuch einer Bilanz: Eine Ausstellung der Berliner Festspiele GmbH, 15. August–15. November 1981, Gropius-Bau (ehemaliges Kunstgewerbemuseum) Berlin. Katalog in fünf Bänden. 1981. Reinbek bei Hamburg: Rowohlt.

Roberts, Adam, and Timothy Garton Ash, eds. *Civil Resistance and Power Politics: The Experience of Non-violent Action from Gandhi to the Present*. Oxford: Oxford University Press.

Schivelbusch, Wolfgang. 2001. *Die Kultur der Niederlage: Der amerikanische Süden 1865, Frankreich 1871, Deutschland 1918*. Berlin: Fest.

Schröder, Klaus. 1998. *Der SED-Staat: Partei, Staat und Gesellschaft 1949–1990*. Munich: Hanser.

Seibel, Wolfgang. 2005. *Verwaltete Illusionen: Die Privatisierung der DDR-Wirstchaft durch die Treuhandanstalt und ihre Nachfolger 1990–2000*. Frankfurt am Main: Campus.

Smolar, Aleksander. 2009. "Towards 'Self-limiting Revolution': Poland, 1970–89." In Roberts and Ash 2009, 127–43.

Weitz, Eric D. 2007. *Weimar Germany: Promise and Tragedy*. Princeton, NJ: Princeton University Press.

Williams, Kieran. 2009. "Civil Resistance in Czechoslovakia: From Soviet Invasion to 'Velvet Revolution,' 1968–89." In Roberts and Ash 2009, 110–26.

Wolle, Stefan. 1998. *Die heile Welt der Diktatur: Alltag und Herrschaft in der DDR 1971–1989*. Berlin: Chr. Links Verlag.

Zatlin, Jonathan R. 2007. *The Currency of Socialism: Money and Political Culture in East Germany*. Cambridge: Cambridge University Press.

2: Reconstituting the Federal Republic? Constitutional Law and Politics before and since 1989

Andreas Niederberger

The German Basic Law

CONSTITUTIONS ARE AMONG the most important yet peculiar political inventions of the modern age. They are agreements that, in most respects, do not differ at all from other political agreements or declarations of intent. Nevertheless, and strangely enough, constitutions make it possible for political orders to be established, directed, maintained, and controlled. Unfortunately, the establishment of a constitution is not always sufficient for its implementation, and there are many examples of constitutions that have not succeeded. They are, generally, declarations of intent written at a specific historical moment such as the end of a war, a revolution, or even the death of a long-time ruler. Furthermore, it is not the "will of the powerful" that implements the constitution. This is important because otherwise, the powerful would simply make use of constitutions to perpetuate their advantage over the weaker members of society. Following Hannah Arendt, successful constitutions might be understood as examples of "communicative power." They exercise a unifying force and bind everyone in a given polity (including the powerful) to a common structure by "founding a new authority" (Arendt 2006, 174). This force and authority cannot be reduced to the amount of resources the "willing" have at their disposal.[1]

The Basic Law has been the constitution of western Germany for more than sixty-five years now, and of eastern and unified Germany for over twenty-five years. Debate about a new German constitution is almost entirely absent in German politics today, despite the fact that the global economic crisis, the threat of international terrorism, and the development of the European Union have presented and present challenges that were unknown to the authors of the Basic Law. On the contrary, the political parties mutually accuse one another of violating the foundations of the Basic Law with respect to particular policies: for instance, in the areas of domestic security, military operations abroad, fiscal policy, or the increasing integration of Europe. This situation is fundamentally different from the debates in 1989/90. At that time, the controversy over the constitution of unified Germany and especially over the establishment of a common constitution was one of the central issues both in the public sphere as well as in the unification negotiations between the Federal Republic of Germany and the German Democratic Republic. This chapter highlights some of the important characteristics of the Basic Law and then examines key topics in the constitutional debates of 1989/90. It concludes with some considerations on the current status of the Basic Law in German politics and how this status has evolved since 1990.

In the chapter I present two main arguments: First, I argue that it is overly simplistic to describe the unification of the FRG and the GDR without a new constitution as a mere continuation of the West German constitutional order before 1989. The wording of the Basic Law, in fact, was changed only in a few essential passages. Nevertheless, as a result of both—of the debates that took place during the unification process and of the unification process itself—the Basic Law was in certain respects "newly" constituted. This "new" constitutionalization took the form of the acknowledgment that a kind of constitutionalism, a removal of certain constitutive and essential features of the political process from everyday politics, was necessary for maintaining the political order. Second, and in view of the situation since 1990, I claim that the transition from constitution to constitutionalism has not only increased the visibility of the Basic Law and its importance for politics but has also entailed the growing importance of "constitutional politics," in contrast to normal or everyday politics. Constitutional politics, in turn, runs the dual risk of either politicizing the constitution or depoliticizing and juridifying politics—two tendencies that have been observed in German politics since unification. Against this backdrop, the current, supposedly unquestioned status of the Basic Law turns out to be much more precarious than it may at first appear.

It is already clear from these initial statements that the concept of the constitution is ambiguous and multidimensional. In a debate central to German constitutional thought, Hans Kelsen ([1931] 2008) and Carl Schmitt ([1931] 1996) clearly demonstrated in the early 1930s, despite the fundamental differences in their arguments and opinions, that there are two important dimensions to a constitution, which are independent of each other. A constitution is, on the one hand, the act by which a political community or state forms itself or emerges as such. Without a community or state referring to itself, there can be no political order and no legal structure. A type of (at least symbolic) unification qua constitution (and this means qua constituting act) is thus required for any polity. On the other hand, this constitution is not merely a contingent fact that (powerful or charismatic) actors are able to bring about at will. The persons affected or involved must know on which principles and rules the polity is based. For it is only on such grounds that they can identify the polity not only as a context established by obligations to a specific person or party or by mutual obligations among persons currently living within a given territory but as a common *polity*. The ability to identify (with) the polity as such (and not only with the actors who embody it at a given time) is an essential prerequisite if a community is to preserve its continuity in the face of changing political personnel and across succeeding generations of the population.

A *constitution* is therefore usually a *document* that establishes the foundations of a political system.[2] These foundations may consist of the allocation of responsibilities to institutions and actors, the regulation of relationships among these institutions and actors (i.e., through the separation or structuring of powers), and the establishment of fundamental rights as well as other principles judged to be important by and for the political system.[3] *Constitutionalism*, on the other hand, refers to a specific form of political system. This form is distinguished by the fact that the political actors or authorities involved recognize or are forced to recognize that certain conditions are necessary for the functioning and upholding of the political system, which must remain apart from everyday politics (see Elster and Slagstad 1988, among others). This does not, however, exclude the possibility of arguments about what exactly these conditions are, or what they should or must consist of; such debates can be understood, in contrast to everyday politics, as *constitutional politics*.[4]

This chapter, thus, will use important distinctions in constitutional law and theory to provide for a more adequate understanding of the transformation the German constitution underwent during the unification process and in the wake of this process. In contrast to common readings of the Basic Law as primarily setting up a value order (*Werteordnung*), it is argued that even though the constitution contains strong normative entitlements and obligations and limits state power with regard to these requirements, it is more important to understand the constitutionalist democracy that emerged with the confirmation of the Basic Law in 1990. The result of this confirmation was not simply the extension of the values contained in the constitution to the former East Germany but the acknowledgment of the necessity of a constitutional order going along with the opening of a space for constitutional politics.

The Basic Law from 1948 to 1989: From "Foreign Domination" to "Constitutional Patriotism"

The Basic Law was developed between July 1948 and May 1949, rather against the will of German politicians than on their initiative. The occupying Western powers had an interest in forming a West German state in order to alleviate the tensions with the Soviet Union. Accordingly, they pressured the newly emerging West German political elite into working out a constitution and reserved for themselves the right to approve or reject it in the end. Other than this final say, however, the Western Allies only specified a few direct requirements, such as their insistence on a "consistently federalist state structure" (Winkler 2000, 131). The Basic Law was drafted on this basis, first in August 1948 at a small conference on the island of Herrenchiemsee in Bavaria and then from September 1948 onward in the Parliamentary Council in Bonn.[5] A point of departure, as well as an essential point of reference, was provided by the Weimar Constitution. On the one hand, its weaknesses were understood to be important factors in the rise of the Nazis. On the other hand, in many respects it represented the political coordinate system of the Parliamentary Council's members, many of whom had been politicians or lawyers during the Weimar period and had joined the Parliamentary Council in part because so many of the younger generation had been compromised by their involvement in the Nazi regime.[6]

Five aspects of the Basic Law were particularly important for West German politics. First, the Basic Law begins with a catalog of fundamental individual rights, which it explicitly states are applicable law. This is a departure from earlier conceptions of fundamental rights, such as those expressed in the Paulskirchenverfassung, the constitution developed by the revolutionary assembly in Frankfurt in 1848 (Grimm 2001, 91–106), or in the Weimar Constitution. It means that they are not only rights of defense against the state, but, in accordance with their "third-party effect" (*Drittwirkung*),[7] they also oblige the state to provide its citizens with goods and services and even to ensure that fundamental rights are not violated in interactions between citizens. The Basic Law is thus a reaction to the serious violations of fundamental rights that occurred during the Nazi period. But it also turns German constitutional thought upside down by giving fundamental individual rights priority over the state and even over their own legal specifications (which previous constitutional theories had considered to be the main reason for the priority of the state over fundamental rights).

Second, the Basic Law establishes a parliamentary democracy in which the president is largely a symbolic figure, while the parliament (specifically, the lower chamber of parliament, the Bundestag) elects the most important authority in the executive branch, the chancellor. This secures the legislature a central position in the political system and strongly ties the executive branch to the law. Moreover, with the "constructive vote of no confidence" (*konstruktives Misstrauensvotum*), the Basic Law sets up a mechanism designed to limit the instability of government. The government—or more precisely, the chancellor—can be voted out of office only if the new chancellor is able to come up with a parliamentary majority within a period of forty-eight hours. Simply voting a government out of office is therefore impossible.

Third, the form of federalism in Germany remains to this day one of the most controversial points of the Basic Law. The controversies surrounding this issue concern, above all, questions regarding the aptly named *Finanzverfassung*, the federal regulation of finances, and the distribution of responsibilities between the union and the Länder, for example, with respect to science and education policies. Further points of contention in this context include the rules that give the Federal Council (*Bundesrat*), the upper chamber, veto power with regard to legislation that affects both the federal and the individual state levels. Another major deviation from earlier German political and legal structures is, fourth, the creation of the Federal Constitutional Court, to which Article 93 of the Basic Law explicitly assigns the function of "judicial review," that is, determining whether laws and executive decisions are compatible with the Basic Law. The Basic Law establishes this court as an authority designed to safeguard the existence of the constitution. At the same time, it intentionally excludes measures allowing for a state of emergency, which might protect the existence of the state in a crisis. Fifth, the establishment of the Constitutional Court finds its counterpart in the so-called eternity clause (*Ewigkeitsklausel*) of Article 79(3) of the Basic Law. This clause holds that any significant change to the essential tenets of the Basic Law—i.e., fundamental rights, the separation of political powers, as well as the principle of federalism—is prohibited. This has played an important role in the increasing significance of the Federal Constitutional Court in (West) German politics, and it can be seen in the court's ruling on the European Union's Lisbon Treaty, in which the court sets limits on the extent to which sovereignty can be handed over from Germany to the EU. We will return to the latter toward the end of this chapter.

In summary, it can be stated that, despite all of the ways in which the Basic Law reacts to the supposed or real expectations of the Allied occupying forces, it outlines a structure without precedent either in the Allied political systems or in German history. One key characteristic of this political structure is that the Federal Republic is first and foremost a *Rechtsstaat* (constitutional state under the rule of law), a democracy, a federal state, and a welfare state; that is, before it is a state that can itself claim value and protection, it first serves certain functions on behalf of its citizens and their interactions.

Between 1949 and 1989, the Basic Law was subject to serious challenges only a few times. Such challenges occurred, for instance, in the context of the debate over West Germany's rearmament and especially during the student protests and the Red Army Faction terrorist attacks in the late 1960s and throughout the 1970s. During this period, in 1968, the West German parliament adopted emergency acts (*Notstandsgesetze*) in fulfillment of the expectations of the Allied forces, who saw the acts as a condition for the protection of their presence on West German territory. At the same time, these acts relativized a core principle of the Basic Law, namely the fundamental primacy of law over the state. On the other hand, and in some sense contrary to the aforementioned decision, the Federal Constitutional Court had been asserting its relevance to West German politics as early as the 1950s, primarily by rendering pioneering judgments in various crucial cases dealing with fundamental rights.[8]

One effect of the West German political order established by the Basic Law was the increasing juridification of politics and state administration, which in turn was an essential precondition for their democratization and for parliamentary control. Article 24 and especially Article 25 also established that international legal norms were directly applicable in German law. This was to prevent the Federal Republic from ever waging war on its own.

Overall, the rule of law, the establishment of democracy, the strong role given to and general applicability of fundamental rights, and the integration of the FRG into the international order formed a propitious environment for West Germany's moderate left to promote the idea of "constitutional patriotism" in the 1970s and 1980s. This concept was first developed in 1979 by Dolf Sternberger (1990) and then prominently taken up by Jürgen Habermas (1987, 135).[9] The reference to constitutional patriotism attempts to establish a particular form of obligation and even loyalty to a polity. It derives from the fact that citizens identify with their political system, which in the case of West Germany essentially consisted of a constitutional and democratic structure that was ultimately fully integrated into international law and also allowed for a critical reflection on German history. Particularly in the context of the so-called historians' quarrel (*Historikerstreit*) of the mid-1980s, constitutional patriotism—and with it, the idea of a republican-democratic state—became the core of a distinctly West German political identity. It stood in opposition to a cultural or ethnic nation-based understanding of the state's fundamental elements and meant abandoning the goal of uniting the two German states.

The Provisional Arrangement is Past: Constitutional Debates during the *Wende-Zeit*

At least since the first and only free and general election of the People's Chamber (*Volkskammer*) on March 18, 1990, it was clear that, given the economic pressures created by East German citizens eager to emigrate,[10] the unification of the GDR with the Federal Republic would occur sooner rather than later. In light of this anticipation, the debate about the form of unification took center stage. This also meant debating the question of whether Germany would adopt a new constitution or whether the GDR would come under the purview of the Basic Law. The background of this discussion was, on the one hand, the constitutional debate, which was initiated primarily by the East German civil rights movement and took place from December 1989 through March 1990 at the so-called Central Round Table (*Zentraler Runder Tisch*). On the other hand, the provisions of Articles 23 and 146 of the Basic Law framed the issue. As already mentioned, in 1948/49 there was initial resistance in West Germany to the establishment of a distinct state on the territory of the Western Allied occupying forces, which politicians feared would render any future German unity impossible. As a result, they stressed the provisional character of the West German constitution, despite the fact that this did not become apparent in the content of the Basic Law. In this respect, the Basic Law was, from the beginning, a full constitution in the legal and political sense. Its provisional character was expressed by its name ("Basic Law" rather than "Constitution") and, even more important to the debates of 1990, in the Preamble along with Article 146. The Preamble held that the Basic Law also acts "on behalf of those Germans to whom participation was denied"[11] and that "the entire German people is called upon to accomplish, by free self-determination, the unity and freedom of Germany" (Basic Law, version of May 23, 1949, Preamble). Accordingly, the Basic Law ended with Article 146, which stated: "This Basic Law shall become invalid on the day when a constitution adopted in a free decision by the German people comes into force." At the same time, Article 23 offered the opportunity for nonparticipating German territories to later come under the purview of the Basic Law: "For the time being, this Basic Law shall apply in the territory of the Länder Baden, Bavaria, Bremen, Greater Berlin, Hamburg, Hesse, Lower Saxony, North Rhine-Westphalia, Rhineland-Palatinate, Schleswig-Holstein, Württemberg-Baden and Württemberg-Hohenzollern. It shall be put into force for other parts of Germany on their accession." The Saarland became part of the Federal Republic in this way in 1957.

In the debates of spring and summer 1990, the East German civil rights movement, with partial support from the West German Green Party, defended the view that the new Germany should be built on a new consensus or new common identity, that is, on a new constitution, as envisioned in Article 146. On the one hand, this view was based on the consideration that East Germans' new "civil rights" self-confidence should also be expressed as an explicit act of civil society establishing a new political system. Accordingly, a referendum on a new constitution was a critical priority. At the same time, the civil rights movement, along with other forces of opposition to state socialism in the GDR as well as various political factions in West Germany, called for certain deficiencies in the Basic Law to be corrected and missing points added. The constitutional draft developed by the Round Table came very close to the structure and political order already established by the Basic Law. But it also included a series of new rights and state functions, as well as limits to state authority, which went beyond the rights and distribution of powers found in the Basic Law. These entailed the obligation of the state to actively promote equal rights and opportunities for men and women (as opposed to merely preventing the creation of inequalities),[12] the right of women to abortion,[13] the right of all citizens to have their personal information protected and to be given access to information collected by the state about them,[14] the freedom of the arts[15] and sciences,[16] special rights for the elderly and for disabled persons,[17] the right to a free education (i.e., the obligation of the state to provide education free of charge),[18] the right to affordable housing (i.e., the obligation of the state to provide affordable housing),[19] the right to work including further rights regarding the organization of the workplace (Articles 26–32), the obligation of the state to protect the environment,[20] special rights for civic associations,[21] and the right to petition for referenda (Article 98). Moreover, the draft constitution contained a number of more detailed rules that were not present in the Basic Law for the organization of the courts, criminal law, and codes of procedure (Articles 12–14), and for the regulation of television and radio broadcasting (Article 15), as well as articulating the principle that there must be a parliamentary opposition.[22] These were all reactions to the particular experiences of East Germany. Finally, the draft constitution declared its support of the aim of German unity, while adding specific instructions regarding how a common constitution would have to be developed, including specifically requiring a referendum for any new common constitution to be considered valid.[23]

In addition to the civil rights movement and other left-progressive forces in East and West Germany, conservative politicians also promoted unification based on a new constitution. In their view, this would "overcome" the precarious situation of the West German state and add legitimacy to the Basic Law. In this way, the new Germany, sovereign once again, would approach the supposed normality of other European nation-states. Considered superficially, both this desire for "normality" as well as the civil rights movement's and the left's striving for a more (fundamentally) democratic, social, and ecological constitution were thwarted. With the Treaty of Unification (*Einigungsvertrag*), the East German states joined the Federal Republic in accordance with Article 23.[24] Certain changes were made to the Basic Law (see Article 4 of the Treaty of Unification), but these concerned only the references to the provisional character of the Basic Law contained in the Preamble and in Article 146, as well as the integration of new Länder into the federal structure. After unification, Article 23 was repealed to emphasize that united Germany would make no further claims to the formerly German territories of Poland and what was then Czechoslovakia. The Treaty of Unification also demanded that deliberations be held regarding a more extensive revision of the Basic Law. This demand has, however, remained largely unmet.

Formally, the GDR joined the FRG; no constitutional convention convened, and no popular vote on the constitution took place. It remains difficult to judge the process in either political or legal terms. The standard interpretation is that most West German politicians had no interest in a constitutional debate and, moreover, were not willing to expose either the constitution or themselves to the danger of a referendum. Lawyers like the former justice at the Constitutional Court Dieter Grimm, who argued for the necessity of a referendum on the basis of Article 146, however, had maintained even at the beginning of the discussion in 1989/90 that there were good reasons not to decide in light of a false juxtaposition of Articles 23 (accession) and 146 (new constitution). In his view, the Basic Law in its current form could well be submitted to a referendum and possibly supplemented by additional articles generally recognized to be necessary or desirable (Grimm 2001, 35).

Looking at the composition of the united German parliament after the election on December 2, 1990, one can scarcely deny that, in a referendum on whether the unchanged or only slightly modified Basic Law should be adopted as a constitution for all of Germany, a majority would have voted in its favor.[25] Such a reconstruction of the process is, however, admissible only if one accepts the premise that the act of constitution-making, which is often taken to be the symbolic founding moment of a polity, is not necessary for the assumption that a constitution is legally valid. Many reject this premise, either highlighting the unifying and ultimately constitutive character of symbolic constitutional acts or pointing to the necessity of a democratic process in constitutional design for the validity of the constitution or at least of its principles (Arato 1995).

But even with—and probably particularly in—its presumably democratic perspective, this rejection neglects a premise of its own argumentation: Republics can only claim legitimacy for their laws, measures, and institutions if they assure that the constitutional order allows the participation of everyone subjected to them, both in the process of lawmaking and in the selection of those who exercise power. This also applies to the process of constitution-making. Here too, it is essential—especially when constituting political structures and institutions in heterogeneous and pluralistic societies—to make it clear that everyone who will later live under the constitution is able to get involved in the process. Accordingly, one must always presuppose a more fundamental political or legal structure that guarantees that everyone has the opportunity to make himself or herself heard in all relevant respects. This cannot be ensured by a democratic procedure of constitution-making, because the procedure as such does not and cannot decide who will or will not be involved in it. Including everyone who is or might be significantly affected by the ensuing constitution requires the observation of a principle creating obligations for such inclusion. Such a principle cannot itself be subject to a democratic decision, and its validity cannot depend on any decision of a constitutional convention. It can only be realized within a constitutionalist structure in which those deliberating and making decisions always acknowledge a priori that they do not dispose of the constitutive principles for their political order. Empirically, constitutions might arise from democratic decisions (most still do not), but from a normative point of view, this cannot be the (sole) source from which the constitution draws its validity.

Viewed from this perspective, the decision in 1990 not to call up a constitutional convention and thus not to perform a symbolic establishment of the new Germany was correct. Constitutions are without a doubt the result of empirical decisions based on actual convictions and interests in specific historical circumstances. This is why they are in many respects bound to their time and eventually require revisions—revisions that must result from democratic deliberations and decisions.[26] There is no ideal constitution. But if constitutions are considered systematically and from a republican perspective, they cannot be understood as the expression of a specific decision if they want to claim legitimacy. In other words, they cannot be understood this way unless it is already clear from the very outset of the process for prepolitical, possibly cultural or racial, reasons who the citizens of the polity will be, or unless a people already forming an admissible unit creates a constitution for itself. These are the only cases in which one could establish "empirically" whether everyone "was asked." But this only shifts the focus. It does not answer the ultimately decisive question: Under which conditions is a particular group legitimized to form a common political order excluding others who may still be subjected to the decisions of this order? Obviously, the will of those forming the order cannot be sufficient.

This leads to the first thesis of this chapter: Germany's decision not to call a constitutional convention or hold a referendum can be understood as an acknowledgment of the need for a constitution if a legitimate political order is to exist at all. At the same time, it was also an acknowledgment that nearly all parts of the constitution could be amended. Therefore, the "particular obligation" of the symbolic act of explicitly establishing a new constitution could be forgone in the case of the creation of the new Germany. Accordingly, Germany's constitution was transformed during the process of unification into a kind of constitutionalism; the Basic Law's importance and necessity were emphasized and renewed, yet at the same time, a space for constitutional politics was created.[27]

The Basic Law since Unification:
A More Prominent Constitution and More
Constitutional Change than Ever Before

Developments since 1990 offer strong support for the thesis that the process of German unification implied the transition from a narrow concept of the constitution to a more generally constitutionalist political structure. As noted at the beginning of this chapter, discussion of the need for or desirability of a new constitution has largely disappeared since unification. At the same time, there has been a significant increase in political and institutional debates about the limits that the Basic Law (rightly or wrongly) sets for politics and about further refining its principles and precepts. This can be demonstrated by two important examples showing how (parts of) the legislature and the Federal Constitutional Court have come into conflict.

A controversy about the right to abortion occurred in 1992/93, still in the aftermath of the constitutional discussions of the unification process. As mentioned briefly above, the draft constitution produced by the Round Table included the continuation of the GDR's practice of essentially leaving decisions about abortion to pregnant women themselves. With unification, this practice became illegal, and women in the former East Germany were subject to the much more restrictive rules of paragraphs 218 and 218a of the West German Criminal Code. These paragraphs allowed abortions mostly for medical reasons or reasons relevant to criminal law (e.g., pregnancy resulting from rape). The Treaty of Unification obligated the Bundestag to create rules that were closer to those of the GDR; the Bundestag thus amended §218a of the Criminal Code in 1992, codifying the so-called *Fristenlösung*, or time-limit solution, according to which a woman would be legally allowed to have an abortion up to the twelfth week of a pregnancy, following an obligatory consultation.[28]

In 1993, the Federal Constitutional Court decided that this amendment did not conform to the principle of human dignity laid down in Article 1(1) of the Basic Law.[29] It held that, according to the Basic Law, the state has a fundamental duty to protect human life and thus is prohibited from allowing the deliberate killing of one human being by another. The court instead "derived" an alternative regulation from the Basic Law, which the Bundestag largely adopted in 1995 and which in essence corresponded to the amendment of 1992, particularly with respect to the consequences for women and medical doctors. The alternative regulation, however, changes the nature of the consultation, which is supposed now to steer women toward giving birth. And it does not declare impunity but rather changes the legal framework by shifting cases of abortion within the first twelve weeks of pregnancy away from the penalization of (other cases of abortion in) Article 218.[30] This decision met with massive criticism from the German public for three major reasons. First, many Germans (including Rita Süssmuth, member of the Christian Democrats and then president of the Bundestag) viewed the decision as expressing a paternalistic understanding of society, since according to the ruling, women were deemed incapable of making their own decisions, while (male) experts were presumed to know altogether more about the well-being of women than women themselves. Second, East Germans who increasingly had the impression that they were the losers in unification considered the ruling a sign of contempt. They saw it as a decision conceived from the point of view of some kind of eternal (religious) order for the world, not as the result of deliberate decisions in the social and political process of unification. Along these lines, many critics read the decision as an expression of the arbitrariness of judges with respect to the parliament's legislative procedures, which they viewed as the real site of democracy.[31]

Interestingly enough, these criticisms were almost exclusively directed at the justices of the Constitutional Court, as opposed to the Basic Law itself. At no time did critics of the decision demand a revision of Article 1(1) of the Basic Law or the acknowledgment that it is an "empty signifier" open to politicization. Rather, they claimed that the justices had projected religious content onto this article and thus engaged in constitutional politics by shifting the political terrain relevant to the abortion issue. Most critics accepted the Basic Law as a frame and limit, yet rejected the justices' claim to know better than either the legislature or individual women when the Basic Law had been violated.

The Federal Constitutional Court's decision to modify the right of asylum was greeted with the opposite response. As early as the 1980s, there were debates within the Federal Republic about the need to limit the right of asylum, which Article 16(2) of the Basic Law unequivocally protected. It granted asylum to everyone who was politically persecuted, and it was included in the Basic Law owing to the experiences of many emigrants during the Nazi period who had encountered difficulties obtaining long-term legal status in their host countries. Since the right of asylum was one of the few ways for non-Germans to receive residence permits in the FRG, over the years more and more people who were not political refugees applied for asylum.

There were many attacks on immigrants in east and west Germany in the early 1990s following unification. Many politicians and journalists explained these attacks as resulting from the German population's disapproval of the "abuse of asylum," despite condemnation of the attacks by local politicians (who were, in fact, responsible for the police who in some cases failed to intervene). In 1993, under pressure from the CSU and with significant parts of the SPD supporting the ruling CDU/CSU/FDP coalition, a two-thirds majority of the Bundestag voted to amend Article 16(2). The new Article 16a largely divests the right of asylum of its nature as a fundamental right, transforming it into a voluntary act of benevolence on part of the German state that the Bundestag can change at will. In addition, the change introduced the so-called third-state regulation, which allows the Federal Republic to refuse access to asylum procedures to persons who have entered Germany via "safe third states." The question of the rights of asylum seekers is therefore no longer a constitutional issue but is now dependent on everyday politics or on the political realities of the capacities and reach of the state.

Opponents of this change to the Basic Law filed a complaint with the Constitutional Court. This led to the decision in 1996 that changing the Basic Law with the aim of limiting the right of asylum was in fact permissible.[32] According to the court's decision, Article 1(1) does not protect the right of asylum, which is a fundamental right in some respects, but not one that the state must guarantee in all circumstances. Therefore, the third-state regulation is also valid, as in these cases the German state is not necessarily the addressee of the legal claim that the asylum seekers make. In contrast to the decision on abortion, most Germans agreed with the court's opinion in this case because it pointed out the limitations of the constitution and thus left room for political action. Yet critics argued that in this case the interpretation of the Basic Law ought to have been more restrictive.[33] In their view, the reasons for flight and migration are often life-threatening situations and therefore frequently constitute the danger of a violation of human dignity. In the eyes of these critics, the Basic Law must not allow the question of whether the state should or should not grant asylum in life-threatening situations to be decided *politically*.

The discussions that preceded the Bundestag's decisions about abortion and the right of asylum, as well as those that followed the respective decisions of the Federal Constitutional Court, highlight the fact that unification has not created a clear division between politics and the Basic Law. Instead, the tension between the two has moved to the center of the debate. While some consider a given issue to be a matter of constitutional politics, requiring special procedural consideration, for others, the same issue is a matter of "normal" politics for which a simple parliamentary majority should suffice. Interestingly enough, since the end of the 1990s it has primarily been the political left—i.e., many of those who argued in 1990 for a new, common constitution—that has tried, with varying levels of success, to stop political decisions by asking the Constitutional Court to rule on the issues at stake. Examples of this include the so-called Great Wiretapping Operation (*Großer Lauschangriff*), the foreign deployment of Germany's armed forces, measures adopted for the tightening of domestic security since September 11, 2001, and the extension of life spans of nuclear power plants. For the left, the Basic Law—given its origins in the period of overcoming the Nazi era as an attempt to prevent any reversion to Nazism—ought to serve in its basic elements as a protection against the "sovereign normalization" of Germany and the return of the security state.

Recent developments in the debate show how far Germany has come on the way from constitutional state to constitutionalist republican polity. In the summer of 2009, the Federal Constitutional Court rendered a decision on the EU Lisbon Treaty, declaring that the treaty was valid but also pointing to severe threats to the sovereignty of the German people if the integration of the EU were to go any further. The court developed a detailed view of the foundations of democracy in Germany and highlighted limits on permissible delegation of political responsibilities—a core subject in any conception of a constitution.[34] This decision has, in turn, led to a far-reaching political, legal, and theoretical debate. Are the arguments of the Federal Constitutional Court against the transfer of responsibilities convincing? Is the model of a constitutionalist democracy as a single state with its own constitutional court still legitimate in a transnational order as represented by the EU? And, finally, what is the future of the principles and procedures of a constitutionalist democracy in an age of globalization and transnational order in general?[35]

The Basic Law has in a certain sense survived unification intact and has contributed in many ways to the integration of the new Länder into the order of the old Federal Republic. At the same time, it must be acknowledged that the German constitution no longer represents an enshrined framework beyond the reach of politics with which a "militant democracy" (*wehrhafte Demokratie*) can protect itself against those who wish to destroy its presumably humanistic political system. The importance, scope, and content of the Basic Law have themselves become subjects of politics—not always of *everyday politics* but of *constitutional politics* as well, which perpetuates the debate about the foundations of the German political system.

Notes

[1] Regarding the understanding of power as "communicative power," see Niederberger (2009).

[2] The cases of Great Britain and Israel, which do not have a written constitution, show that the existence of such a document is not a necessary condition for the constitution of a polity in the two dimensions discussed above. See Tomkins (2005).

[3] One issue, for instance, which will not be central in this chapter, is the tendency seen during the creation of new constitutions for the East German *Bundesländer* in the early 1990s to declare ecological sustainability a major constitutional goal. See Denninger (1994).

[4] On the difference between "normal" and "constitutional" politics, see Ackerman (1991).

[5] On the historic steps toward the creation of the Basic Law, see Bommarius (2009) and Möllers (2009, 18–38).

[6] Möllers (2008) suggests more generally that constitutional law theory in West Germany after 1945 was dominated by theories developed during the German Empire and the Weimar Republic, whereas constitutional law as such was characterized by pragmatism and reservations to theory.

[7] See footnote 8 on the "third-party effect."

[8] One should mention the so-called Lüth decision, which established the "third-party effect" of fundamental rights, that is, their applicability in private legal relations and the duty of the state to enforce them in interactions among "private parties" (BVerfG 7, 198, January 15, 1958), and the first broadcasting decision, which acknowledged the importance of free media for a democratic public sphere (BVerfG 12, 205, February 28, 1961).

[9] For more general remarks on this debate, see Müller (2007).

[10] For more on this idea, see Fulbrook (2001, 275–79).

[11] The constitutional lawyer Isensee (1992) refers to this in order to justify why it is desirable that the GDR join the FRG.

[12] Art. 3(2): "The state has the duty to work toward the equal status and treatment of women in their professional and public life, in education and in job training, in the family as well as in the domain of social security." For the German text see http://www.documentarchiv.de/ddr/1990/ddr-verfassungsentwurf_rundertisch.html (last consulted on December 28, 2016).

[13] Art. 4(3): "Women have the right to take their own decisions on their pregnancy. The state shall protect unborn life by offering social support."

[14] Art. 8(2): "Everyone has the right to their own personal data and to access files and documents that concern them. Without voluntary and explicit consent of the rights holder, no personal data may be collected, saved, used, processed, or forwarded. Limitations to this right require a law and rights holders must be notified of them."

[15] Art. 20: "(1) The arts are free. (2) Cultural life as well as the conservation and transmission of cultural heritage shall be supported. Necessary means to do so must be reserved in the federal, Länder, and communal budgets."

[16] Art. 19(1): "Science is free. The state shall protect the exercise of freedom in research and teaching."

[17] Art. 23: "(1) The polity shall respect old age. It shall respect disability. (2) Every citizen has the right to social security against the consequences of illness, accidents, invalidity, disability, the need for long-term care, old age, and unemployment. (3) Public insurance systems will guarantee this right. Everyone has the right and obligation to participate in these systems."

[18] Art. 24(1): "Every citizen has the right to equal and free of charge access to public education and job training institutions."

[19] Art. 25: "Every citizen has the right to adequate housing. There must be legal protection against rent cancellations. In balancing the interests of the tenant and the owner of an apartment, the state must attribute special weight to the overriding importance of an apartment to leading a human life in dignity. Evictions can only be carried out if there is an alternative. (2) Social housing and the preservation of housing must be subsidized."

[20] Art. 33(1): "The protection of the natural environment as the basis of life for current and future generations is a duty of the state and of all citizens. State environmental policy must take precautions against the occurrence of harmful environmental effects and it must work toward the economical use and reuse of nonrenewable resources and toward an efficient use of energy."

[21] Art. 35: "(1) Associations devoting themselves to public affairs and contributing to the formation of public opinion (civil rights movements) shall benefit from the special protection of the constitution, as actors in the realm of open societal creation, critique, and control. (2) Civil rights movements whose activities extend to a certain domain of a Land or the federal level have the right to present and to have a fair discussion of their concerns in the commissions of the People's Chamber or of the parliaments of the Länder. They are entitled—if no third parties' person and privacy are affected—to access information held by the public administration that is relevant to their concerns, after proper weight has been granted to conflicting public interests."

[22] Art. 51(2): "The opposition is a necessary component of parliamentary democracy. It confronts the governing majority as an alternative and has a right to equal opportunities."

[23] Art. 132: "(1) If unification is realized by accession to the Federal Republic of Germany, the conditions under which the Basic Law applies to the current territory of the German Democratic Republic must be regulated by agreement. . . . (2) To be valid, the agreement requires the consent of two thirds of the members of the People's Chamber and confirmation in a referendum. (3) This agreement should contain rules on the accelerated adjustment of the economic productivity of the parts of the state on the current territory of the GDR and the living conditions of their inhabitants to the conditions on the current territory of the FRG. In order to guarantee the rights of the citizens of the GDR to participate in the democratic self-determination of the German people, attempts should be made to form a constitutional convention for all of Germany. (4) In addition, the agreement must ensure that the human and civic rights guaranteed by this constitution will continue to apply to the current territory of the GDR, even if they are not included in the Basic Law."

[24] The Treaty between the Federal Republic of Germany and the German Democratic Republic to establish German Unification, Article 1.

[25] A poll by the Wickert-Institutes in February 1990 showed that almost 90 percent of West Germans and approximately 84 percent of East Germans wanted the Basic Law as the constitution for unified Germany.

[26] Cf. on this issue the American debate among constitutional lawyers since the 1930s on the idea of a "living constitution," for instance in Strauss (2010).

[27] For a more detailed description of this transformation from constitution to constitutionalism, see Niederberger (2008, 183–206).

[28] Cf. Bundesgesetzblatt 1992, Part I, p. 1402: "§ 218a. Exception to liability for abortion —(1) The abortion is not unlawful if 1. the pregnant woman requests the termination of the pregnancy and demonstrates to the physician by certificate pursuant to section 219(3) 2nd sentence that she obtained counseling at least three days before the operation (Counseling to a pregnant woman in a situation of hardship and conflict); 2. the termination of the pregnancy is performed by a physician; and 3. no more than twelve weeks have elapsed since conception."

[29] Cf. BVerfGE 88, 203-Schwangerschaftsabbruch II, May 28, 1993.

[30] Cf. the current version of §218a: "§ 218a. Exception to liability for abortion— (1) The offence under section 218 shall not be deemed committed if 1. the pregnant woman requests the termination of the pregnancy and demonstrates to the physician by certificate pursuant to section 219(2) 2nd sentence that she obtained counseling at least three days before the operation; 2. the termination of the pregnancy is performed by a physician; and 3. no more than twelve weeks have elapsed since conception."

[31] See Hermes & Walter (1993) on the debate regarding the Federal Constitutional Court's decision on abortion.

[32] Cf. BVerfGE 94, 49—May 14, 1996.

[33] See also the Committee for Fundamental Rights and Democracy's comment on the judgment: http://www.friedenskooperative.de/komitee/komit014.htm (last consulted on December 28, 2016).

[34] Cf. BVerfG, 2 BvE 2/08—June 30, 2009.

[35] For an overview of this debate, consult the *Zeitschrift für europarechtliche Studien* 4 (2009), and in a more systematic perspective, Niederberger (2014).

Works Cited

Ackerman, Bruce. 1991. *We the People: 1. Foundations.* Cambridge, MA: Harvard University Press.

Arato, Andrew. 1995. "Forms of Constitution Making and Theories of Democracy." *Cardozo Law Review* 17: 191–231.

Arendt, Hannah. 2006. *On Revolution.* London: Penguin.

Bommarius, Christian. 2009. *Das Grundgesetz: Eine Biographie.* Berlin: Rowohlt.

Brunkhorst, Hauke, Regina Kreide, and Cristina Lafont, eds. 2009. *Habermas-Handbuch. Leben—Werk—Wirkung.* Stuttgart: Metzler.

Denninger, Erhard. 1994. *Menschenrechte und Grundgesetz.* Weinheim: Beltz Athenäum.

Elster, Jon, and Ruth Slagstad, eds. 1988. *Constitutionalism and Democracy.* Cambridge: Cambridge University Press.

Fulbrook, Mary. 2001. *History of Germany 1918–2000: The Divided Nation.* Malden, MA: Blackwell.

Grimm, Dieter. 2001. *Die Verfassung und die Politik: Einsprüche in Störfällen*. Munich: Beck.

Habermas, Jürgen. 1987. *Eine Art Schadensabwicklung*. Frankfurt am Main: Suhrkamp.

Hermes, Georg, and Susanne Walther. 1993. "Schwangerschaftsabbruch zwischen Recht und Unrecht-Das zweite Abtreibungsurteil des BVerfG und seine Folgen." *Neue Juristische Wochenschrift* 37: 2337–47.

Isensee, Josef. 1992. *Braucht Deutschland eine neue Verfassung?* Cologne: Schmidt.

Kelsen, Hans. 2008. *Wer soll der Hüter der Verfassung sein?* Tübingen: Mohr Siebeck.

Kreide, Regina, and Andreas Niederberger, eds. 2008. *Transnationale Verrechtlichung: Nationale Demokratien im Kontext globaler Politik*. Frankfurt am Main: Campus.

Möllers, Christoph. 2008. *Der vermisste Leviathan: Staatstheorie in der Bundesrepublik*. Frankfurt am Main: Suhrkamp.

———. 2009. *Das Grundgesetz: Geschichte und Inhalt*. Munich: Beck.

Müller, Jan-Werner. 2007. *Constitutional Patriotism*. Princeton, NJ: Princeton University Press.

Niederberger, Andreas. 2008. "Konstitutionalismus und Globale Gerechtigkeit in der Theorie Transnationaler Demokratie." In *Transnationale Verrechtlichung: Nationale Demokratien im Kontext globaler Politik*, edited by Regina Kreide and Andreas Niederberger, 183–206. Frankfurt am Main: Campus.

———. 2009. "Macht-Diskurse." In Brunkhorst, Kreide, and Lafont 2009, 69–71.

———. 2014. "Die politische Philosophie des Bundesverfassungsgerichts: Demokratie und Europa vom Maastricht- zum Lissabon-Urteil." In *Grenzen der europäischen Integration*, edited by Claudio Franzius, Franz C. Mayer, and Jürgen Neyer, 211–31. Baden-Baden: Nomos.

Schmitt, Carl. 1996. *Der Hüter der Verfassung*. Berlin: Duncker & Humblot.

Sternberger, Dolf. 1990. *Verfassungspatriotismus*. Frankfurt am Main: Insel.

Strauss, David A. 2010. *The Living Constitution*. Oxford: Oxford University Press.

Tomkins, Alan. 2005. *Our Republican Constitution*. Oxford: Hart.

Winkler, Heinrich August. 2000. *Der lange Weg nach Westen II: Deutsche Geschichte 1933–1990*. Munich: Beck.

Part II.

What and How Do We Remember?
Literature, Film, and Exhibitions

Part II

3: East German Literature and Reunification: Continuities and Discontinuities

Stephen Brockmann

What Is "East German Literature," and Who Are "East German Authors"?

THE TITLE CONTAINS A KEY TERM that may need clarification: "East German literature." This was already a relatively problematic term prior to 1989, since it was so difficult to define. Did "East German literature," for instance, include the literature of former GDR citizens who went to the west, such as Uwe Johnson, Günter Kunert, Sarah Kirsch, or Wolf Biermann? And even when it was written by citizens of the GDR who remained in the GDR, to what extent could one speak of "East German literature" as something separated from that larger sphere of literary activity known as "German literature?" These were not easy questions to answer even before 1989. Now, almost three decades later, they have become doubly complicated, since the GDR no longer exists as a state. A writer like Thomas Brussig (born in 1965), who has had a major impact on the literary picture of East Germany since reunification, does not even want to be called an East German writer. He would like to think of himself primarily as a German writer.[1]

No doubt for Brussig part of the reluctance to be seen as an "East German" writer comes from resistance to the GDR literary establishment's attempt to create a canon of "DDR-Literatur," as exemplified most prominently in the eleventh volume of the history of German literature put out by the Marxist think tank Institut für Gesellschaftswissenschaften beim ZK der SED (Institute for Social Sciences of the Central Committee of the SED) in 1976. In that volume Horst Haase designated GDR literature as "sozialistische Nationalliteratur der Deutschen Demokratischen Republik,"[2] arguing that this literature was "fest gegründet auf das Leben und Wirken der werktätigen Menschen in der sozialistischen Deutschen Demokratischen Republik und auf die Existenz des internationalen Sozialismus/Kommunismus"[3] and that it existed in energetic opposition to the purported imperialism of the Federal Republic of Germany and other capitalist states (Haase et al. 1976, 21, 28). Writers like Christa Wolf, whom Brussig sees as having supported the East German state in a conformist way, may have found entry into this volume as part of the East German canon, but Brussig would hardly like to see himself in such company. On the contrary, he has established his career at least in part precisely as a critic of the former East German literary establishment; his most famous novel, *Helden wie wir* (1995), includes, in its final chapter, a relentless critique of Christa Wolf.[4] And yet Brussig's topic, perhaps even more so than Wolf's, is certainly East Germany, at least in his second and third novels, *Helden wie wir* and *Am kürzeren Ende der Sonnenallee* (1999), and to a large extent also in his later novels, *Wie es leuchtet* (2004), which set out—unsuccessfully, I would argue—to establish itself as *the* novel of German reunification, and his 2015 novel, *Das gibts in keinem Russenfilm*, an alternative history based on the conceit that the GDR state persisted long after 1990.

How, then, does one classify Thomas Brussig and quite a few other midgeneration authors like him, writers who had not published prior to 1989 but who were socialized and came of age in the GDR and whose topic, to a large extent, *is* the GDR? One could include an author like Kerstin Hensel, who in the years following reunification published a number of well-received novels and novellas, including the remarkable *Falscher Hase* (2005), which, to make matters even more confusing, is set largely in Pankow, Berlin, in the capital of the German Democratic Republic and later of the Federal Republic of Germany, but whose chief character is originally a West Berliner who escapes his troubles by going to the other side of the Wall. Just as important is a writer like Uwe Tellkamp, born and raised in Dresden, whose novel *Der Turm* (2008) created a literary sensation, garnering its author the German Book Prize for its re-creation of an East German world now lost to history. Almost as influential for his literary coming to terms with the GDR past is Ingo Schulze, whose works, from *Simple Storys* (1998) to *Neue Leben* (2005) and *Adam und Evelyn* (2008), have created a panorama of life in the late GDR and in postunification eastern Germany. Other key authors who have emerged in the period following 1990 include Lutz Seiler, who won the German Book Prize in 2014 for his novel *Kruso*, about the GDR's final year; Eugen Ruge, who had previously won the German Book Prize for *In Zeiten des abnehmenden* Lichts (2011), a novel spanning four generations and covering several decades before the end of the GDR as well as the period following the end of the East German State; Antje Rávic Strubel, with her 2011 novel *Sturz der Tage in die Nacht*, an Oedpial story about the persistence of East German history and mentalities long after the end of the GDR; and Clemens Meyer, whose novel *Als wir träumten* (2006) was a depiction of the very generation to which Meyer himself belongs: the generation born in the 1970s that experienced the end of the GDR in their teenage years. Can authors like Brussig, Hensel, Schulze, Tellkamp, Seiler, Ruge, Strubel, and Meyer meaningfully be called "East German" authors, and can their books be called "East German literature"?

The answer to both questions, I would submit, is yes, but only if "East German" is defined in a capacious and liberal way. Such authors are indeed East German authors to the extent that they grew up and were socialized in the GDR; and their books are "East German literature" to the extent that their action takes place in the GDR (or in the space once occupied by that state), depicts the GDR (or the social and cultural structures that emerged after the disappearance of that state), and deals with the problems of life in the GDR, as well as contemporary problems resulting from GDR history. Such a liberal definition, which is in accordance with the approach developed in 2011 by Ulrike Kalt Wilson, says nothing about whether the book was written during or after the existence of the GDR, nor does it specify the author's attitude to the GDR—whether she or he thinks the GDR was a good or a bad idea, for instance. It is important to stress this point, since implicitly or explicitly some previous definitions of GDR literature, and particularly definitions of GDR literature coming from the East German establishment, required that an author's attitude toward the East German state and toward socialism be positive. The aforementioned eleventh volume of the GDR's official literary history, for instance, had managed to exclude Wolf Biermann from the GDR's "sozialistische Nationalliteratur" by arguing that Biermann's lyrics, allegedly full of "Sensualismus und . . . Genußstreben . . . glitten in einen anarchistischen Individualismus ab, der sich objektiv außerhalb politisch-gesellschaftlicher Verantwortlichkeiten stellt,"[5] thus functioning "als ein Instrument der DDR-feindlichen Politik des Imperialismus" (Haase et al. 1976, 491).[6] The argument was clear: in order to be considered real GDR literature, an author and his or her books had to be for the real-existing GDR and its gerontocratic leaders. In my definition that is no longer the case. An author can be extremely, indeed devastatingly critical of the once actually existing GDR, like Brussig, Hensel, Schulze, Tellkamp, Gert Neumann, and Eugen Ruge, or like the late Wolfgang Hilbig, and still be an East German author writing East German literature.

Postunification Literature Takes a Critical Look at the Former GDR

The postunification productivity of what might be termed the new East German literature is, I would submit, the most positive development and a genuine, productive discontinuity in "East German literature" since reunification. For well over two decades it has been possible to be an eastern German author, even to remain in eastern Germany, and to publish fiercely critical and honest books about the GDR and its problems. There is no more censorship, and authors are free to write whatever they want. Of course, one could argue that now there is the censorship of the market, and that, in fact, some authors find it difficult to get their works published. But I would contend that this argument is simply wrong. A wide range of works is now published, far wider than prior to 1989, and because of Germany's extensive system of literary prizes and writer-in-residence programs it is possible for many authors to more or less make a living as writers, always assuming that they can convince a jury that they have at least a modicum of literary talent.[7] Germany has a great many cities with writer-in-residence programs and various literary prizes, and some writers move from city to city and from prize to prize working on their novels, poems, stories, and articles. This system enables a significant level of independence from the demands of the marketplace: authors do not necessarily have to sell books in order to make a living as writers. I do not know of any comparative systematic sociological studies on the matter, but I suspect that there are more people per capita making a living off of their writing in Germany than anywhere else in the world, or at least in the Western world, with the possible exception of Austria. This system is a significant aid, particularly to younger authors trying to make their name. Well before he even published his novel *Der Turm* in 2008, Uwe Tellkamp had already won the Ingeborg Bachmann Prize, one of Germany's most coveted literary awards, in 2004 for excerpts from an as-yet-unfinished novel, *Der Schlaf in den Uhren*, and this prize helped to increase anticipation for Tellkamp's subsequent work. The prize also brought in a significant amount of money in its own right: 22,500 euros, which is enough for a young author of modest means to live on for a year, possibly more, if she or he is careful with her or his money.[8] Writers like Seiler, Tellkamp, and Ruge have earned money not just by selling their books but also through such significant prizes (which also, of course, tend to increase the sales of books).

Writers Who Were Already Established before 1989

As for the older East German authors, the ones already established prior to 1989, they continue to be influential and important. Loyal and unapologetic socialists like Hermann Kant (born in 1926) did not stop writing and publishing after the end of the GDR, and they continued to enjoy an audience and publishers; Kant published his memoirs, *Abspann*, in 1991, and his death in 2016 was commented on respectfully even in the nonleftist German press. Kant was generally recognized as an important

German author, regardless of his problematic politics. Other East German authors of the older generation also continued their activities: writers such as Volker Braun (born in 1939), Monika Maron (born in 1941), and Christoph Hein (born in 1944), all of whom have been consistently productive in the years since 1990, as well as Stefan Heym (born in 1913), Peter Hacks (born in 1928), Christa Wolf (born in 1929), Heiner Müller (born in 1929), and Wolfgang Hilbig (born in 1941) before their deaths. All of these authors continued publishing after 1989, in spite of all controversies surrounding their names, and no matter what their individual political attitudes may have been: most were devastatingly critical of the GDR, but an author like Kant defended it. The controversies surrounding some of them, particularly Christa Wolf and Monika Maron, who were accused of having worked with the East German secret police, the Stasi, at various times, were certainly painful to many of the authors, but none of these authors' critics succeeded in toppling them from their status as significant writers.[9] In fact, paradoxically, the attacks against them helped to cement their fame; after all, nothing succeeds like controversy in the contemporary media market. The work of authors like Wolf, Braun, Hein, and Maron since reunification has often been at a very high level; it might even be argued that some of these authors' best work has occurred in the post-1989 period. For instance, Volker Braun's 1990 poem "Nachruf"— retitled "Das Eigentum" (1996)—has now established itself as *the* canonical poem about the collapse of the GDR and the dream of democratic socialism in Germany, and it is cited routinely in many books and articles about literature and German reunification.[10] I would argue that for writers like Braun and Wolf there has been a great deal of literary continuity between 1989 and the present: they were major figures prior to 1989, and they continued to be major figures in the two decades after German reunification. They were already established as representatives of GDR literature during the GDR's existence, and once the GDR had disappeared, they became important as living representatives of a lost culture. They emerged, to cite the title of Christa Wolf's controversial 1990 book, as *Was bleibt* (what remains). In the year before her death Wolf published her literary memoir *Stadt der Engel oder The Overcoat of Dr. Freud*, which went over some of the same ground as *Was bleibt* but from a different perspective and with even more skepticism toward the idea of socialism; this book reconfirmed Wolf's status as one of the key authors of GDR literature. In it, she wrote even more honestly about life in the GDR than she had previously, citing a friend of the autobiographical protagonist as telling her that the East German state "ist wie jeder Staat ein Herrschaftsinstrument. Und diese Ideologie ist wie jede Ideologie: Falsches Bewußtsein" (is like every state an instrument of power. And this ideology is like every ideology: False consciousness; Wolf 2010, 121). It is hard to imagine such a sentence getting by East German censors prior to 1989.

In addition, even some of the works that these authors produced in the GDR itself are now generally recognized as a fascinating, lasting record of GDR life. No less a source than Germany's most respected weekly newspaper, *Die Zeit*, published an article in the autumn of 2009, coinciding with the twentieth anniversary of the fall of the Berlin Wall, proclaiming that, in fact, East German literature was more interesting than West German literature: "Die Wunde DDR produzierte vielleicht nicht immer die bessere, aber allemal die aufregendere deutsche Literatur" (Cammann 2009, 6).[11] This is a remarkable turnaround in literary valuation, when one considers that two decades earlier, at the moment of German unification itself, *Die Zeit* and other major West German media outlets were busy attacking prominent East German authors like Christa Wolf for their purported complicity with the East German state.[12] The last two decades or so have seen the beginning of a new critical reexamination even of earlier East German literature.[13]

A New Generation of East German Writers

In addition to these older writers, however, the German literary scene is now teeming with many younger authors like Brussig, Hensel, Ruge, Schulze, Seiler, Meyer, and Tellkamp who have been able to establish successful careers over the course of the last two decades under the new, postreunification political, cultural, and economic conditions. An influential 2012 book referred to the youngest of these authors—those born in the 1970s, who experienced national reunification in their childhood or teenage years—as the *Dritte Generation Ost* (Third Generation East).[14] At the 2014 conference of the German Studies Association in Kansas City there were no fewer than three sessions devoted to "East Germany's Third Generation," as well as a session on "Remembering and Forgetting the German Democratic Republic."[15] A somewhat older generation, to which Tellkamp and Hensel belong, has also emerged in the post-1990 years, however. Sometimes such authors do not even have to have published or sold much in order to be successful, as Uwe Tellkamp's already mentioned receipt of the Bachmann prize in 2004 demonstrates. As a result of the new freedom to publish, we now have excellent and honest depictions of life then and now in the former GDR from younger and older authors alike: Brussig's *Helden wie wir* (1995), Hensel's *Falscher Hase* (2005), Hilbig's *"Ich"* (1993), Reinhard Jirgl's *Abschied von den Feinden* (1995) and *Hundsnächte* (1997), Michael Kumpfmüller's *Hampels Fluchten* (2000), Irina Liebmann's *Die freien Frauen* (2004), Gert Neumann's *Anschlag* (1999), Ruge's *In Zeiten des abnehmenden Lichts* (2011), Klaus Schlesinger's *Die Sache mit Randow* (1996), Ingo Schulze's *Simple Storys* (1998) and *Neue Leben* (2005), and Tellkamp's *Der Turm* (2008), to mention only a few of the most prominent.[16] In the cases of Brussig, Hensel, Jirgl, Neumann, Ruge, Schulze, and Tellkamp, it is probable that without the collapse of the GDR and the elimination of censorship we would not have seen these novels in this form. In other words, the collapse of the GDR has made possible the development of an entirely new, very honest, and sometimes stylistically quite ambitious East German literature, a literature that was impossible or suppressed under official definitions of "sozialistische Nationalliteratur" and official insistence on the tenets of socialist realism. Moreover, books that actually were suppressed at the time of their creation in the GDR have also been able to appear in the last two decades. The most prominent recent example is Werner Bräunig's novel *Rummelplatz* about life in and around an East German uranium mine, which was suppressed in the mid-1960s in the wake of the Socialist Unity Party's notorious eleventh plenum, in which major politicians attacked both literary figures like Christa Wolf and filmmakers like Kurt Maetzig. *Rummelplatz*, an important milestone in the evolution of socialist realism, was finally able to appear in 2007. One might even argue, provocatively, that a real, unfettered, uninhibited, and uncensored East German literature has come into existence only with the collapse of the GDR. This literature does what literature is supposed to do: it processes reality and consciousness via language, one of the key media of consciousness. These books, some of them difficult and some of them easy to read, make it possible for us to enter the German Democratic Republic as a life-world and to participate in its effects on consciousness. This was possible prior to 1989, too, of course, but not in the same uninhibited, uncensored way. In 2005, a young East German entrepreneur started marketing canned "Trabi-Duft" for nostalgic East Germans who missed the smell of their old Trabant automobiles.[17] For a while, one could purchase Trabi-Duft on the World Wide Web. Picking up one of the books of these authors is, however, a far more effective way of transporting oneself back to the GDR.

Representing Two Competing Perspectives on the GDR

In my 1999 book *Literature and German Reunification* I argued for the relevance of Friedrich Meinecke's old concept of a *Kulturnation* in understanding the national significance of literature in Germany prior to German reunification (Brockmann 1999, 6–10). Meinecke had argued that in the absence of political unity, which he defined as the *Staatsnation*, the sphere of culture, and in particular literature, serves as the focal point for people's feelings of national identity. Meinecke's argument, of course, was intended to apply to all of Germany, not just a part; the point for Meinecke, after all, was precisely to overcome German division and achieve German unity. I would argue, however, that one can make Meinecke's argument in reverse, for a part of Germany, namely the former GDR. Now that the GDR no longer exists as a state, East German culture, and in particular East German literature, serves as a focal point for people's feelings of East German identity. This is certainly no longer, if it ever was, a national identity. But I accept Ursula Heukenkamp's argument that it is a regional identity with significant staying power (Heukenkamp 1995, 22–37). In fact, East German identity is probably far more attractive, and "cooler," now than it ever was, as a result of the work of authors like Brussig, Schulze, or even Tellkamp, or of nostalgic movies like Leander Haußmann's *Sonnenallee* (1999) or Wolfgang Becker's *Good Bye, Lenin!* (2003).[18] Toward the end of Brussig's novel *Am kürzeren Ende der Sonnenallee* comes Brussig's summary of life in the GDR: "*Es war von vorn bis hinten zum Kotzen, aber wir haben uns prächtig amüsiert*" (Brussig 1999, 153).[19] This is certainly not a defense of the GDR or of socialism, but it *is* a defense of a life-world and of memories. This new GDR literature, of which Brussig is one of the most prominent and popular representatives, often treats the GDR almost as if it were the former Austro-Hungarian Empire. A famous joke about the difference between the Prussians and the Austrians goes that for the Prussians "Die Lage ist ernst, aber nicht hoffnungslos," while for the Austrians "Die Lage ist hoffnungslos, aber nicht ernst."[20] A bit of this jaded Austrian levity has now entered into East German literature, the literature of what used to be Prussia: Brussig's statement comes structurally very close to the purported Austrian attitude: "von vorn bis hinten zum Kotzen," but not really serious. "Mein Gott, waren wir komisch, und wir haben es nicht einmal gemerkt," Brussig (1999, 153) writes.[21] One of Brussig's subsequent projects was the movie *NVA*, released in 2005, created together with Leander Haußmann, Brussig's partner for the movie *Sonnenallee*, one of the key works in the development of filmic Ostalgie. *NVA: Der Film* let its viewers know how ridiculous and stupid but also funny and perhaps even cool it was to be a member of the GDR's Nationale Volksarmee. One can hardly imagine so much grudging affection for the state institutions of the GDR during its actual existence. If there had been a movie entitled *NVA* in 1985, no one would have gone to it. In Brussig's work the GDR has become a kind of operetta state, a silly and buffoonish but fun place to be. In the first seven years after reunification, there were heated debates for and against comparing the GDR to the Nazi dictatorship.[22] A film like *NVA* is concrete evidence as to exactly who won those debates: like it or not, Germans have not accepted the direct comparison between the GDR and the Nazi dictatorship. Or can one imagine a German film comedy entitled *Wehrmacht: The Movie?*

Of course, Brussig's approach is not the only one, and the approach of writers like Hein, Jirgl, Neumann, Tellkamp, Wolf, Strubel, Ruge, and

Seiler is quite different and far more serious—perhaps even more Prussian in the sense of the joke cited above. Even Tellkamp's *Der Turm*, however, a devastating critique of late GDR society, is filled with admiration for the literary culture of the GDR, which is presented as a last bastion of the German *Bildungsbürgertum*. For many of the characters in this novel, the GDR is a state full of people "beseelt von der Liebe zur Literatur, zum Wort, zum gutgemachten Buch" (Tellkamp 2008, 852).[23] Schulze's protagonist in *Neue Leben* proclaims to his East German tormentors, who have accused him of wanting to leave the GDR: "Jemand wie ich verläßt nicht freiwillig ein Land, in dem Literatur das Wichtigste ist!" (Schulze 2005, 230).[24] In these and other works, the GDR continues to enjoy the status of a country in which literature and literary intellectuals play a privileged role. As the sociologist Heinz Bude remarked as early as the mid-1990s, for many Germans in east and west the GDR has gradually become the secret "Wunschbild einer kulturellen Heimat, die der Nationalsozialismus zerstört hat" (cited in Cammann 2009, 6).[25] This is a country in which the love of culture, and of *Bildung*, are sometimes capable of standing up against the worst kind of dictatorship—a picture famously developed, for instance, in Florian Henckel von Donnersmarck's Oscar-winning debut film *Das Leben der Anderen* (2006), which shows how the love of culture ultimately overcomes the machinations of the Stasi itself.

These two competing postunification perspectives on the GDR—the funny, disrespectful one typified by Brussig and the serious, reflective one of authors like Tellkamp, Ruge, and Wolf—are clearly very different from each other. But both perspectives suggest that East German culture, for all of its problems, preserved something that is worthwhile. This, more than two decades after German unification, is a remarkable continuity with GDR culture's own vision of itself. Postunification literature about the GDR in the last two decades represents a genuine enrichment of German literature as a whole.

Notes

[1] See, for instance, Brussig's interview with Silke Schoppe in May 2000: http://www.planet-interview.de/interviews/thomas-brussig/33394/.

[2] Translated as: socialist national literature of the German Democratic Republic.

[3] Translated as: firmly based on the life and work of the working people in the socialist German Democratic Republic and on the existence of international socialism/communism.

[4] Thomas Brussig, *Helden wie wir* (1995, 277, 288).

[5] Translated as: Sensualism and pursuit of pleasure . . . slipped into an anarchist individualism, which is objectively beyond political and social responsibilities.

[6] Translated as: as an instrument of anti-GDR policy of imperialism.

[7] Not much has been written yet about Germany's system of literary prizes, but at least it comes under consideration in Sean McIntyre's article "The Literary Public Sphere: A Case for German Particularity?" in Katharina Gerstenberger and Patricia Herminghouse, *German Literature in a New Century: Trends, Traditions, Transitions, Transformations* (2008, 23).

[8] On the 2004 Bachmann prize, see http://archiv.bachmannpreis.orf.at/bachmannpreis/information/stories/14564/.

[9] On such controversies, see Brockmann (1999, 64–79), as well as Anz (1991) and Grub (2003, 196–239).

[10] See, for instance Grub (2003, 457–463) and Schlenstedt (1992, 124–132).

[11] Translated as: The sore spot GDR did not always produce the better, but definitely the more exciting German literature.

[12] On the various literary debates of unification, see my articles "The Politics of German Literature" (1992, 46–58) and "A Literary Civil War" (1993, 69–78).

[13] See in particular Ohlerich (2005), Barck (2003), and Peitsch (2009). In English, see Brockmann (2015). A younger generation of North American scholars of East German literature has also begun publishing fascinating work in the last decade. See, for instance, Urang (2011) and Swope (2009). The reexamination of pre-1960 East German literature still has a long way to go, but Bivens (2015) provides a fascinating prolegomena to this reexamination; and Peitsch's book (2009) pushes it forward. My own book *The Writers' State* (2015) also addresses this period.

[14] See, for example, the Michael Hacker-edited volume *Dritte Generation Ost: Wer wir sind, was wir wollen* (2012).

[15] The 2014 GSA program can be uploaded at: https://www.thegsa.org/conference/documents/GSA_program_14.pdf. See also: https://thirdgenerationost.wordpress.com/publicationsconferences/gsa-2014/.

[16] The authors in this list who could be considered part of the "older" generation are Klaus Schlesinger, born in 1937, who died in 2011; Wolfgang Hilbig, born in 1941, who died in 2007; Gert Neumann, born in 1942; and Irina Liebmann, born in 1943. Reinhard Jirgl, born in 1953, stands between the older and younger generations. Kerstin Hensel was born in 1961, Ingo Schulze in 1962, Lutz Seiler in 1963, Thomas Brussig in 1964, and Uwe Tellkamp in 1968. Among the authors of the so-called third generation are Antje Rávic Strubel, born in 1974, and Clemens Meyer, born in 1977. The so-called third generation, however, emerged not long after the previous generation, and, in fact, Meyer's *Als wir träumten* (2006) appeared before Tellkamp's *Der Turm* (2008). Even though these may be distinct generations, their appearance on the literary scene overlaps to some extent.

[17] See http://www.tagesspiegel.de/weltspiegel/ddr-nostalgie-trabi-duft-aus-der-dose/626126.html.

[18] On the phenomenon of Ostalgie in this context and in other contexts, see Cooke (2005).

[19] Translated as: It really sucked but we had a great time.

[20] Translated as: The situation is serious but not hopeless. / The situation is hopeless but not serious.

[21] Translated as: My God, were we funny, and we did not even realize it.

[22] For an overview of some of these debates, see Bill Niven's useful *Introduction: German Victimhood at the Turn of the Millennium* (2006, 1–25).

[23] Translated as: inspired by the love of literature, by the word, by the well-written book.

[24] Translated as: Someone like me does not leave a country voluntarily where literature is the most important thing.

[25] Translated as: desired image of a cultural homeland that was destroyed by National Socialism. From Heinz Bude, "Bilder vom Osten: Wie die Westdeutschen ihre Sehnsüchte projizierten" (1996, 81).

Works Cited

Anz, Thomas, ed. 1991. *"Es geht nicht um Christa Wolf": Der Literaturstreit im vereinten Deutschland*. Munich: Spangenberg.

Barck, Simone. 2003. *Antifa-Geschichte(n): Eine literarische Spurensuche in der DDR der 1950er und 1960er Jahre*. Cologne: Böhlau.

Bivens, Hunter. 2015. *Epic and Exile: German Novels of the Popular Front, 1933–1945*. Evanston, IL: Northwestern University Press.

Brockmann, Stephen. 1992. "The Politics of German Literature." *Monatshefte* 84 (1): 46–58.

———. 1993. "A Literary Civil War." *Germanic Review* 68 (2): 69–78.

———. 1999. *Literature and German Reunification*. Cambridge: Cambridge University Press.

———. 2015. *The Writers' State: Constructing East German Literature, 1945–1959*. Rochester, NY: Camden House.

Bude, Heinz. 1996. "Bilder vom Osten: Wie die Westdeutschen ihre Sehnsüchte projizierten." *Transit—Europäische Revue* 11: 78–86.

Cammann, Alexander. 2009. "Im Osten ging die Sonne auf." *Die Zeit* 49 (Zeit Literatur): 4–16.

Cooke, Paul. 2005. *Representing East Germany since Unification: From Colonization to Nostalgia*. Oxford: Berg.

Gerstenberger, Katharina, and Patricia Herminghouse, eds. 2008. *German Literature in a New Century: Trends, Traditions, Transitions, Transformations*. New York: Berghahn.

Grub, Frank Thomas. 2003. *"Wende" und "Einheit" im Spiegel der deutschsprachigen Literatur: Ein Handbuch*. Vol. 1. Berlin: Walter de Gruyter.

Haase, Horst, Hans Jürgen Geerdts, Erich Kühne, and Walter Pallus. 1976. *Geschichte der Literatur der Deutschen Demokratischen Republik*. Vol. 11 of *Geschichte der deutschen Literatur von den Anfängen bis zur Gegenwart*, edited by Klaus Gysi. 12 vols. Berlin: Volk und Wissen, 1960–83.

Hacker, Michael, ed. 2012. *Dritte Generation Ost: Wer wir sind, was wir wollen*. Berlin: Christoph Links.

Heukenkamp, Ursula. 1995. "Eine Geschichte oder viele Geschichten der deutschen Literatur seit 1945? Gründe und Gegengründe." *Zeitschrift für Germanistik* 5 (1): 22–37.

McIntyre, Sean. 2008. "The Literary Public Sphere: A Case for German Particularity?" In Gerstenberger and Herminghouse 2008, 17–33.

Niven, Bill, ed. 2006. *Germans as Victims: Remembering the Past in Contemporary Germany*. Basingstoke, UK: Palgrave Macmillan.

Ohlerich, Gregor. 2005. *Sozialistische Denkwelten: Modell eines literarischen Feldes der SBZ/DDR 1945 bis 1953*. Heidelberg: Winter.

Peitsch, Helmut. 2009. *Nachkriegsliteratur 1945–1989*. Göttingen: V&R Unipress.

Schlenstedt, Dieter. 1992. "Ein Gedicht als Provokation." *Neue Deutsche Literatur* 40 (480): 124–32.

Swope, Curtis. 2009. "Building Materialism: Architecture, Interior Space and Urbanism in East German Literature, 1949–1973." Diss., University of Pennsylvania.

Urang, John Griffith. 2011. *Legal Tender: Love and Legitimacy in the East German Cultural Imagination*. Ithaca, NY: Cornell University Press.

Wilson, Ulrike Kalt. 2011. "East German Literature after the Wende: Kerstin Hensel, Angela Krauß, and the Weiterschreiben of GDR-literature." PhD diss., University of Virginia.

Literary Sources

Braun, Volker. 1990. "Nachruf." In *Neues Deutschland*, August 4–5: 1. Republished under the title "Das Eigentum." 1996. In *Lustgarten: Preußen*, 141. Frankfurt am Main: Suhrkamp.

Bräunig, Werner. 2007. *Rummelplatz*. Berlin: Aufbau-Verlag.

Brussig, Thomas. 1995. *Helden wie wir*. Berlin: Verlag Volk und Welt.

———. 1999. *Am kürzeren Ende der Sonnenallee*. Berlin: Verlag Volk und Welt.

———. 2004. *Wie es leuchtet*. Frankfurt am Main: S. Fischer.

———. 2015. *Das gibts in keinem Russenfilm*. Frankfurt am Main: S. Fischer.

Hensel, Kerstin. 2005. *Falscher Hase*. Munich: Luchterhand.

Hilbig, Wolfgang. 1993. *"Ich."* Frankfurt am Main: S. Fischer.

Jirgl, Reinhard. 1995. *Abschied von den Feinden*. Munich: Hanser.

———. 1997. *Hundsnächte*. Munich: Hanser.

Kant, Hermann. 1991. *Abspann: Erinnerungen an meine Gegenwart*. Berlin: Berlin-Verlag.

Kumpfmüller, Michael. 2000. *Hampels Fluchten*. Cologne: Kiepenheuer & Witsch.

Liebmann, Irina. 2004. *Die freien Frauen*. Berlin: Berlin-Verlag.

Meyer, Clemens. 2006. *Als wir träumten*. Frankfurt am Main: S. Fischer.

Neumann, Gert. 1999. *Anschlag*. Cologne: DuMont-Buchverlag.

Ruge, Eugen. 2011. *In Zeiten des abnehmenden Lichts: Roman einer Familie.* Reinbek bei Hamburg: Rowohlt.

Schlesinger, Klaus. 1996. *Die Sache mit Randow.* Berlin: Aufbau-Verlag.

Schulze, Ingo. 1998. *Simple Storys: Ein Roman aus der ostdeutschen Provinz.* Berlin: Aufbau-Verlag.

———. 2005. *Neue Leben: Die Jugend Enrico Türmers in Briefen und Prosa.* Berlin: Aufbau-Verlag.

———. 2008. *Adam und Evelyn.* Berlin: Aufbau-Verlag.

Seiler, Lutz. 2014. *Kruso.* Frankfurt am Main: Suhrkamp.

Strubel, Antje Rávic. 2011. *Sturz der Tage in die Nacht.* Frankfurt am Main: S. Fischer.

Tellkamp, Uwe. 2008. *Der Turm.* Frankfurt am Main: Suhrkamp.

Tellkamp, Uwe, and Iris Radisch. 2004. *Klagenfurter Texte: Die 28. Tage der deutschsprachigen Literatur in Klagenfurt.* Munich: Piper.

Wolf, Christa. 1990. *Was bleibt.* Berlin: Aufbau-Verlag.

———. 2010. *Stadt der Engel oder Der Overcoat von Dr. Freud.* Berlin: Suhrkamp.

4:   The Afterlife of the GDR in Post-Wall German Cinema

Mary-Elizabeth O'Brien

DESPITE THE COLLAPSE of the SED regime and unification, the German Democratic Republic continues to live on in the social imaginary, especially in contemporary German cinema. Since 1989 a plethora of feature films set in the GDR have graced the silver screen, and while they employ different perspectives, conventions, and aesthetic approaches, they share a fundamental interest in the past that coalesces them into a genre. Genre is notoriously difficult to characterize definitively. Predictable storylines, recurring characters, and familiar visual cues form a distinct connection between texts, but "genres do not consist only of films, they consist also, and equally, of specific systems of expectation and hypothesis which spectators bring with them to the cinema, and which interact with films themselves during the course of the viewing process" (Neale 2000, 46). Genre encompasses more than a set of texts with shared formal characteristics and themes. It is also a discursive network, in which the expectations of multiple and often competing stakeholders (filmmakers, viewers, and critics) are presented, interpreted, negotiated, and contested. Genre is distinguished by a continuous process of transformation, which entails a messy course of articulation, disruption, and renewal rather than a smooth evolution. Rick Altman (1999, 195) has suggested that "genres are regulatory schemes facilitating the integration of diverse factions into a single unified social fabric. As such, genres operate like nations and other complex communities. Perhaps genres can even teach us about nations." The history-film genre can be seen as a bellwether of how the German nation seeks to integrate competing discourses on the GDR past into a single unified social fabric.

Over the last few decades the history film has gained increasing credence as a valid source of historical knowledge. Robert Rosenstone (1992, 1138) offers a broad definition of the history-film genre by suggesting that its primary salient feature "is its willingness to engage the discourse of history—that is, the facts, the issues, and the arguments raised in other historical works." Like many historians and cultural critics, however, Rosenstone (1995, 11–12) presents a twofold classification that segregates what he calls standard or mainstream history films from the serious inquiry found in postmodern history films. Whereas standard films "deliver the past in a highly developed, polished form that serves to suppress rather than raise questions," the postmodern film is "a work that, refusing the pretense that the screen can be an unmediated window onto the past, foregrounds itself as a construction" and "utilizes the unique capabilities of the media to create multiple meanings." A theoretic cornerstone for this twofold approach to history on film can be found in the work of Fredric Jameson, who differentiates between nostalgia and history films. Jameson (1992, 179) maintains: "In nostalgia film, the image—the surface sheen of a period fashion reality—is consumed, having been transformed into a visual commodity" that represents "a formal compensation for the enfeeblement of historicity in our time." Jameson contends that the history film, by contrast, rejects surface imagery over challenging narratives and vexing styles that present "history with holes, perforated history, which includes gaps not immediately visible to us." Much of the scholarly debate on the merits of the history film is characterized by this distinction between films that focus on visual splendor that reportedly engenders a reactionary perspective of history and films that employ innovative styles that are potentially radicalizing and allow them to evaluate social and political issues effectively (See Higson 2003 and Landy 2001).

The preference for art-house over mainstream history films limits our ability to see the whole picture. Mainstream films often depict the past as coherent, meaningful, and concluded and offer immediacy, vivid audiovisual effects, and potential for identification and emotional involvement. Art-house films generally challenge viewers by refusing to grant narrative closure and by drawing attention to the artistic edifice to question history as a well-made story that ends in resolution rather than doubt. Instead of privileging one over the other as more fruitful to the study of history on film, it is important to see mainstream and art-house films as varying degrees along a spectrum of approaches to history and recognize that cinematic conventions have a history of their own that deserves investigation. Marnie Hughes-Warrington (2007, 191) suggests an approach that understands the genre of history film as a discursive network. She argues that what makes a film historical "is its location in a timebound network of discussions—more or less explicit—on what history is and what it is for." Thus, "any film may be historical because it is viewed as offering indexical markers—on-screen phenomena seen as capturing or connected with past phenomena—or because it suggests something about how and why histories are made."

Numerous articles and several recent monographs have begun to explore the fundamental questions of why so many German filmmakers have been drawn to GDR history and why viewers have readily embraced certain types of history while rejecting others.[1] In order to gauge which conventions are repeated and circulated, to identify which storylines are resilient, and to determine whether there is a resistant popular practice, it is essential to examine a wide variety of films ranging from blockbusters to low-budget films with modest audience figures, from motion pictures that received artistic acclaim to those that failed to gain critical or public approval. Genre analysis allows us to move beyond the individual text to analyze exemplary films in the context of their production, exhibition, and reception, thereby elucidating the persistence of certain models and formulas for GDR history. If we view the history film as a distinct, though by definition messy, genre, then an examination of the GDR's celluloid afterlife can reveal much about the German nation's past and present, shared communal values, and ongoing disputes over what historical legacies are worth preserving, reproaching, and commemorating.

The GDR on the Post-Wall Screen

In the fall of 1989, when demonstrators were taking to the streets in the hopes of reforming socialism in the GDR, the official state-owned film studio DEFA (Deutsche Film-Aktiengesellschaft) was in the process of shooting a motion picture about the growing disillusionment of an entire generation and the mass exodus to the West. Peter Kahane's *Die Architekten* (*The Architects*, 1990) depicts the struggles of a young architect who attempts to fight a stagnant bureaucracy and create a truly socialist urban living space. He loses both professionally and personally: his innovative designs are rejected, and his wife and child defect to the West. The approval of such a socially critical filmscript in 1988 seemed to signal the long-awaited glasnost in GDR cinema, but the reform came too late. What at the time of filming was seen as a remarkably open portrayal of the current state of affairs quickly became overshadowed by the sheer magnitude of revolutionary change. Shooting in Berlin from October 1989 to January 1990 and thus confronted on a daily basis with history in the making, Kahane first began to document the demonstrations and rewrite the script to reflect the rapidly changing situation.[2] Faced with a nearly unfathomable transformation of reality, he eventually decided to return to his original script and record the historical moment that led to the GDR's collapse.

From this dramatic start until today, the GDR has been a steady theme in post-Wall German cinema. In the wake of the peaceful revolution, filmmakers on both sides of the German divide began to make motion pictures about the GDR. In the early nineties, the dividing line was drawn by geography and genre. Films made in the west were primarily mainstream comedies, road movies, and horror films about east-west encounters after unification, while films made in the east were a

long-awaited reckoning with GDR history and the constricts of socialist realism. Over the course of the next two decades, the dividing line
between east and west became less distinct, but the choice of genre continued to signal divergent interpretations of the past. Melodramas, biop-
ics, and docudramas generally portray the GDR as a prison state and
illustrate the brutal repression of dissent. The growing Ostalgie can be
seen as a reaction that worked against this dominant discourse. Comedies
and tragicomedies tend to depict a more ambivalent view of the GDR
by focusing on positive memories of a normal, happy life in the East and
advocating the preservation of certain aspects of this past. Regardless of
the generic approach, cinematic depictions of the GDR have contributed
to public debates on how the past informs the present and helps define a
shared national identity.

This essay begins with a survey of DEFA films made from 1989 to
1992, because these films and the dismantling of the GDR film industry
deserve more scholarly attention. What follows is an overview of films that
exemplify developments in the GDR memory landscape at distinct historical junctures. The persistent afterlife of the GDR in post-Wall German
cinema reveals that the past is anything but over, mastered, and departed.

The Transitional Period: From the Fall of the Wall to Unification

In the transitional period from the fall of the Wall to unification, the East
German film industry was completely restructured. On June 1, 1990, the
day of the currency reform, DEFA Studio für Spielfilme (DEFA movie
studio), a nationally owned enterprise (Volkseigener Betrieb, VEB),
became a limited-liability company, DEFA-Spielfilm GmbH im Aufbau.
The last GDR government passed a law on June 17, 1990, to transfer all
state-owned companies to the *Treuhandgesellschaft*, a holding company
responsible for the privatization of all GDR property. Despite the reorga-
nization that led to nearly half of the 2,400 employees losing their jobs
or being paid minimal wages while clocking zero hours, a select group
of DEFA filmmakers were given the opportunity to make a feature film
fully subsidized by the GDR's last state budget.[3] These early films made
during or shortly after the Wende at the DEFA studios concentrate on
the disillusionment and despair of individuals who no longer have the
strength to fight against the persistent corruption, bureaucratism, surveillance, and repression in the GDR. Collectively they mourn the loss of a
utopian vision to create a democratic, just, and classless society.

Films that center on the collapse of the GDR were the most common, although the generic and aesthetic approaches differed greatly.
First-time directors Jörg Foth and Andreas Höntsch as well as seasoned

filmmaker Egon Günther captured the surreal nature of the turbulent year 1989 when the familiar old world was suddenly turned upside down. Foth embraced the tradition of political cabaret for his episodic satire *Letztes aus der Da Da eR* (Latest from the Ge De aR, 1990), which follows the clowns Meh and Weh from the GDR prison to the garbage dump of the FRG. In a series of irreverent satirical songs and sketches, the clowns make their way through various stations of the GDR and the new world of the FRG: piercing each other with medals for their contributions to socialism until they collapse from the pain, walking through the slaughterhouse of capitalism, and mesmerized by a hypnotic display of German patriotism in a graveyard that leaves little optimism for the prospects of unification. Höntsch, by contrast, opted in *Der Straß* (Rhinestone, 1991) for a highly stylized aesthetic that flew in the face of DEFA realism. Photojournalist Georg Bastian becomes fascinated by the erotic, acrobatic dancer, Miss Albena, who beguiles and ultimately rejects him. As the film's tagline reads, "Wo man Leben nicht leben kann, bleibt nur die Flucht in den Traum" (Where one cannot live life, the only thing left is escape into dreams), Bastian's encounter with Miss Albena awakens him to the oppressive state of existence in the GDR. Dreaming about this unreachable, ideal woman, Bastian emancipates himself through fantasy just as the Berlin Wall falls (Höntsch had captured documentary footage on November 9, 1989, and incorporated it into the final film version (McGee 1998). *Der Straß* won the audience prize at the Max Ophuls Festival in Saarbrücken but had an extremely limited cinematic release and received little critical notice.

Former DEFA director Egon Günther, best known for his literary adaptations, had left the GDR in 1978 and returned in 1990 to make the brooding drama *Stein* (1991). Whereas Höntsch touts the emancipatory potential of fantasy for individuals faced with an authoritarian system, Günther explores the topic from the tragic perspective of a man forced into inner exile for decades and wavering between dream and insanity. The loosely bound, episodic narrative depicts the unstable emotional life of Ernst Stein, an elderly actor who left the stage in 1968 to protest the Soviet invasion of Prague and withdrew to an isolated villa on the outskirts of Berlin. In 1989 Stein welcomes to his refuge children and a host of outcasts who refuse to accept the sociopolitical order. In this alternative community where everyone is welcome—except those who threaten his precarious position politically and sexually—Stein plays the dissident but makes no concrete gesture of rebellion beyond detachment. Günther's film does not present a realistic chronology of the GDR's demise. Instead, it focuses on the theme of the nonconforming artist and withdrawal as a political strategy that is ultimately ineffective (Steingröver 2014). Various devices draw attention to the broader political issues. In a surrealistic scene depicting protestors being arrested, Stein hypnotizes and humiliates a policeman in a grand, if delusional, manner. Documentary footage of the changing of the guard and the dismantling of the Berlin Wall is also sporadically embedded into the film without narrative motivation. The soundtrack likewise features intermittent gunshots heard in the garden that hint at the fortified border and armed suppression of demonstrations. The fact that these gunshots continue after the Wall falls, however, suggests that the peril lies deeper than the SED regime and that the newly unified state holds an equally formidable threat to the individual.

Heiner Carow and Helmut Dziuba adopted a much more realistic narrative, but their films about the Wende have open endings, leaving the viewer with unease about the future. These established directors were indebted to the DEFA traditions of realism and literary adaptations, and their films center on the lives of individuals subjected to the arbitrary power of the socialist state. Heiner Carow, vice president of the GDR Academy of Arts (1982–91) and prizewinning director of such films as the cult classic *Die Legende von Paul und Paula* (The legend of Paul and Paula, 1973), adapted a short story by Werner Heiduczek. Carow's *Verfehlung* (The mistake, 1992) depicts a love affair destined for tragedy owing to the inner-German border in early 1989. Jacob, a dockworker from Hamburg, visits relatives in an East German village and falls in love with the cleaning woman Elisabeth, but Germany's political division prevents them from being together. When Jacob arrives without a visa to celebrate his engagement to Elisabeth, the town's mayor, who is also in love with her, has his rival arrested and deported. Elisabeth kills the mayor, but her rebellion on the eve of the revolution is ultimately self-destructive, forcing her to go from the petty and restrictive cage of the GDR to an even smaller prison cell in unified Germany.

Helmut Dziuba, educated at the distinguished Gerasimov Institute of Cinematography in Moscow and best known for his children's films, adapted a short story by Manfred Härtel. *Jan und Jana* (1992), a drama about young love evolving in a GDR juvenile-detention center in 1989, presents the viewer with a closed world governed by disenfranchised youths who terrorize each other in an authoritarian system that mirrors the SED state. After Jana becomes pregnant, she and Jan decide to keep the baby, but they must endure ostracism by fellow inmates enraged by their potential happiness. The historic Monday demonstrations in Leipzig and the dismantling of the Wall are shown on television but have little impact on the teenagers' lives. After the GDR collapses, the lovers escape from the detention center and make their way to the West. The film's ending is disjointed and unsettling. Jana begins to give birth in an abandoned guard tower at the deserted border, but suddenly her screams echo as the camera cuts to a shot of the fog-covered no man's land and then to Jana alone in a hospital bed crying out in pain. The suspended birth in the borderland in a period of upheaval is a fitting metaphor for the uncertain prospects of unification.

The First Years after the Wende

The pervasive surveillance system and culture of fear propagated by the Ministry for State Security became an important theme in East German cinema after the Wende. Focusing on the crimes committed by the Stasi and the power exerted on ordinary citizens to keep them in line, veteran filmmakers Frank Beyer and Roland Gräf returned to the DEFA tradition of literary adaptation. In 1989 Gräf received the go-ahead for an adaptation of Christoph Hein's controversial novel *Der Tangospieler* (Tango player), published only months earlier. *Der Tangospieler* features the unwitting dissident Hans-Peter Dallow. Sentenced to twenty-one months in prison for playing the piano at a cabaret where students maligned the state, Dallow experiences momentary paralysis and cannot sign his name on his release papers as the film opens. Leaving prison in early 1968, the former historian wants to be left alone to ponder the injustice done to him. Stasi officers promise restitution of his position at the university if he will become an informant, but Dallow refuses to cooperate. Never fully liberated from his wrongful imprisonment, he floats through life passive and unable to forget the past. Dallow has become so distant that he is numb to the news that Soviet tanks have violently crushed the Prague Spring. Despite his attempts to maintain a position as an outsider, he eventually surrenders himself to the system in a moment of opportunism. When an unsuspecting colleague tells students that it is unthinkable that Soviet and GDR troops would ever invade Czechoslovakia and that the news must be Western propaganda, Dallow is suddenly needed again. Upon his triumphant return to the university, he waves to the Stasi officer, suggesting that collaboration is the price he has paid for rehabilitation. The cost is nothing less than his identity, for the film ends on the same note on which it began: Dallow is unable to make his arm work and sign his name legibly on his new employment papers.

Frank Beyer's *Der Verdacht* (Suspicion, 1991), with a screenplay by Ulrich Plenzdorf based on Volker Braun's *Die unvollendete Geschichte* (Unfinished story, 1977) continues this trend. *Der Verdacht* is set in the GDR in the seventies and treats the absurd lengths to which the SED went to preserve the illusion of consensus. Karin, the daughter of a high-ranking party official, is persuaded by her parents to break up with her boyfriend, Frank, because the young man plans an escape over the border. She bows to pressure and breaks off the relationship. When Frank attempts to commit suicide and lies in a coma, the truth comes out that the only evidence against him is that a friend who defected wrote him a letter encouraging him to leave—a letter Frank never received. Beyer prefigures Frank's suicide attempt and the theme of petty-bourgeois acquiescence to social pressures by having the characters attend a performance of *Die neuen Leiden des jungen W.* (The new sorrows of young W). He creates critical distance to the topic through self-reflectivity by having Ulrich Plenzdorf, the author of both the drama and this film's script, prominently seated in the theater. Frank's recovery, the family's remorse, and Karin's return to her lover do not represent a comfortable, reassuring return to normalcy, since Frank has no memory of the events. He laughs at the story the nurses tell him that he supposedly tried to kill himself over a failed escape attempt and betrayal. He puts his arms around Karin, whose awkward smile and searching look speak volumes for the suppressed history lying just below the surface.

Herwig Kipping made one of the most notable stylistic breaks with the GDR's aesthetic heritage, earning him the sobriquet "aesthetic anarchist" (Vollmer 1992). *Das Land hinter dem Regenbogen* (The land beyond the rainbow, 1992) is based loosely on his childhood growing up in the Stalinist era and is a nightmare vision of collectivism, heavily influenced by Russian masters Tarkovsky and Dovzhenko.[4] The story takes place in 1953 in the fictional village of Stalina. Kipping makes use of parable in a dreamlike fantasy world and employs haunting imagery to depict the GDR as an absurd state of existence. From the opening scene, where Pegasus stands guard next to a giant tree filled with life-sized dolls, it is clear that symbolic imagery takes precedence over plot. The story is told through the eyes of a boy called Rainbow-maker, whose grandfather is the devoted Stalinist mayor of the village. The children play in a forest that is as beautiful and as wicked as any imagined by the Brothers Grimm. The adults fight over power using common methods of tyranny, including denunciation and indoctrination of the youth as informants. After the death of their godlike leader, the inherent brutality of the regime bursts out into the open. The June 17, 1953, revolt is depicted in apocalyptic tableaux of fiery destruction that end in the grandfather's being crucified on a black-red-gold border stake and crying out, "Stalin, why have you forsaken me?" Despite the destructive force of extreme political idealism, the hope of finding utopia is resilient. The last scene features the entire village marching out into the wasteland past the lonely Karl Marx monument in search of the land beyond the rainbow. The film failed at the box office and received mixed reviews but was awarded the German Film Prize in Silver.

In this brief period from 1989 to 1992, despite all hopes for a cinematic renaissance, the last DEFA films played to empty houses. Various factors contributed to their box-office failure. The films were either beholden to an outdated tradition of realism or were eccentric avantgardist visions that failed to find an audience in either east or west. Bärbel Dalichow (1994, 336) argued convincingly that many DEFA films from this period are an explosion of pent-up ideas that ultimately failed to hit the mark: "Freewheeling imagination leads to eclecticism and grandstanding, narrative structures are overdone and destroyed. Touching images drown in an orgy of citations, music, camera, and lights. This produces patchwork quilts that keep no one warm."[5] For western viewers unfamiliar with DEFA's foreign styles, historical topics, stars, and directors, the films remained uncharted territory. For eastern audiences, economic factors played a significant role in keeping them away. The end of the GDR affected not only production but also distribution and exhibition. The eight hundred cinema houses in the new federal states were public property put up for sale by the Treuhand. Roughly half of all cinema houses were closed, with small towns and rural areas hit hardest ("Ende der Vorstellung" 1994). The remaining cinemas were generally modernized, and many were converted to multiplexes that favored Hollywood and mainstream genre films. Thus, while DEFA directors in the GDR could count on the centralized distribution of their films, after the Wende cinemas exhibited films according to market demand. After decades of limited access to films from the West, moviegoers had backlog demand for Hollywood fare. In addition, the currency reform raised the price of general admission from 1.50 East Marks to 6 DM (Wiedemann 1991). Whereas in 1988 the average GDR citizen went to the movies four times a year, by 1992 the number had fallen to once a year. The introduction of cable and satellite television, video recorders, and video rental stores further contributed to a dire situation that the press frequently labeled *Kinosterben*, the death of cinema.

Dark, retrospective DEFA films with characters who suffer from ailments ranging from disillusionment to madness appeared in cinemas at the same time as western comedies. Christoph Schlingensief's satirical horror film *Das deutsche Kettensägenmassaker* (The German chainsaw massacre, 1990; released in English as *Blackest Heart*) showcases a West German family that butchers East Germans as they come over the border and turns them into sausage. Schlingensief's low-budget underground film found some critical acclaim as a swift and biting commentary on the uncanny nature of unification, but its slasher aesthetics and scathing humor failed to win large audiences.[6] Light-hearted comedies like *Go Trabi Go* (directed by Peter Timm, 1991), its sequel *Das war der wilde Osten* (That was the wild East, directed by Wolfgang Büld and Reinhard Klooss, 1992), and *Wir können auch anders...* (No More Mr. Nice Guy, directed by Detlev Buck, 1993) were far more popular with viewers. These amusing road movies made at west German studios explore the culture clash when East meets West in a post–Cold War world and contributed to a comedy wave that dominated German cinema for a decade.

Go Trabi Go was one of the first comedies about the open German border to become a box-office hit, with 1.5 million viewers, and to receive critical recognition by being nominated for the German Film Prize. The movie features German teacher Udo Stuutz from Bitterfeld, who travels with his family to Rome in his beloved sky-blue Trabant armed with a copy of Goethe's *Italian Journey*. The film's production benefited from a blended East-West pedigree. Western commercial expertise was provided by successful producer Günter Rohrbach at Bavaria Studios with ample funding from the Federal Subsidy Board (Filmförderungsanstalt, FFA) and television stations as well as a wide distribution by Bernd Eichinger's profitable Neue Constantin Film (for details on the production history, see Naughton 2002). Eastern cultural expertise came from director-screenwriter Peter Timm, who was born and educated in East Berlin but expelled from the GDR in 1973. The three main actors, including television star and popular cabaret artist Wolfgang Stumph, hailed from the East, and this casting choice lent a sense of authenticity to the story. What could have been an open field for ridiculing inexperienced Easterners turned out to be an amusing and affectionate look at a naïve but adaptable family exploring unknown territory. Stumph emphasized that having Easterners involved was essential: "We didn't want our fellow East Germans to be laughed at, let alone mocked . . . nor did we want, as far as possible, Wessis playing Ossis. If anyone's going to make fun of us, let it be us" (quoted in Hodgin 2011, 36). Self-deprecation by former GDR citizens meant that the humor was not mean-spirited, and it gave audiences in both east and west permission to laugh at cultural stereotypes. Easterners are presented as unsophisticated, but despite their Saxon dialect, outdated clothing, and toylike car, they seem to be the rightful inheritors of the German cultural heritage embodied in Goethe and display the positive social values of amiability, industriousness, and adaptability. Western relatives, by contrast, are depicted as arrogant, overweight, and obsessed with money. The Trabi nicknamed George is the star of the film, and its adventures highlight the pitfalls of central planning (eager consumers waiting years owing to a production shortage for a car sporting a plastic body and a two-stroke engine that was neither fuel efficient nor environmentally friendly) and the resilience of Eastern products (the car's design remained relatively unchanged for thirty-four years, its resale value was higher than new, and its average lifespan was twenty-eight years). *Go Trabi Go* celebrates the open borders, the long-awaited freedom to travel, a modest introduction to consumerism, and an optimism that learning to deal with capitalist economics can be relatively painless, if not fun.

A sweeping history of the inner-German border would take some six years to come to German cinemas. Margarethe von Trotta's *Das Versprechen* (The promise, 1995), based on a screenplay cowritten with Peter Schneider, was the first feature film to address German division in a story spanning the entire duration of the Berlin Wall.[7] The film centers on young lovers Sophie Sellmann and Konrad Richter, who attempt to escape the GDR in 1961. Only Sophie makes it to the West, but Konrad promises to join her as soon as circumstances allow. The couple continues to love each other and has a child together, but the family reunion is only possible when the Wall falls in 1989. *Das Versprechen* was only a moderate box-office success, with 203,860 tickets sold. Von Trotta's choice of melodrama to depict the Cold-War division was lambasted in the press. Numerous critics complained that she focused too much attention on political repression in the GDR. *Der Spiegel* magazine was particularly vitriolic, commenting that "without a doubt beyond reproach is the political correctness: German finger-pointing cinema par excellence for all the knowledge-hungry people in all the Goethe Institutes of the Third World."[8] Perhaps what actually disturbed critics is that *Das Versprechen* is not so much about political oppression in the GDR as about separation: the separation of lovers because of political decisions beyond their control and the imposed division of Germany by the postwar victors. Von Trotta renders the story of the Wall in true melodramatic fashion as an act beyond an individual's control ("Filmfestspiele" 1995). The collective powerlessness of the German people to determine their own national borders is illustrated in the microcosm of a family torn apart by the Wall. Von Trotta's steadfast reliance on some of the more obvious components of melodrama—a prominent, often intrusive musical score, extreme sentimentality, the aesthetically pleasing rendition of pain, domestic conflict amid societal pressures—stands in stark contrast to her refusal to offer narrative closure (see Foell 2001, 246). *Das Versprechen* seeks to elicit an emotional reaction using such heavy-handed methods that one wonders whether the attention to artifice is intentional, meant to encourage viewers to adopt a critical stance.[9] The film does not give viewers an easily identifiable position as morally clean winners of German history and the Cold War. Nor does it end on a happy note with the resolution of conflicts and the joyous restoration of the nuclear family. There is no emotionally fulfilling embrace between Konrad and Sophie but rather an arrested moment in the in-between. The family meets on a bridge between the two states, and its future is uncertain. The division of Germany, like that of this exemplary family, has been so disruptive that it is impossible to visualize Konrad, Sophie, and their son, Alex, in the same frame, let alone see the bigger picture of a unified people. The bittersweet smile frozen on Sophie's slightly out-of-focus face reflects both the pain of historical losses and the resilient hope for reconciliation in the future.

The First Decade after the Wende

In the first decade after its official demise, the German Democratic Republic unexpectedly began to flourish as a popular trend. As if resurrected devoid of political content and manifest primarily in its material culture and rituals of daily life, the GDR was suddenly hip and gave rise to Ostalgie.[10] At stake in the debate over Ostalgie is the question of whether the GDR should be understood as real-existing socialism, a failed experiment, repressive totalitarianism, a welfare dictatorship, or simply a relatively normal state. Depending on one's answer, the popular fascination with everyday life in the GDR, especially rituals and texts that celebrated a happy, fulfilling life in the SED state, could be met with approval, bewilderment, or outrage. Many critics initially dismissed Ostalgie as the domain of naïve romantics, party loyalists, or capitalist entrepreneurs seeking a market niche. Others deemed nostalgia irresponsible because it failed to recognize the GDR's human-rights violations and the suffering of its victims. In 1999 anthropologist Daphne Berdahl argued against the notion that Ostalgie was merely restorative desire or escapism. She maintained that such dismissals were "part of a larger hegemonic project to devalue eastern German critiques of the politics of re-unification." Allegations that Ostalgie trivialized history represented broader "struggles over the control and appropriation of historical knowledge, shared memories, and personal recollections" (Berdahl 1999, 205). Cultural ethnologist Ina Merkel (1999, 401) saw Ostalgie primarily in terms of its ability to satisfy emotional needs in a period of social upheaval. Merkel maintained that the consumption of retro Eastern products was not evidence that post-Wall consumers wanted to reestablish the GDR or that they had idealized the political world of the past. She cautioned "that even a retrospectively romanticized view should not be seen as longing for the past system but rather for the daily experiences that cannot be repeated, for the long-lost tastes, colors, and forms."[11] Ostalgie afforded a psychological anchor in a world of constant change. Holding onto physical reminders of the past gave consumers access to feelings of certainty and stability they associated with such objects. Ostalgie can thus be seen as a reaction against the pervasive media portrayal of the GDR as a fortified prison state.

The comedy *Sonnenallee* (*Sun Alley*, 1999), directed by Leander Haußmann and written by Thomas Brussig,[12] tapped into the Ostalgie wave and became a box-office hit, with 2.5 million viewers in its first full year in release.[13] Unlike *Die Stille nach dem Schuss* (The silence after the shot, 2000; released in English as *The Legend of Rita*), which was marketed explicitly as an East-West production uniting Western director Volker Schlöndorff with Eastern scriptwriter Wolfgang Kohlhaase, *Sonnenallee* was promoted as the first film since unification made by East Germans to achieve mass appeal throughout Germany. Publicity materials touted the production's authentic Eastern heritage, stressing that the director and screenwriter grew up in the GDR. They highlighted the care with which former DEFA set designer Lothar Holler created historically accurate backdrops for filming at the site of the former DEFA

Studios, now renamed Studio Babelsberg. The contributions of popular West German actor Detlev Buck were downplayed, although he assisted on the script, starred as the policeman, produced the film together with Westerner Claus Boje, and distributed the film through their co-owned company, Delphi. The emphasis on an East German pedigree was important because it validated the notion that Ostalgie was a reaction against a perceived hegemonic discourse defining the GDR as a dictatorship. Daniela Berghahn (2005, 260) argues that by celebrating positive memories of the past while simultaneously making fun of the Ostalgie industry itself, the film attempts "to counteract the process of historical elision and the devaluation of their life experiences that have been lamented by many East Germans ever since unification" (see also Cormican 2007).

Sonnenallee is set in the 1970s and is a coming-of-age story about teenager Micha Ehrenreich, who lives on the short end of Sun Alley, which is divided by the Berlin Wall. As one of the first films to look at the GDR from the perspective of someone who was generally satisfied with his family, friends, and community, *Sonnenallee* can be seen as an attempt to overcome the individual's loss of legitimacy and value in a denigrated common past. Many reviewers criticized the film for portraying the GDR as a normal state. Viewers, however, found it appealing for its humorous take on adolescence: its sympathetic teenage protagonists falling in love for the first time, trying to score the elusive original rock-'n'-roll LP, and rebelling against authority in amusing and relatively harmless ways. The film is filled with stereotypes of both East and West: the perpetually paranoid Eastern mother who wants her son to volunteer for a three-year stint in the army and study in the Soviet Union because she thinks that will guarantee his security, and the condescending, if well-intentioned, Western Uncle Heinz, who smuggles in noncontraband items like nylons and underwear so that he can play the hero.

Neither the West nor the East escapes unscathed. Westerners look down on Easterners from their viewing platforms or air-conditioned tour buses. Acutely aware of the probing, disapproving, and pitying Western eyes that follow him, Micha plays for his audience. He runs after a Western travel bus, sucking in his cheeks and crying "Hunger!"; and when taunted by gawkers looking over the Berlin Wall, he notes that things are not all that bad in the GDR. The East may be his home and a relatively happy place, but it is far from perfect. A policeman shoots at a teenager who gets too close to the Wall, students are interrogated by the Stasi, Micha reckons with limited career options because he refused military service, and Mario admits to selling out when he is greeted at the army recruiting office by the Stasi. Unlike *Das Versprechen*, which presents individuals with limited options, *Sonnenalle* is populated by characters who knowingly play the system to their own advantage. Micha volunteers to undergo a public self-critique to get closer to Miriam, his mother offers to house party delegates from Dresden to look like a patriot to the neighbor she believes works for the Stasi, and his father falsely claims to have epilepsy so that he can get a telephone. It is, however, the power of fantasy that emerges as the most effective strategy to deal with both personal and political challenges. In order to win Miriam's affections, Micha falsifies his own personal history, stylizing himself as a rebel who tried to escape to the West and founded an underground resistance group. He writes in his make-believe diary: "This country pinches like a pair of tight shoes. You can't move, you can only dream."[14] At the film's conclusion, the power of fantasy is depicted as essential to political change. When Wuschel's long-sought-after Rolling Stones album turns out to be a counterfeit, Micha convinces him to accept it as real. They silently agree to pretend that the record is actually unpublished, forbidden Stones music. As they play air guitars on the balcony, their rebellious energy becomes infectious, and the entire neighborhood begins to dance to the beat. Although an undercover Stasi officer reports the delinquent behavior, the crowd happily dances up to the Wall, hinting at the future turn of events. When one border guard asks whether this is allowed, another replies that they are powerless against such a thing. Like *Der Straß* and *Stein*, made nearly a decade earlier, *Sonnenallee* presents characters who pretend that the reality they want is the one they have. All three films argue that the mindset of fantasy and freedom of thought eventually toppled the GDR.

The Second Decade after the Wende

Thirteen years after unification, a fairytale about bringing the GDR back to life became the most popular German film of the year. Some 6.5 million viewers flocked to see *Good Bye, Lenin!* (2003), directed by Wolfgang Becker, and it achieved a level of popularity and critical acclaim rare for German films. It joined the ranks of international blockbusters, was released in seventy countries around the world, and won thirty awards, including the German Film Prize and European Film Prize for best motion picture.[15] This tragicomedy about the Kerner family spans more than a decade, but the main action takes place from the Wende to unification. Christiane Kerner suffers a massive heart attack after seeing the police beating peaceful demonstrators and arresting her son Alex. She wakes up from an eight-month coma with amnesia and in such a fragile condition that Alex decides to spare her the shocking news about the collapse of socialism and re-create the GDR in her bedroom.

Good Bye, Lenin! is less concerned with an accurate historical picture of political developments than with the loss of utopian ideals and the reconstruction of national identity. What this film shares with various forms of Ostalgie is a profound sense of loss; but unlike the more sensational television shows that celebrate GDR material culture while conveniently neglecting its totalitarian legacy, Becker's film takes a nuanced approach to socialism's checkered past. It pokes fun at the frenzied attempts to reconstruct Eastern consumer products as a means to preserve and validate the ideal of a state that no longer has a material, political, or geographic existence. Yet, it also mourns the missed opportunity of the GDR, the utopian aspirations that were never truly brought to fruition. *Good Bye, Lenin!* is a response to recent history that constantly shifts strategies: alternately ridiculing futile attempts to recapture a bygone era, wallowing in regrets over irretrievable loss, and then celebrating the power of imagination to create the past we need for the present. It highlights the postmodern preoccupation with ruptures, discontinuities, and absences in order to question the master narrative that sees the period 1989–90 as the inevitable triumph of capitalism over communism.

Memory, more than history, is the central concern in this film. Because Christiane cannot remember her immediate past, Alex is forced to recall what it was about the former GDR that is worth preserving. The things that Alex remembers are his mother's activism, her attempts to make constructive criticism, her love of homeland, and her steadfast belief that a better world is possible. With his mother playing the leading role in his memories of the GDR, it becomes a community where people helped each other and a childhood state that provided unconditional love, well-being, and security. After the Berlin Wall turns into historical debris, Alex becomes an archaeologist of memory, recovering traces of the past and imbuing them with meaning. Relentlessly digging around in trash barrels, scouring flea markets, and exploring abandoned flats in search of the artifacts of GDR daily life, he attempts to salvage something from his past that has significance for the present. Alex uses the media to create a simulacrum of reality capable of deceiving his mother. His fictional *Aktuelle Kamera* news reports[16] are hilarious attempts to shelter his mother from the truth. But Alex's growing obsession with creating an alternate reality starts to be more about his own insecurities than about his mother's health. He uses the media to suit his own agenda, mobilizing everyone he can to playact for the good of the mother(land). Yet in this compelling drama, where the family is a synecdoche for the nation, it is out of love for his mother and her ideals that Alex looks to the stars and imagines a past he can be proud of. Alex creates a what-if scenario that reflects a willful lie and a deep-rooted wish, a maneuver that Roger Hillman (2006) has fittingly termed "history in the subjunctive mood." As a counter to the historical amnesia represented by his mother, Alex writes the history he would have liked to experience and argues that this shared fiction is the most satisfying and the most authentic foundation for the united German nation.

In 2003 *Good Bye, Lenin!* became a prominent topic for film critics, cultural observers, and even politicians. On the evening of April 3,

2003, the film reached a milestone in the annals of German politics. For the first time in history, members of the Bundestag went together to the movies. On the invitation of Minister of Culture Christina Weiss, over 200 members of parliament representing all the political parties collectively watched *Good Bye, Lenin!* at the International Kino in the Karl-Marx-Allee, which had been the premiere cinema in the former GDR. This ceremonial act was staged and paid for by X Filme Creative Pool to promote its own production, but the participation of lawmakers indicates that cinema can contribute to reconciliation. Critic Kerstin Decker (2003) suggested that a true unification was finally taking place in the cinema thirteen years after the political reality: "*Good Bye, Lenin!* is in fact a funerary film for the GDR. And that is important. Because no one has buried it yet, there was no farewell, it was suddenly just gone like the Spreewald pickles in Alexander's grocery store, from one day to the next. The cinema is making up for something for which there was no time in reality."[17] This film participates in a discourse of recovery—not the history of a perfect state but the memory of a communal hope that a better world is possible. *Good Bye, Lenin!* restores dignity to the people who lived decent lives in the GDR and provides a projection screen for those who desire the preservation of a utopian socialist agenda. Ending with a death and an imminent birth, the film reassures us that life goes on; and with the return of the father, it implies that some lost things can be recovered. The film's self-reflective irony encourages spectators to view the world from dual perspectives at the same time, mourning the passing of an era in which a perfectible world was believed to be achievable while simultaneously celebrating the fantasy that universal ideals survive and can come true.

After an array of comedies and years debating the merits of Ostalgie, many critics welcomed *Das Leben der Anderen* (*The Lives of Others*, 2006) for its serious treatment of the GDR as a surveillance state. Set in East Berlin in 1984, *Das Leben der Anderen* is a tale of idealism, betrayal, and the power of art to awaken the soul. Equal parts melodrama, thriller, and historical drama, the story revolves around the notion that individuals can change. Hard-line Stasi officer Gerd Wiesler conducts surveillance on playwright Georg Dreyman based on false charges of sedition. Wiesler quickly learns that a top-ranking party official wants to discredit Dreyman so that he can continue to sexually exploit the writer's lover, actress Christa-Maria Sieland. The more Wiesler watches and listens, the more he becomes enamored with the playwright's life, with poetry, music, affection, and love, until he is willing to defy his long-held beliefs and act against the state. The committed socialist Dreyman likewise undergoes a transformation and illegally publishes a regime-critical essay in the Western press. Despite Wiesler's attempts to shield the couple, he cannot help Sieland, who becomes an informant and commits suicide. After the

Wende, Dreyman learns about Wiesler's intervention and dedicates his novel, *The Sonnet of a Good Person*, to the former Stasi officer. Written and directed by newcomer Florian Henckel von Donnersmark, the film became an international success and was awarded the German Film Prize, the European Film Prize, and an Oscar for best foreign-language film.

Right in the opening scene, von Donnersmarck reveals the perverse logic of a dictatorship against which there is no defense. When a young man being interrogated for crimes against the state protests his innocence, Wiesler counters: "So you believe that we simply incarcerate upstanding citizens on a whim? . . . If you think our humanistic state capable of such a thing, then we would have been right to arrest you for no other reason than that."[18] In a cross-cut Wiesler uses the tape of this interrogation to teach young Stasi recruits standard cross-examination techniques. After a student questions whether it is humane to grill a suspect for forty hours straight, Wiesler conspicuously marks a cross next to his name in the seating chart. The omnipresent surveillance system upholding the SED dictatorship is directed against its opponents and supporters with equal force and works precisely because the irrational fear of being secretly watched is constantly substantiated as real. In a masterful use of Orwellian doublethink, Wiesler demonstrates that no one is beyond suspicion and that there is no safe refuge against the eyes and ears of Big Brother in the GDR of 1984.

More than any other film in recent years, *Das Leben der Anderen* stimulated a heated debate in Germany about the Stasi legacy.[19] Joachim Gauck (2006), former federal commissioner for the Stasi files (and federal president from 2012 to 2017), was moved by the film and exclaimed enthusiastically: "Yes, it was like that!" He conceded that it was unlikely that there had ever been a Stasi officer like Wiesler, "but a feature film is not contemporary documentation, it can treat history in a freer manner."[20] Former GDR dissident Wolf Biermann (2006) was impressed with von Donnersmarck's film: "The basic story in *Das Leben der Anderen* is crazy and true and lovely—which means utterly sad. The political sound is authentic, the plot moved me."[21] Biermann acknowledged that some aspects of the story and setting seemed inaccurate, but this was of little consequence in the end. Noting that Alexander Solzhenitsyn's novel *One Day in the Life of Ivan Denisovich* did more to sensitize the world to the plight of political prisoners in Soviet gulags than any historical account detailing all the atrocities committed under Stalin ever could, Biermann maintained that fiction can reveal important historical truths. Objections to the film targeted von Donnersmarck's choice of a Stasi officer as the hero and the fact that he wrapped up a complex political reality in the guise of a personal love story. Director of the Hohenschönhausen prison memorial site Hubertus Knabe refused to allow von Donnersmarck to film in the prison because the storyline heroicized a Stasi officer who became enlightened and converted. Since there was no evidence that such a case ever happened, Knabe considered the film a falsification of history that insulted the memory of those who suffered at the hands of the Stasi. Knabe stated that it would have been unacceptable to allow the crew to film "in a place where people suffered and which they would perhaps recognize in the cinema, to misuse as a backdrop for a film that handles the past in such a casual manner" (Ddp/mar 2006).[22] Film critic Rüdiger Suchsland (2006) notes: "That is the curious thing about this film: the surveillance the film describes and uses to expose the true nature of the surveillance state is driven by the purely personal motive of jealousy and not by political motives. . . . Henckel von Donnersmarck invents the Stasi good person and one wonders where this need for exoneration comes from that is satisfied in these kinds of scenarios?"[23] Because this film has a visual code that looks historically accurate, and it draws the viewer, like Wiesler, emotionally into the life of others, it has the potential to be a powerful, if not the representative version of the GDR past in the minds of many viewers. The ramifications are potentially far-reaching if we concentrate on the notion of a shared national past in which the perpetrator turns into a victim. As a national narrative, *Das Leben der Anderen* shifts culpability for the SED dictatorship's crimes from the Stasi rank and file to the informants they coerced.

Over the last two decades, numerous filmmakers have set their stories in the GDR, embracing nearly every possible genre and stylistic approach. Until recently, the only field unrepresented was the Berlin School, celebrated for its stylized aesthetics, formal experimentation, and nonpsychological-based narratives. One of the most prominent Berlin School filmmakers, Christian Petzold, the son of refugees from the GDR in the 1950s, wanted to make a motion picture that did not present the East as a dreary gray world filled with the ubiquitous Honecker portrait, national flags, and hidden microphones. Petzold wrote and directed *Barbara* (2012), the story of a doctor from Berlin banished in 1980 to a small Baltic town for having applied for an exit visa. Forced to start over in a provincial hospital where she suspects everyone of being a spy and is constantly subjected to house and body searches by local Stasi officials, Barbara plans an escape to the West to join her lover. In contrast to *Das Leben der Anderen*, which portrayed the Stasi from within the rank and file as they interrogated suspects, installed surveillance equipment, and intimidated the populace through open threats while embroiled in their own internal power struggles, *Barbara* addresses the human toll of living in a system of uncertainty and paranoia, always wondering who is watching and who will betray a trust. The sparse soundtrack captures unseen barking dogs, screeching seagulls, and a stiff wind blowing through the trees and accompanies Barbara on her lonely bike rides on deserted roads, illustrating her detachment and the ghostly fear of being alone and vulnerable to hidden forces. Emotionally detached and suspicious of the chief surgeon, Andre Reiser, who may or may not be an informant, she relates to her patient, the rebellious pregnant teenager Stella, who has repeatedly run away from a work camp and desperately needs her help. The value Barbara finds in her work as a doctor becomes a key factor in her decision to stay in the GDR and let Stella take her place on the boat to the West. In a brief but pivotal scene, Barbara and Andre study Rembrandt's painting *The Anatomy Lesson of Dr. Tulp*, where the artist has rendered the corpse's arm incorrectly to draw attention to the fact that it is a depiction from an anatomy book that all the doctors in the painting can see but the outside observer cannot. Andre interprets Rembrandt's constellation of figures within the fiction who look at something unseen that is made visible through distortion as a self-reflective device that allows viewers to focus on the victim. Rather than aligning the perspective with the authorities or the subjective position of the character, Petzold finds a middle ground that forces viewers to fill in the gaps and come to their own conclusions.

Final Remarks

In reviewing the discursive network of the GDR history film, one finds that two primary trends emerge. Firstly, a pervasive, recurring story-line focuses on the struggles of individuals against an iniquitous system and on the collective mission of bringing about a fair social order. This grand national narrative pits average citizens against a repressive government conceived as a police state—and unlike the passivity of the masses during the Third Reich, which is a prominent component in the retelling of German history, these more contemporary national heroes fight back against tyranny. In films about the GDR decent, average citizens want to escape, become victims of a corrupt bureaucracy that either destroys their initiative or robs them of their creativity, and are often driven to suicide. The heroes in this modern saga are overwhelmingly rebels who fight against injustice in all its forms. The most common figure is the courageous person who refuses to be held captive behind a wall, risking imprisonment and possible death to gain liberty. Those who stay are convinced socialists but fall prey to a regime demanding the type of compliance and conformity that depletes the human spirit. One-dimensional villains with no redeeming values exploit the vulnerable or mindlessly serve the powers that be. The rather clear-cut divide between upstanding heroes and self-serving scoundrels is symptomatic of mainstream cinema. Such a simplistic opposition of good and evil, however, comes to define not merely the storyline for popular movies. Increasingly, it contributes to a prevalent discourse on national history as more and more people learn about the past in the cinema, and motion pictures are endlessly reproduced.

For all their flaws, the films under consideration capture significant historical lessons on the dual legacies of the GDR: the attempt to better humanity, on the one side, and the force employed to achieve such noble goals, on the other. When assembled together into a whole, these films give a faceted picture of the past, one that is constantly evolving. The cinematic GDR is most often portrayed as a collective united in the utopian desire to contribute to a better world. The enduring belief in the promise of socialism to create a more equalitarian system for all, however, comes at a price. The genre not only depicts the pain of German division and forced separation of an entire nation. It also demonstrates how the drive for a just society ironically engenders a police state that demands absolute adherence to its dogma, fosters mistrust and paranoia among its citizens to enforce conformity, and deploys the openly secret, omnipresent Stasi surveillance system to eradicate opposition to the party line and destroy vulnerable individuals who dare to voice dissent. The most prominent filmic national narrative is a tragedy illustrating that the seeds of self-destruction lie in a system that used violence to promote peace. The most remarkable element of this grand narrative is that despite all the missteps in implementation, the utopian dream of socialism remains inextinguishable.

Secondly, since 1989 there has been a small but steady stream of feature films about the GDR that highlight the power of fantasy, dreams, and art as both a coping mechanism under communistic dictatorship and a strategy for political resistance today. Whereas the majority of history films depict the GDR as a totalitarian regime, there is a countervailing discourse that displays an ambivalence toward the past and argues that there is at least as much that needs to be preserved as forgotten. These films rail against the notion that the GDR was little more than a police state and question the master narrative that sees the period 1989–90 as the inevitable triumph of capitalism over communism. While relatively few in number, history films that promote fantasy over fact include some of the most successful feature films in recent years and are valuable for understanding the need to uncover what has been forgotten in the transition to a unified Germany if one is to build a common future. The genre also features heroes who willfully disregard reality and grant their imagination free rein to conjure up a personal and collective history that better suits their values and beliefs. While some critics have argued that this type of history film should be dismissed as mere entertainment, it is important to recognize that the genre makes a strong case for remembering and preserving the utopian ideals at the core of GDR history. Heroes who embrace an openly fictitious version of history nonetheless expose authentic wishes that remain hidden behind real events that never matched the desired outcome. History films, even the most blatantly fictional ones, poignantly chronicle how, despite persistent acknowledgment of political oppression, the GDR continues to represent a resilient collective dream of a perfectible world.

Notes

[1] For a variety of approaches to depictions of the GDR in post-Wall German cinema, see Cooke (2005), Hodgins (2011), O'Brien (2012), Frey (2013), Wagner (2014), and Steingröver (2014).

[2] Peter Kahane discusses how his contemporary social critique suddenly became a historical drama in *Sylvester* (1990). For a detailed analysis of the film, see O'Brien (2012) and Steingröver (2014).

[3] DEFA was sold on August 25, 1992, to the French group Compagnie Générale des Eaux (renamed Vivendi Universal in 1998). For an overview, see Dalichow (1994).

[4] Horst Seeman also turned to the Stalinist era in *Zwischen Pankow und Zehlendorf* (1991), which treats a traumatized soldier returning from a Russian POW camp who terrorizes his family in a country divided not merely by politics but also by a fascist, authoritarian legacy.

[5] "Der Freilauf der Phantasien führt zu Eklektizismus und Effekthascherei, Erzählstrukturen werden überfrachtet und zerstört. Berührende Bilder ertrinken in Zitaten, Musik-, Kamera- und Lichtorgien. So entstehen Patchwork-Decken, die niemanden wärmen" (Dalichow 1994, 336).

[6] For a detailed analysis of the theme of unification in horror films, see Halle (2003).

[7] The theme of lovers divided by the Wall features in the eighties punk drama *Wie Feuer und Flamme* (Like fire and Flame, directed by Connie Walter, 2000; released in English as *Never Mind the Wall*), the made-for-television *Der Tunnel* (*The Tunnel*, directed by Roland Richter Suso, 2001), and the historical drama *Der rote Kakadu* (*The Red Cockatoo*, directed by Dominic Graf, 2006). A much lighter touch can be found in a Prince and the Pauper-type love story, *Kleinruppin Forever* (directed by Carsten Fiebler, 2004).

[8] "Doch über alle Zweifel erhaben ist die politische Korrektheit: Deutsches Zeigefinger-Kino schlechthin für alle Wissensdurstigen in allen Goethe-Instituten der Dritten Welt" ("Festspiele" 1995).

[9] Jutta Brückner (1995, 153–54) argues that von Trotta's melodramatic excess is intentional. By drawing attention to artifice, she forces the audience to adopt a critical perspective.

[10] In the summer of 2003, four Ostalgie variety shows flooded the airwaves: *Die Ostalgie-Show* (ZDF, August 17), *Ein Kessel DDR* (MDR, August 22), *Meyer & Schulz—die ultimative Ost-Show* (SAT. 1, August 23 und 30), and *Die DDR Show—von Ampelmann bis zum Zentralkomitee* (RTL, 4 episodes, starting September 3).

[11] "daß sich selbst ein retrospektiv verklärender Blick nicht als Sehnsucht nach dem vergangenen System verstanden wissen will, sondern nach nicht mehr

wiederholbaren Alltagserfahrungen, nach verloren gegangenen Geschmäckern, Farben und Formen."

[12] Thomas Brussig adapted his novel *Helden wie wir* for a film directed by Sebastian Person (1999).

[13] For statistics, see the Federal Film Subsidy Board, www.ffa.de.

[14] "Dieses Land drückt wie enge Schuhe. Man kann sich nicht bewegen, nur träumen."

[15] Audience statistics for Germany are available at http://www.ffa.de. For worldwide grosses, see *Box Office Mojo*, http://www.boxofficemojo.com/movies/?pag e=main&id=goodbyelenin.htm.

[16] The *Aktuelle Kamera* was the main (in fact, the only) daily news show in East Germany, the equivalent of the *Tagesschau*.

[17] "*Good Bye, Lenin!* ist in der Tat ein DDR-Begräbnisfilm. Und das ist wichtig. Denn es hatte sie ja keiner begraben, da war kein Abschied, sie war plötzlich einfach nur weg wie die Spreewald-Gurken in Alexanders Kaufhalle, von einem Tag auf den anderen. Das Kino holt nach, wozu in Wirklichkeit keine Zeit war" (Decker 2003).

[18] "Sie glauben also, daß wir unbescholtene Bürger einfach so einsperren, aus einer Laune heraus? . . . Wenn Sie unserem humanistischen Staat so etwas zutrauen, dann hätten wir ja schon recht, Sie zu verhaften, auch wenn sonst gar nichts wäre."

[19] Like *Good Bye, Lenin!*, *Das Leben der Anderen* enjoyed a special showing exclusively for the German Bundestag (see Kurtz and Mösken 2006).

[20] "aber ein Spielfilm ist keine zeitgeschichtliche Dokumentation, er kann freier mit Geschichte umgehen" (Gauck 2006).

[21] "Die Grundgeschichte in *Das Leben der Anderen* ist verrückt und wahr und schön—soll heißen: ganz schön traurig. Der politische Sound ist authentisch, der Plot hat mich bewegt" (Biermann 2006).

[22] "[Man kann] einen Ort, in dem Menschen gelitten haben und den sie vielleicht im Kino wiedererkennen, nicht als Kulisse für einen Film missbrauchen, der so lässig mit dieser Vergangenheit umgeht" (Ddp/mar 2006).

[23] "Das ist das eigentlich Kuriose an diesem Film: Die Überwachung, von der er erzählt, und mit dem er die wahre Natur des Überwachungsstaats bloßlegen will, ist rein persönlich durch Eifersucht motiviert und gar keine politische. . . . Henckel von Donnersmarck erfindet sich den guten Stasi-Menschen—und man möchte schon wissen, woher das Entlastungsbedürfnis eigentlich kommt, das sich in solchen Szenarien befriedigt?" (Suchsland 2006).

Works Cited

Altmann, Rick. 1999. *Film/Genre*. London: British Film Institute.

Berdahl, Daphne. 1999. "'(N)Ostalgie' for the Present: Memory, Longing, and East German Things." *Ethnos: Journal of Anthropology* 64 (2): 195–211.

Berghahn, Daniela. 2005. *Hollywood behind the Wall: The Cinema of East Germany.* Manchester, UK: Manchester University Press.

Biermann, Wolf. 2006. "Die Gespenster treten aus dem Schatten: *Das Leben der Anderen:* Warum der Stasi-Film eines jungen Westdeutschen mich staunen läßt." *Die Welt,* March 22. https://www.welt.de/print-welt/article205348/Die-Gespenster-treten-aus-dem-Schatten.html.

Brückner, Jutta. 1995. "Für Margarethe von Trotta." In Peter Schneider and Margarethe von Trotta, *Das Versprechen oder Der lange Atem der Liebe: Filmszenarium,* 150–59. Berlin: Verlag Volk und Welt.

Cooke, Paul. 2005. *Representing East Germany since Unification: From Colonization to Nostalgia.* Oxford: Berg.

Cormican, Muriel. 2007. "Thomas Brussig's Ostalgie in Print and on Celluloid." In *Processes of Transposition: German Literature and Film,* edited by Christina Schönfeld and Hermann Rasche, 251–68. *Amsterdamer Beiträge zur neueren Germanistik* 63. Amsterdam: Rodopi.

Dalichow, Bärbel. 1994. "Das letzte Kapitel 1989–1993." In *Das zweite Leben der Filmstadt Babelsberg, 1946–1992,* edited by Ralf Schenk, 328–55. Berlin: Henschel.

Ddp/mar. 2006. "Historiker Knabe kritisiert Stasi-Film *Das Leben der Anderen.*" *Basisdienst,* April 6.

Decker, Kerstin. 2003. "Das wahre Ende der DDR: Wolfgang Beckers wundersame Komödie *Good Bye, Lenin!*" *Der Tagesspiegel,* February 28.

"Ende der Vorstellung: Die Filmbranche boomt, aber im deutschen Osten dauert das Kinosterben an." 1994. *Der Spiegel* 28: 68–70.

"Filmfestspiele: 'Es darf geweint werden.'" 1995. *Der Spiegel* 6: 188–90.

Foell, Kristie A. 2001. "History as Melodrama: German Division and Unification in Two Recent Films." In *Textual Responses to German Unification: Processing Historical and Social Change in Literature and Film,* edited by Carol Anne Costabile-Heming, Rachel J. Halverson, and Kristie A. Foell, 233–52. Berlin: Walter de Gruyter.

Frey, Mattias. 2013. *Postwall German Cinema: History, Film History and Cinephilia.* New York: Berghahn.

Gauck, Joachim. 2006. "*Das Leben der Anderen*: 'Ja, so war es!'" *Stern* 12, March 23. http://www.stern.de/kultur/film/-das-leben-der-anderen---ja--so-war-es---3495674.html.

Halle, Randall. 2003. "Unification Horror: Queer Desire and Uncanny Visions." In *Light Motives: German Popular Film in Perspective,* edited by Randall Halle and Margaret McCarthy, 281–303. Detroit: Wayne State University Press.

Higson, Andrew. 2003. *English Heritage, English Cinema: Costume Drama since 1980.* Oxford: Oxford University Press.

Hillman, Roger. 2006. "*Goodbye Lenin* (2003): History in the Subjunctive." *Rethinking History* 10 (2): 221–37.

Hodgin, Nick. 2011. *Screening the East: Heimat, Memory and Nostalgia in German Film since 1989.* New York: Berghahn.

Hughes-Warrington, Marnie. 2007. *History Goes to the Movies: Studying History on Film*. London: Routledge.

Jameson, Fredric. 1992. *Signatures of the Visible*. London: Routledge.

Kurtz, Andreas, and Anne L. Mösken. 2006. "Abgeordnete im Dunkeln: Der Kulturstaatsminister lud ins Kino—die Grünen konnten sogar zwischen zwei Filmen wählen." *Berliner Zeitung*, March 15.

Landy, Marcia. 2001. "Introduction." In *The Historical Film: History and Memory in Media*, edited by Marcia Landy, 1–22. New Brunswick, NJ: Rutgers University Press.

McGee, Laura. 1998. "'Genau so schlimm wird es noch kommen': Ein Gespräch mit Andreas Höntsch und Carmen Blazejewski." *GDR Bulletin* 25: 62–63.

Merkel, Ina. 1999. *Utopie und Bedürfnis: Die Geschichte der Konsumkultur in der DDR*. Cologne: Böhlau.

Naughton, Leoni. 2002. *That Was the Wild East: Film Culture, Unification, and the New Germany*. Ann Arbor: University of Michigan Press.

Neale, Steve. 2000. *Genre and Hollywood*. London: Routledge.

O'Brien, Mary-Elizabeth. 2012. *Post-Wall German Cinema and National History: Utopianism and Dissent*. Rochester, NY: Camden House.

Rosenstone, Robert A. 1992. "Film Reviews." *American Historical Review* 97 (4): 1138–41.

———. 1995. *Visions of the Past: The Challenge of Film to Our Idea of History*. Cambridge, MA: Harvard University Press.

Steingröver, Reinhild. 2014. *Last Features: East German Cinema's Lost Generation*. Rochester, NY: Camden House.

Suchsland, Rüdiger. 2006. "Mundgerecht konsumierbare Vergangenheit: Was ist eigentlich dran am Hype um Disneys DDR-Melo *Das Leben der Anderen*?" *Telepolis*, March 28. http://www.heise.de/tp/r4/artikel/22/22334/1.html.

Sylvester, Regine. 1990. "Leidenschaft und Überlebungskämpfe: Drehreport über den neuen DEFA-Film *Die Architekten* von Thomas Knauf (Autor), Peter Kahane (Regie), Andreas Köfer (Kamera)." *Filmspiegel* 9: 4.

Vollmer. Antje. 1992. "Endlich: Ein neuer deutscher Film." *TAZ*, July 3: 15.

Wagner, Brigitta B, ed. 2014. *DEFA after East Germany*. Rochester, NY: Camden House.

Wiedemann, Dieter. 1991. "Wo bleiben die Kinobesucher? Daten und Hypothesen zum Kinobesuch in der neuen deutschen Republik." In *Medien der Ex-DDR in der Wende*, 81–99. Beiträge zur Film- und Fernsehwissenschaft 32 (40). Berlin: Vistas.

5: Exhibiting 1989/2009: Memory, Affect, and the Politics of History

Kerstin Barndt

AFTER THE FALL of the Wall in 1989, Germany entered a veritable exhibition boom. The frenzied pace of exhibition and museum openings peaked at the turn of the millennium, when an average of more than one new museum opened its doors to the public every other day (Rauterberg 2002, 43). The end of the Cold War brought a windfall to economic and cultural globalization. At the same time, new digital technologies revolutionized the way we communicate, trade, and go about our lives. While digital technologies also impacted museum culture, where they enabled the creation of new immersive environments, object-based history exhibitions and art exhibitions soared as well, attracting ever more visitors through special events and other innovative programs.[1] This explosive growth, in some respects a permutation of what came to be known globally as the "Guggenheim effect" of the 1980s,[2] had specific resonances in postunification Germany. After 1989, the reconfigured state and its regions turned to the medium of exhibition to work through the divided past—including the differently lived legacies of World War II, Nazism, and the Shoah—and to reflect on the transformation of the present. Across the newly unified nation-state, museum and memory culture during the 1990s worked with an array of new exhibition concepts in regional museums and *Gedenkstätten* (memorial sites) devoted to Nazi militarism and perpetration. The *Topography of Terror* exhibit in Berlin that opened in 1987 on the site of the former Gestapo headquarters, for instance, has since grown into a full-scale museum and documentation center. While still considered a "difficult heritage" overdetermined by trauma, mourning, guilt, and shame, the history of Nazism and the genocide of European Jewry now have a firm place in virtually every contemporary regional or history museum in Germany.[3] The aesthetics of these proliferating exhibitions, however, have varied greatly, from the *Topography of Terror*'s sober documentary style, to the experiential, *Erlebnis*-oriented presentation at the Historisch-Technisches Museum Peenemünde, to the concept of the Nazi Bunker Valentin in Bremen-Fargo as *Denkort*, "a place to think but also to remember" (Heckner 2016, 369).

In her review of recent site-specific exhibitions with a focus on Nazi militarism, Elke Heckner (2016) sheds light on the installations of the Bremen Bunker, the site of a former Nazi submarine wharf. The info stations treat the architecture of the bunker as a witness to military and material history, including the history and memory of forced labor. While Heckner positively reviews the curatorial work in Bremen-Fargo, she faults the curators for failing to consider the "affective impact of the bunker space on visitors" (372). Against the curators' bracketing of affect, Heckner insists that Nazi architecture's enduring "fascination" has to be confronted head-on to guide visitors from "reactionary" to "productive" affect. "Critical thinking must be able to accommodate an affective response, that is, the very claims of the Bunker Valentin as *Denkort* ought to be inclusive of an affective experience" (376). In keeping with recent developments in literature and film, it has become clear that museum culture, too, needs to confront the complex affective layerings of any engagement with the stories of both victims and perpetrators in Nazi and postwar Germany.

Outside of Germany, the shifting memory of atrocities and violent conflict has similarly yielded new and explicitly emotional strategies of exhibiting. Paul Williams (2007) has coined the term "memorial museums" for such institutions around the globe. The new museum genre has been inspired by institutions that focus on the memory of the Shoah, particularly by the affect-laden approach spearheaded by the United States Holocaust Memorial Museum, which opened in 1993. Not only is the outer and inner architecture of the museum evocative of the space of a Nazi concentration camp, but the visitor is also asked to closely follow the biography of a victim and to confront the politics of genocide in the present.

After 1989, German museum culture had to confront the fact that the history and memory of Nazi Germany and the Shoah had themselves been divided over the past forty years. The memory of the Shoah, to take only the obvious example, functioned differently in relation to the GDR's antifascist foundational myths than it did in the historiographies of victims and perpetrators in the West. In this respect, postunification memorial museums constitute just a subset of the broader need to confront the divided histories of Germany and to articulate the place of GDR history, in particular, in the narrative of a newly unified nation. Unlike the Nazi past, which is receding from memory to history, the GDR past is still bound to the biographies and individual and collective memories of many visitors to German museums. Looking closely at the curatorial goals of German history exhibits and how they address their audience emotionally confirms not only that one cannot sever affect from curatorial aim but also that the study of affect in contemporary exhibition culture provides rich material for the history of emotions more generally.[4]

Over twenty-five years after 1989, museum representations of the history of the GDR are still contested and vary greatly depending on public or private patronage and on national or regional outlook. Just over a quarter century after unification, Germany boasts a fascinating and diverse set of exhibitionary engagements with the history of division, which extends well beyond the walls of the museums and into the very landscape of Germany. On the national level, new history museums in Bonn, Berlin, and Leipzig have opened with the explicit purpose of shaping public history and memory discourses of both postwar German states, tending to cast the FRG as the triumphant victor over state socialism and the GDR as a repressive state.[5] Meanwhile, other exhibitions and land-art projects have reckoned with the legacy of the GDR as part of a larger history of industrialization. Former factories, mines, and power stations have hosted history and art exhibitions, and even the renaturation of devastated landscapes in the industrial heartland of the former East Germany in Lusatia has been cast as a large-scale "exhibition project" in the Internationale Bauausstellung (International Building Exhibit, or IBA) *Fürst-Pückler-Land* (1999–2009).

I suggest that we read these and other modes of GDR "musealization" not only for the ways in which they have represented the rupture of 1989 and the history of the GDR but also for the kinds of historical imagination and affect these events have projected. In the following case studies, I deliberately focus on unconventional temporary exhibitions outside of the institutional museum, thus shifting our attention from the historical authenticity and emotional appeal of official architecture and exhibition culture to public places, world's fairs, and postindustrial landscapes as witnesses to history. The display aesthetics and the event character of these exhibits, I contend, have marked time and heightened the role of affect in peculiar ways, offering provocative configurations of emotion and temporality quite different from the hegemonic narratives that have begun to emerge in the nation's larger museums and their permanent exhibits.

In my analyses of an open-air exhibition on Berlin's Alexanderplatz, the German pavilion at Hannover's 2000 world's fair, and land-art projects in Lusatia, I consequently ask how affect and temporality—the order through which we relate past, present, and future—are linked. How do these exhibitions work through memory and its own forms of affect? How do they capture the emotional underpinnings of change? And what feelings do they attach to the possible futures they project?

As I have already suggested, scholars have found that many public museums and Gedenkstätten representing GDR history mainly focus on the repressive state apparatus and that they still fall short of rendering visible the multiplicity of everyday GDR lived experiences, or *Alltag*, including the importance of labor and material culture in the socialist state

(Paver 2016, 402). On the other hand, some private GDR museums have rescued items of GDR everyday life that they display in terms of what has been lost, and also as a counter-image to the new capitalist consumer culture. In this context, Chloe Paver has pointed to the importance of differentiating between two temporal levels of emotional attachment and their historicization: on the one hand, she notes the foregrounding of feelings of optimism or terror that bound citizens to state socialism between 1945 and 1989; and on the other hand, she aligns retrospective memories of the GDR with post-'89 affective states of "sorrow, resentment, intergenerational conflict, and, in more recent years, *Betroffenheit*" (399). I would add to this list the complex and often contradictory emotions that the events of 1989 themselves evoked in Germans with biographical roots in the GDR and the FRG—emotions that Paver pointedly describes as *asymmetrical* across East and West Germany (404).

We can certainly see these asymmetries play out in the case studies discussed below. Exhibitions and large-scale landscape projects such as the IBA *Fürst-Pückler-Land* in Lusatia, I argue in the following, have projected a range of competing historical affects associated with 1989 and the first decades of a new, unified Germany. Depending on the specific place, mode of address, and aesthetic of display, the exhibitions' emotional tenor fluctuates between the pathos of revolution and democracy and the joyful but inevitably empty celebration of a new "brand" of Germany; but also between loss and melancholia, on the one hand, and a self-reflexive and emphatically future-oriented mode of place-making facilitated by art and landscape architecture, on the other hand. These unusual exhibitions open up a space for reflecting on a complex and varied landscape of affect on which to map memory and history of the GDR and 1989.

Social History and the Pathos of Democracy

Among the many local and national exhibitions commemorating the events of 1989 twenty years after, the open-air show *Wir sind das Volk! Friedliche Revolution 1989/90* on Berlin's Alexanderplatz clearly stood out: On the wide-open and windy platforms of the famous public square, amid hundreds of pedestrians and surrounded by traffic day and night, rows of panels filled with photographs and texts reflected on the civil rights movements of the GDR. On view from May 2009 to October 2010, the displays highlighted individual and collective acts of courage against the backdrop of larger geopolitical developments (USSR glasnost and perestroika, Solidarność in Poland, and the opening of the border between Hungary and Austria, among others). The show was coorganized by the Robert-Havemann-Foundation, which houses an archive of documents relating to GDR opposition and resistance and promotes political education about GDR history, and the city's own event agency

(Kulturprojekte Berlin GmbH, financed by the German lotto foundation and federal funds). The exhibition project paid particular tribute to the citizen actors of the political sea change: political and artistic dissidents, oppositional collectives, environmental and church groups, demonstrators, and refugees. A compelling assemblage of photos, texts, and a few objects represented the complex and diverse nature of the protest movement. Documentary photos invited former East Germans to identify and remember friends and foes. The juxtaposition of the official festivities for the GDR's fortieth anniversary, on the one hand, and the civil protests, on the other, highlighted the growing rift between the "official" world of SED party politics and the "unofficial" politics of the street. The displays also reflected on the passage of time since the events: typewriters and moving images from a handheld video camera documenting a demonstration served as reminders that this mass protest movement organized itself without the help of text messaging, computers, and cellphone photography. The location of the exhibition, meanwhile, itself the site of mass protests twenty years earlier, provided a historic panorama of 1960s socialist modernist architecture and iconic structures: Hermann Henselmann's *House of the Teacher*, the TV Tower, the World Time Clock, the Fountain of Friendship between People. Demonstrators had flooded the Alexanderplatz and its surroundings on November 4, 1989, when more than half a million people came together for the largest public protest in GDR history. Photographs in the exhibition recalled this event in situ, reinfusing the contemporary space with a tangible connection to its urban and social history.

The exhibition's emphasis on citizen actors, the authentic location of the Alexanderplatz, and the public space of the exhibition, its 24/7 accessibility without entry fee or museum threshold, fostered a democratic pathos of engagement and reminiscence. As a work of remembrance, the project aimed to strengthen identity—especially that of the East Germans who collectively overturned the authoritarian state apparatus of the GDR. But the show also called upon "the people" of today, the passersby and visitors of the Alexanderplatz, to bring the ethics of active citizenship into the present. The latter became especially apparent in the stylized metal banners that crisscrossed the exhibit panels and other parts of the square. Reiterating words and fragments of slogans that were shouted in unison by demonstrators in 1989—"we," "people," "get involved," "act," "one people," "together not against each other," and "privileges for all," among others—the placards turned pedestrians into actors and interpolated them into the "we" of "the people." If the varied landscape of affect on which to map memory and history of the GDR and 1989 engaged in critical memory culture with democratic pathos, it also perpetuated a historical ethos that linked the past to the present and thus integrated the historical rupture into the here and now of contemporary Berlin.

The Birth of a Nation

The democratic interpolation into a sociopolitical collective on Alexanderplatz reverberated historically not only with the mass demonstrations of 1989 but also with prior exhibitions that reenacted the 1989 revolution. The show in the German pavilion at the 2000 World's Expo in Hannover, however, offered a very different mediascape. Articulating a far more abstract but no less emotional point of view, the show aimed to imbue history with a festive aspect to offer a highly aestheticized foundational narrative for the reunified nation.

The German pavilion reenacted the historical moment of 1989 with a view toward generating an emotional catharsis for visitors from near and far. To this end, the show worked to suspend temporality altogether with the help of a film spectacle designed to emulate the zero hour of historical transformation. This strategy was structured on the exclusion of the collective movement that brought about the change. Instead, the show celebrated individual creativity and openness as cornerstones for a new national community of inclusion.

The exhibit was structured in three successive parts organized as a one-way street, channeling a seemingly endless stream of visitors (5.3 million). Accordingly, the first part, entitled "Workshop of Ideas," served above all as a waiting room and antechamber for the main show, "Bridges to the Future." While standing and waiting in the construction-zone-like "Workshop of Ideas," the visitor was invited to contemplate forty-seven representative plaster heads in different sizes: side by side, one encountered former chancellor Ludwig Erhard, Dr. Motte of Berlin's "Love Parade," East German soccer star Jürgen Sparwasser, potter Hedwig Bollhagen, nuclear scientist Lise Meitner, author Thomas Mann, a few East Germans demonstrating for political change, and tennis legend Steffi Graf (German Pavilion 2005, 17–26). In postmodern fashion, the playful eclecticism of the assembled personalities ironized the traditional historical narrative of "great men" and its presentation in the national portrait gallery.

As soon as the queue had wound its way over the scaffolding and passed the big heads to reach the doors to the "main show," visitors entered quite a different space: a large rectangular room without any objects or windows other than some bridges criss-crossing the interior. Advertised by the show's producers as a "720-degree experience room," the installation used every wall, as well as the ceiling and the floor, for the projection of moving images. The audience, standing on the bridges, became part of the spectacle and found itself immersed in images, sounds, artificial light, and decorative elements that moved through space.

According to Milla & Partner, the marketing firm that produced both rooms, the video show formed the "heart" of the German pavilion.

The visitors were to feel as if they were right "in the middle of Germany" (in Deutschland mittendrin). The spatial conception of the video installation facilitated this notion of immersion. The multidimensional video itself, which was only six minutes long, employed a vaguely narrative framework that was filled with and rhythmically interrupted by a number of associative nonnarrative elements. At the beginning, we see an aerial view of Berlin. In a movement reminiscent of the opening shots of Wim Wenders's *Wings of Desire* (1987) or Tom Tywker's *Run Lola Run!* (1998), the camera singles out one house and moves down window by window. We see glimpses of everyday life behind the windows and catch a word or two. The soundtrack is mostly nonverbal, almost all music, but the word "Mama!" sticks out, uttered by a child we see through one of the windows. The child's affectionate cry adds emotional authenticity to the scene and invites primordial identification.

The core of the narrative plays in a courtyard party with food and live music, and everybody appears to be having a good time. The happy family/community that is portrayed here is mostly German middle-class, some younger, some older, and one child—a girl—in a wheelchair. From the party, the film images fade to the red dress of a moving dancer and then to the quintessential 1989 scene: at a border crossing, a Trabi and its female driver are greeted enthusiastically by a crowd. The soundtrack and the following fireworks mark that moment as one of several emotional climaxes in the piece. Before the scene moves from the courtyard back up the house wall, past the windows and into the sky, we see more dance scenes, hands playing a piano, a girl swinging through space and across the different screens; then some animated computer art conjuring up the freedom of thoughts, and a waterfall. At the very end, the wall of the house that we encountered at the beginning of the show becomes transparent, and its windows, now floating in space, open up into a night sky. Framing darkness and nothing else, the windows yet again invite the viewer's projection, implying a multitude of possible dreams and transitions. This multitude is cloned, however. Window frames look alike, and the imagination is prescribed by the images preceding this "open" end. Nightmares are left outside of the frame, so to speak, and a positive mood prevails even in the darkness of the night. As mere surface phenomenon, these frames, then, only toy with the idea of openness and contingency and represent the mass-media counter-image of the more self-reflexive media frames that Lutz Koepnick (2007, 10–11) reveals in his work on windows in German culture.

Besides the technological refinement and fetishization of the film, besides the spatial experience of the 720-degree media projection of beautiful (and moving) images—what is at stake here? Is there a message in the medium and its branding aesthetics? If so, and to the degree that this message is to be understood referentially, it appears to center on 1989: the image of the Trabi is the only one with a recognizable historical referent, and it is dramaturgically highlighted in the construction of the film itself. The moment of reunification in 1989, the film installation insists, stands as a founding moment for the new national community. Besides functioning as a vehicle for nation branding, the show frames this community in ways that do not rely on conventional patriotic semantics: no flags in sight, no anthems or hymns audible. Instead, the intimate setting of the courtyard suggests a seamless translation of nationalism into community in one multidimensional, continuous affective flow. This nonthreatening intimacy is further underscored by the gendered rendition of the story: the initial, anonymous call for "Mama" is followed by images of female beauty and elegance (dancer, girl on swing) and a woman Trabi driver.

In fact, I would argue that the organizers of the German pavilion took on the role of a "national brand steering committee," as it had been advocated by the consulting firm Wolff Olins in a proposal entitled "Branding Germany."[6] In its attempt to "brand" the nation, the German pavilion advanced a new kind of national symbolic politics that has since been employed in a number of social-media campaigns, culminating in broad marketing efforts accompanying the FIFA soccer World Cup in 2006. During the months leading up to this event, large billboards pointed imaginary fingers at German residents: "Du bist Deutschland" (You are Germany), proclaimed an authoritative voice on television; "Du bist Franz Beckenbauer" (the West German soccer star who won the World Cup as a player in 1974 and as a coach in 1990), posters asserted in bold letters. In a concerted effort, an alliance of media companies and public television stations had launched Germany's largest national image campaign. All celebrities appearing in the TV spot and its various spin-off versions participated without charge, and the sponsoring agencies provided free print and TV space to circulate the campaign's message in journals and newspapers, in movie theaters, and on prime-time television.[7] Taken together with the German pavilion at Expo 2000, "You are Germany" indexes a move in public discourse toward a form of populist and "light" nationalism whose specific "party patriotism" characterized FIFA 2006, the World Cup that opened in Berlin. Not only stadiums but also fans on the streets, cars, and houses were wrapped in German flags, proudly exhibiting national colors as in no postwar cultural or athletic event before.

Meanwhile, such political spectacle has become ritualized, reliably returning to mark every half decade that has passed since unification. On November 9, 2009, Berlin commemorated the political struggle of 1989 with yet another playful act: as part of the city's "Festival of Freedom" about a thousand overblown dominos, resembling pieces of the Wall and designed by German high-school students and Goethe Institutes around the world, fell in slow motion along the former border that had divided the city center: history as a domino effect. Five years later, Berlin celebrated the twenty-fifth anniversary of the 1989 revolution with seven thousand helium balloons marking the former border. At sunset, the balloons were released to rise into the night sky. The emotional economies of such nation branding rely on an open and positive horizon of expectation. The affective politics of history and memory in both instances closely knit past and present together to celebrate the historical rupture of 1989 and its actors (*Friedliche Revolution*) and to project the evolution of the new national community as open-minded, inclusive, and nonchauvinistic (German pavilion).

Mourning and Melancholia in Lusatia's Post-1989 Landscapes

In my final example of post-1989 exhibition culture, I turn to a large-scale landscape project, the International Building Exhibit (IBA) *Fürst-Pückler-Land* that began in 2000 and spanned the first decade of the twenty-first century. My reading of this project will bring out the other side of accelerated change. Embedded in processes of *slow* natural change, the renaturalization of landscapes devastated by opencast lignite mining reveals layers of time and affective temporalities that remain invisible or muted in the celebratory events of the capital and the Hannover pavilion.

In East Germany, the end of the GDR also accelerated a process of rapid deindustrialization that had begun in the West a decade earlier. The shocklike repercussions of this development were clearly visible in the installations and photo and art exhibits in the temporary IBA project *Power Station Plessa*. In 2005, the interior arrangement of instruments, machinery, and furnishings instilled a sense of loss in the viewers: right before their eyes, the forlorn past and its objects were frozen in time. Although they might have been able to reach out and touch the objects of the past, their sense of temporality clashed with the reality of these objects. Visitors found themselves in a different present, and this realization rendered these objects "museal": they had escaped functionality and become historical signifiers. The black-and-white photos that hung from the factory ceiling and on the walls deepened this sense of dislocation and melancholia. Visitors were locked into this space of the past and confronted by the gaze of the *Last Shift*, a photographic series by Christina Glanz. In contrast to the opening and uplifting window frames at Expo 2000, the dark room of the power plant instilled a sense of claustrophobia, and large-scale photographs on brick walls merely mimicked the idea of windows. All one could see on (rather than through) these photo windows were barren, desertlike landscapes. One floor up, the site featured a fully furnished director's suite. As an exhibit modeled on the concept of living-history museums, the room was arranged with attention to detail: The desk was set with pens, a framed personal photograph, and papers. The requisite portrait of Erich Honecker, former GDR head of state, adorned the wall alongside a tapestry with ocher and light-brown patterns that blended in with the other brownish elements in the room: wallpaper, chairs, and other furnishings. Closets and shelves were filled with a collection of objects relating to work and recreation: beer mugs and wineglasses next to books, a yellow safety helmet and pennant, a set of Russian dolls. A blue work jacket hung outside a closet as if casually left there to be retrieved at any moment. An administrative wall calendar from 1975 functioned as a caption to authenticate the historicity of the installation.

Contrary to the installations and photos on the first floor, the director's suite represented not the moment of the plant's closing but a time of GDR economic stability. The display here staged a specific, work-centered GDR life-world that had come to an end. Following Walter Benjamin, we might define the diverging historiographic approaches of the two floors as examples of historicism, on the one hand, and of historical materialism, on the other. The "eternal" and historicist image of one particular GDR work world, hermetically presented on the second floor, stands in stark contrast to the installations on the first floor, which could be described as staging the industrial fall of the region after 1989, in Benjamin's (1998) terms, as the "unique experience" of a "moment of danger." But then again, these installations patently lacked the dialectical "rescue" of the revolutionary experience that is also the object of Benjamin's *Theses on the Philosophy of History*. Melancholia prevailed over any attempt to associate the end of the plant with a new beginning. The installations at Plessa made it look as though the end of the GDR did not occur through the revolutionary uprising of its people in 1989 but rather with the closing of its factories and plants a few years later. As long as the former GDR citizens still had work, it appears, their life-worlds had not changed drastically. Only with the winding down of East German industry did the GDR as everyday experience come to an end: This is what the melancholic space of the Plessa power plant memorialized.

This memorialization significantly elided the GDR's repressive state apparatus, or even its demise: in stark contrast to the emphasis on civil rights on Alexanderplatz, here state security, closed borders, or censorship were not part of the display and did not enter into the consciousness of the visitor. The effect of this elision reinforced the localism of the exhibit as well as its emphasis on the quintessential Lusatian life-world— the everyday work of the lignite miner. The elegiac sense of ruination in Plessa attached not so much to the worker's *state* but rather more specifically to the worker's plant and its culture. The power plant in Plessa confronted us with an industrial and labor regime in demise. Still visible as order, documented in the form of carefully posed workers in uniform in Christina Glanz's photographs or in the staged authenticity of the director's room, this order was relegated to a past era.

One could also read this photo installation as melancholic comment on the energetic attempt of IBA *Fürst-Pückler-Land* to reinvent the destroyed industrial environment of Lusatia. The IBA's logo *see* combines the English verb *to see* and the German noun *See* (lake). While the verb *to see* explicitly stresses the role of aesthetic perception in landscape design, the noun *See/lake* serves as a reminder of the final goal of the reclamation process, that is, the production of a vast lake district. As this goal gradually takes shape through manmade and natural processes, the IBA has chosen to accompany reclamation by exhibiting different stages of this process with a stress on "interim landscapes." Given the fact that these landscapes are currently in the process of submersion, and hence disappearance, the financial and cultural investment in these interim landscapes and the attendant projects appears striking. On the other hand, the decision to accompany the lengthy process of reclamation by aesthetic means is a principled one: During the time of IBA *Fürst-Pückler-Land*, it was clear that the flooding of the lakes would be at least a decade-long process, and the IBA held out hope for constructing a new regional cultural identity for Lusatia. From the perspective of cultural history, these interim landscapes raise fundamental questions about the temporalities of deindustrialization, the demise of the GDR, and cultural memory: If the interim landscapes of the IBA were designed to disappear with time, what have they preserved? What has been laid to rest with their flooding? What forms of mourning have they facilitated? Or must we read the process rather in terms of repression, naturalized again in the process of flooding?

A particularly visible example that allows us to explore the implications of such interim landscapes within the context of the IBA was on view at Großräschen-Senftenberg between 2003 and 2010. Framed by newly built IBA exhibition cubes called the *IBA Terraces*, a former strip mine extended into the distance. Deck chairs invited the visitor to contemplate the open horizon over the enormous pit. Today, this gaping hole has been flooded with water, and the future lake has become visible, submerging any signs of the industrial past in a massive land-art project. Situated in an expanded present in which the echoes of 1989 continued to reverberate, the *IBA Terraces* invited its visitors to contemplate lost chances and possible futures, as well as the function of memory itself.

During the ten-year running time of the project, the three Bauhaus-style white exhibition cubes welcomed visitors to a show entitled *Timemachine Lusatia*. The exhibit concentrated on the major phases of the region's industrialization process. Significantly, it also explored Lusatia's cultural history, spanning from the minority culture of the Sorbes to Count von Pückler-Muskau's landscape gardens, from model workers' colonies to Bruno Taut's architectural legacy in Senftenberg, from local performances of Goethe's *Faust* to the start of the reclamation process of former lignite-mining sites during the GDR. Most striking, however, was the odd place of the GDR itself in the exhibition narrative. After all, the GDR had turned Lusatia's industry into the state's main powerhouse. Having lost the rich coal resources in the Ruhr district to the West, the GDR concentrated its efforts on building up an energy sector of its own around Cottbus, Lusatia. At the heart of these efforts stood an enormous lignite-processing enterprise, the state-owned Kombinat Schwarze Pumpe (Combine Black Pump), that rose to fame as the socialist model plant of GDR postwar reconstruction and that was frequently celebrated in contemporary literature.[8] To accommodate the thousands of workers needed for this enterprise, the new city of Hoyerswerda was built from scratch.

These defining aspects of regional identity, however, played a decidedly subordinate role in the conceptualization of the exhibit at Großräschen. Significantly, the exhibit alluded to the substantial increase in the region's mining activity after 1949 with only two texts (in a fairly dark corner), the official state symbol for the second five-year-plan under which the combine was built, and a few seemingly misplaced pieces of brown coal. Production and its related orders and culture of work were decisively not the focus of *Timemachine Lusatia*; key aspects of local and industrial history, and the forty-four years of the GDR more generally, were easily subsumed in the exhibition narrative as one, comparatively minor, chapter among others. Moreover, rather than tracing the patterns of production that had irrevocably defined the region since the late 1900s, the exhibit stressed forms of recreation and consumption: In well-lit glass cases, it displayed goods from other industries (such as glass and textile), presented the region's soccer association and theater, and drew attention to the sandy beaches of lake Senftenberg, a former lignite-mining site turned into a recreational area during GDR times, as a model for the future of Lusatia.

These curatorial decisions also had implications for the ways in which the *Terraces* engaged visitors on issues of mourning and memory. In clear contrast to the exhibit in Plessa, the space of mourning at the *IBA Terraces* was not centered on a lost mode of production or forms of labor so much as it related to the private sphere. An antique wooden rocking chair, a used trunk, and an old-fashioned children's bed were allowed to stand metonymically for devastated towns and living spaces lost to the ruination of landscape through lignite mining. Although this destruction began in the 1920s, most of the places remembered in the exhibit were destroyed during the time of the GDR between 1960 and 1989. In the mise-en-scène of the exhibit, however, this specific historical time frame once again receded into a broader temporal framework of industrialization from the nineteenth century onward.

A second exhibit at the *IBA Terraces* made this relativizing gesture even more explicit by vastly increasing the temporal horizon. Entitled *Land in Motion*, the 2005 show situated the regional projects of the IBA within a naturalizing narrative of the genesis of coal, reaching back to prehistoric ice ages. In a self-promoting effort to mark the halfway point of the ten-year-long IBA, the exhibit showcased "the transformation of landscape" (Kuhn 2005, 13). Although the curators were at pains to cite notions of industrialization and postindustrialization, these concepts remained empty signifiers within the construction of the exhibit, where they appeared devoid of historic specificity, only integrated into the all-encompassing regime of geological time.

As I have already suggested, the exhibits at the *Terraces* as well as the architectural design of the cubes serve to frame and give perspective to the transformation of the landscape under the aegis of the IBA. While they usefully (albeit problematically) foreground issues of temporality, memory, and working through the ongoing processes of transformation, these processes are best studied in the various IBA projects that took place in, or transformed, the Lusatian landscape itself. These ranged from open-air theater productions to guided walks, from land-art exhibits to the reclamation of former industrial sites for cultural events. Together, they amounted to a set of interventions and practices bound to an interim that anticipated the future flooding of the area. While these events were destined to remain elusive in the larger historical picture, their transitory character arguably heightens their relevance to the overriding issues of time and memory.

An IBA theater production from 2005 serves to illustrate this function of landscape-bound interventions. Staged on the site of the former town of Brückgen, the play symbolically reclaimed one of the destroyed places that *Timemachine Lusatia* had mourned. The buildings and streets that made up Brückgen once stood where the earth now opens up into the deep void of the former mining site. On the grounds of this vast opening, and in immediate view of the *IBA Terraces*, the production entitled *Everything Lost—Everything Gained?* marked in miniature some contours of the former town of four thousand inhabitants that was destroyed in 1988–89. On this "set," twenty people of Brückgen took the stage as witnesses, or *Zeitzeugen*, presenting stories from their past lives and "lost Heimat."[9] The oral histories reflected upon life at the edge of pit Meuro, oscillating between cherished childhood memories and the air pollution of the ever-present coal dust that turned white clothes black in no time. Owing to the immediacy of the lost place, the theatrical reconstruction of its history provided a narrative space easily filled with nostalgic feelings, once again privileging the private site of GDR life-worlds at the expense of public layers associating this microcosm with the totalitarian state. In the end, however, the chorus of Brückgen's former citizens longed for closure and offered a sense that one does not really want to go back in time (i.e., to Brückgen).[10] The theater performance on the ground of pit Meuro points to the intricate layers of memory embedded in the ruins of this particular open-cast mining site: On one level, spectators were asked to engage with the life of a town and its surrounding landscape, whose destruction coincided with the end of a state; on another level, the production drew attention to the end of an industry that affected the (work) lives of many people in the region. The object of the theater production, then, was arguably to work through these layers of memory, laying them to rest and clearing the path for the subsequent flooding of the pit.

If *Everything Lost—Everything Gained?* looked backward to take leave of the past in this sense, then other IBA projects strove to bring places of the past back to life through political and aesthetic means, as conceptual artists discovered the open brown coal pits as premier sites for aesthetic experimentation. Before IBA *Fürst-Pückler-Land* opened its first shows and projects, three international land-art exhibits prepared the ground in Lusatia.[11] The artists' projects provided focal points through which one could observe and experience the transformation of the landscape. While ongoing mining or reclamation activities have already destroyed a number of these land-art projects, a group of works is still on view in Pritzen, a town once destined to fall prey to mining.

The land-art events in Pritzen created the conditions of possibility for the village's postindustrial future through a properly *aesthetic* production of place that eventually put Pritzen back on the map.[12] The new identity of Pritzen rests on a number of land-art installations left by the art fairs. These installations now frame the former pit and its surrounding landscape. One prominent example of these works is Hermann Prigann's *Yellow Ramp*, an artificially constructed earth hill that resembles a pyramid at its highest elevation. At its tip the artist created an observation point marked by granite and concrete slabs previously used for temporary roads through the surface mine. Mimicking spiritually enchanted prehistoric observatories such as the stone circles of Stonehenge, the perpendicular slabs form a circle and leave spaces for the sun to touch the granite slabs at the center on the solstices.[13] Prigann calls his earthworks *geoglyphics*. These spatial signifiers, or "symbols of aesthetic perception,"[14] are supposed to leave an aesthetic mark that eventually links this site to other similarly derelict spaces and places.[15]

For all of their overtly mythical and utopian dimensions, Prigann's programmatic and artistic practices echo some of the central concerns of the IBA *Fürst-Pückler-Land* even as they contribute to a substantive transformation of the area's defunct landscapes.[16] In comparison to the black-coal landscape of the West German Ruhr area with its artistically crowned mining tips as signposts and lookouts (Barndt 2010, 280), Lusatia's lignite-mining landscape scarcely exhibits any natural or artificially mounted hills. The landscape is flat, wide open, and seemingly empty. In this environment, only a few natural or technical structures can be found to elevate visitors to a height from which they can look down upon the landscape and its history.[17] Prigann's observatory atop *Yellow Hill* provides a platform from which locals and visitors can overlook and contemplate the future lake and its surrounding plains. In this respect, it relates to scattered examples of restored machinery that have been left sitting in the postmining landscapes they once turned upside down.

In the small town of Golpa, for example, five excavators frame the open-air arena of Ferropolis, an agglomeration on a peninsula reaching into yet another postmining lake in the Halle/Dessau area. Likewise, the IBA project *F60 Mining Heritage Site* preserves the last of five conveyor bridges used in the coal-mining district in Lusatia. As has become customary with many industrial monuments in the Western Ruhr district, powerful colored beams illuminate the machines on event nights. During the daytime, however, visitors can climb onto the huge machines to experience the defunct technology within and the surrounding scenery on view from atop. Detached from their former function, these machines now stand as the only witnesses of a bygone industrial time in an inverted interim landscape. Where they once helped to unearth the last residue of coal at a vast industrial site, they now provide vistas over a landscape of recreation with lakes, beach life, theater productions, and music festivals. The clash between the gigantic technological machines and the recreational landscape surrounding them is so stark, in fact, that the machines become projection sites for new myths. In Ferropolis one of the five former excavators that frame the open-air event stage at their center is named "Medusa"; other machines are called "Mosquito," "Gemini," "Mad Max," and "Big Wheel." Anthropologization and mythologization go hand in hand here, turning the machine park into a new kind of Jurassic Park. Perceived as industrial dinosaurs, the excavators solicit emotional responses ranging from sublime thrill in the presence of these giants of technological progress to intimate sorrow at their extinction.

As I have been suggesting in various other instances discussed here, the temporality of the postmining landscapes in Ferropolis, Pritzen, or Großräschen oscillates between the locally specific here and now and the *longue durée* of geological time. Again and again, however, these potent temporal vectors seem to leapfrog over defining sociohistorical moments that produced the landscapes in their current, ruinous forms. This process reminds us of Robert Smithson's temporality of "extreme past and future," where visions of prehistoric ice ages meet posthistoric technological futures.[18] In reviewing the constellation of IBA projects over the past decade, it would appear that industrial history, bound as it is to the GDR's past and to current environmental damage, is made to recede either behind the private stories of individual lives or into the background of an all-encompassing geological time in which it appears as a mere blip on the geohistorical radar.

What is striking about the IBA *Fürst-Pückler-Land*, however, is the amount of celebratory and aesthetic energy that the project invested into its interim landscapes, into industrial ruins and artificial lake districts. Interestingly, then, the IBA sites fused melancholy to mourning, allowing overlapping layers of time and affect to coexist during the transitional phase of the interim landscape. The extension of "in between" time and space seemed to capture the human time it has taken to adjust to the political, sociological, and economic changes brought about in 1989.

In this longitudinal approach, the IBA project is to be distinguished from the celebratory presentation of Expo 2000 as well as from the authenticating pathos of the exhibition on Alexanderplatz. The flatness of the branding images in the German pavilion in Hannover, moreover, stand in sharp contrast to the history of resistance on public display in Berlin as well as to the aesthetic reflections on a changing landscape in Lusatia. The latter two exhibitions bring into focus historical actors and their feelings—as subjects who changed the course of history on Alexanderplatz, and as local actors embedded in a broader history of industrialization and mining that includes but is not limited to the history of GDR. Within this history the events of 1989 mark the most important turning point, but these events are complemented by a different temporality that articulates itself in the loss of towns and ways of life to mining.

From the vantage point of 2017, the pasts that these shows revisited, the democratic and economic futures they imagined during the first decade of the twenty-first century, already seem to be receding into distant history. Faced with Brexit and with the rise of right-wing populist power brokers, parties, and ideologies in Germany, other European countries, and the USA, Western democracy and the vision of Europe are in crisis. Histories and memories displayed just a few years ago now carry a changed affective charge as they become overwritten by the present. Past futures become futures past. Exhibition culture, both present and future, will have to confront, incorporate, and work through these competing temporalities and their affective dissonances.

Notes

[1] After a slight dip in the early 1990s, the number of visits to German museums has continuously grown. In 2014, the Institut für Museumsforschung in Berlin counted over 111 million visits to more than six thousand museums. Only the year 2012 had seen higher numbers. See Staatliche Museen—Preußischer Kulturbesitz: Institut für Museumsforschung 2015, 13.

[2] Variations of what has become known as the Guggenheim effect—the economic reinvigoration of abandoned city centers and industrial sites through new museum

buildings and other cultural institutions—can be observed in many German cities, including Bonn, Berlin, Essen, Cologne, and Wolfsburg. On the Guggenheim effect in Spain and worldwide, see Guasch and Guleika (2005).

3 On the notion of "difficult heritage" in Europe generally and in Germany in particular, see MacDonald 2016, 6, 14–19.

4 While related, *affect* and *emotion* are terms that capture phenomenological variants. For the purpose of this article, I understand *affect* as a slightly more diffuse emotional orientation closely related to mood (Stimmung), while *emotion* (Gefühl) captures more specific feelings such as joy or anger.

5 Exemplary in this regard is Daphne Berdahl's critique of the Zeitgeschichtliches Forum in Leipzig, a museum funded by the federal government that reviews GDR history; it appeared in 1999, the year of the museum's opening. Cited in Paver 2016, 400 and 402. In 2007, the Zeitgeschichtliches Forum thoroughly revised its permanent exhibition in dialogue with new scholarship on GDR memory and history.

6 In 1999, the German public TV station ZDF invited Wolff Olins to reconceptualize (or rebrand) the general image of Germany. See Olins 1999, 12.

7 The campaign (TV spot, advertisement boards, and Internet) ran from September 26, 2005, to May 2006.

8 In 1958, a state-controlled cultural initiative asked literary authors to visit the combine and write about it. Brigitte Reimann (1997) participated in this program and critically reflected upon her experiences in her diaries. Heiner Müller's radio play *The Correction* (written in collaboration with Inge Müller) is also based on the combine Schwarze Pumpe (Müller and Müller 1959).

9 *Alles Verloren—Alles Gewonnen*, a play directed by Jörg Montalta, premiered on April 2, 2005, in the Meuro pit in Großräschen.

10 Cf. the account of Ruth Kuring, an actor/witness in the play *Alles Verloren— Alles Gewonnen*: "You know, that place looked just awful by the end. First the Nazis and then the war—and after that, we had nothing left. Not a roof, not a window was replaced. No," she says emphatically, "I would not want to go back" (cited in Heintges 2005).

11 The first *Europa Biennale* took place in 1991 near the Cottbus-North coal mine; *Biennale II* (1993) and *Biennale III* (1995) were staged near Pritzen and its open-cast lignite mine, Greifenhain.

12 The organizers of the land-art projects are well aware of this fact. They stress the biannuals as a "dynamic and sensational ritual of the revival of a site." See "Prologue," in Förderverein Kulturlandschaft Niederlausitz 1997, 7.

13 Ron Graziani (2004, 124–26) discusses Smithson's Dutch restoration project *Broken Circle/Spiral Hill* (1971) in the context of a number of 1970s earthworks that were based on observatories.

14 For a more comprehensive account of geoglyphics in the context of Hermann Prigann's work, see Udo Weilacher's (1996, 173–188) interview with Prigann, "The Mad Dance of Entropy and Evolution—Hermann Prigann."

[15] Part of a larger project by the artist, entitled *Terra Nova*, the *Yellow Ramp* ultimately gestures toward European dimensions. *Terra Nova* consists of a network of deindustrialized zones. It aims to redesign and realign these landscapes aesthetically and ecologically with the help of local citizens whose loss of employment after the end of mining activities sets them free to engage with (or work for) Prigann's projects (Weilacher 1996, 180 and 187). In describing his earthworks, Prigann refers to the same concepts as Robert Smithson, emphasizing metamorphosis, evolution, and entropy. In distinction to Smithson, Prigann's projects emphasize art as a social practice that challenges and changes environmental awareness.

[16] The artificially constructed hill of *Yellow Ramp*, for example, serves as a windbreaker for the town of Pritzen.

[17] The most prominent of these structures is the *Pegelturm* (Water Level Tower), a slim steel staircase that winds itself up from the bed of the postmining lake Goitzsche close to Bitterfeld. The *Pegelturm* was designed by Wolfgang Christ, who also built the *Tetraeder* (Tetrahedron) in the Ruhr district.

[18] For Anthony Vidler (2000, 246–54), Smithson's shortcut of pre- and posthistory speaks to a more general contemporary sensibility marked by the divide of the digital age, a sensibility that undermines historic reflection and favors the screen over the mirror. The dehistoricizing practices of IBA *Fürst-Pückler-Land* might render the reflective surfaces of Lusatia's future lakes into flattened-out screens, a sign of "resignation that the grand narratives of introjection and projection that characterized historicist and modernist space/time models no longer hold" (245).

Works Cited

Barndt, Kerstin. 2010. "Memory Traces of an Abandoned Set of Futures." In *Ruins of Modernity*, edited by Julai Hell and Andreas Schönle, 270–93. Durham, NC: Duke University Press.

Benjamin, Walter. 2003. "On the Concept of History." In *Walter Benjamin: Selected Writings.* Vol. 4: *1938–1940*, edited by Howard Eiland and Michael W. Jennings, 389–400. Cambridge: Belknap Press.

Förderverein Kulturlandschaft Niederlausitz, ed. 1997. *III. Europa Biennale Niederlausitz 1995.* Cottbus: Förderverein Kulturlandschaft Niederlausitz.

German Pavilion. 2000. *Exhibition Catalogue.* Hannover: Trägergesellschaft Deutscher Pavillon.

Graziani, Ron. 2004. *Robert Smithson and the American Landscape.* Cambridge: Cambridge University Press.

Guasch, Anna Maria, and Joseba Guleika, eds. 2005. *Learning from Guggenheim Bilbao.* Reno: University of Nevada Press.

Heckner, Elke. 2016. "Fascism and Its Afterlife in Architecture: Towards a Revaluation of Affect." *Museums & Society*, 14 (3): 363–81.

Heintges, Valerie. 2005. "Da oben war die alte Heimat." *Sächsische Zeitung*, April 13.

Koepnick, Lutz. 2007. *Framing Attention: Windows on Modern German Culture*. Baltimore: Johns Hopkins University Press.

Kuhn, Rolf. 2005. "Landscape Change in Lusatia." In *Bewegtes Land: Internationale Bauausstellung 2000–2010. IBA Werkschau 2005*. Fürst-Pückler-Land, edited by IBA, 4–12. Berlin: Aedes.

Macdonald, Sharon. 2016. "Is 'Difficult Heritage' Still 'Difficult'? Why Public Acknowledgment of Past Perpetration May No Longer Be So Unsettling to Collective Identities." *Museum International* 67: 6–22.

Müller, Heiner, and Inge Müller. 1959. *Die Korrektur: Hinweise zur Regie von H. Konrad Hoerning*. Leipzig: F. Hofmeister.

Olins, Wolff. 1999. *Debatte—Deutschland als globale Marke*. Munich: Econ.

Paver, Chloe. 2016. "Exhibiting Negative Feelings: Writing a History of Emotion in German History Museums." *Museums & Society* 14 (3): 397–411.

Rauterberg, Hanno. 2002. "Selbst die Gegenwart ist bereits eingefroren." *Die Zeit*, September 5.

Reimann, Brigitte. 1997. *Ich bedauere nichts: Tagebücher*. Berlin: Aufbau-Verlag.

Scribner, Charity. 2003. *Requiem for Communism*. Cambridge, MA: MIT Press.

Staatliche Museen zu Berlin—Preußischer Kulturbesitz: Institut für Museumsforschung, ed. 2015. Heft 69, *Statistische Gesamterhebung an den Museen der Bundesrepublik Deutschland für das Jahr 2014*. Berlin: Institut für Museumsforschung.

Vidler, Anthony. 2000. *Warped Space: Art, Architecture, and Anxiety in Modern Culture*. Cambridge, MA: MIT Press.

Weilacher, Udo. 1996. *Between Landscape Architecture and Land Art*. Basel: Birkhäuser.

Williams, Paul. 2007. *Memorial Museums: The Global Rush to Commemorate Atrocities*. London: Berg.

Part III.

A Changing Reception:
Painting, Orchestras, and Theaters

6: Reexamining the *Staatskünstler* Myth: Bernhard Heisig and the Post-Wall Reception of East German Painting

April A. Eisman

Heisig and the Fall of the Wall

WHEN THE BERLIN WALL FELL unexpectedly on November 9, 1989, the East German artist Bernhard Heisig already had many of his most important works hanging in a museum in the West. Just a few weeks earlier, on September 30, a major exhibition containing 120 of his paintings and more than 300 prints and drawings had opened at the Martin-Gropius-Bau in West Berlin. *Bernhard Heisig, Retrospective* was the largest and most comprehensive exhibition of an East German artist ever held in West Germany. It was also the first major exhibition of a postwar German artist—East or West—put together by a collaborative effort of East and West German curators; it would travel to cities in both countries over the course of the next year. At the age of sixty-four, Heisig had made it as a "German" artist—highly praised for his work in both East and West—at a time when a unified Germany still seemed decades away.

Within weeks of the Berlin Wall's collapse, however, Heisig's reception changed drastically. Rather than praising his work for its commitment to the Expressionist tradition and history, the West German press now attacked him for his biography and, in particular, for his connection to the German Democratic Republic (GDR), where he had been both a successful artist and a powerful cultural figure. These often vehement attacks in the press, which lasted for more than a decade, have become known as the German-German *Bilderstreit*, or "image battle,"[1] and were aimed at East Germany's most successful artists. At stake was what role, if any, East German art and artists should be allowed to play in the new Germany.

In these debates the term *Staatskünstler*, or "State Artist," was frequently used as shorthand to dismiss these highly praised artists. In this chapter I will focus on this term with regard to Heisig in order to better understand the tendentious nature of East German art's reception after the Wende and, in particular, the Bilderstreit of the long 1990s. What does the term *Staatskünstler* actually mean, both literally and by implication? Who used the term? And why? Ultimately, I will argue that *Staatskünstler*, when used with East German artists, perpetuates negative stereotypes that undermine a deeper understanding of the artists and the work they created. I begin by tracing the history of East German art's reception in the West before and, especially, after the Wende, before turning briefly to how the Bilderstreit continues to affect exhibitions of East German art in the new millennium—most notably in the 2005 Berlin exhibition, *Bernhard Heisig: Die Wut der Bilder* (Bernhard Heisig: The Anger of Images) and the 2009 exhibition in Los Angeles, *Art of Two Germanys: Cold War Cultures.*

East German Art's Reception in the West

In Anglophone scholarship Heisig—as well as contemporary East German art in general—is virtually unknown, the result, in part, of the Cold War era's politicization of the visual arts, which were divided in two since the late 1940s: abstract and realist, good and bad, Art and non-Art. According to this paradigm, East Germany did not create art, merely political propaganda and kitsch. It is a stereotype that, despite the passage of more than twenty-five years since the end of the Cold War, remains dominant in the minds of most Anglophone academics, who, if asked to describe "East German art," would probably mention "Socialist Realism" and imagine pictures of Communist leaders or happy workers portrayed in an almost photographic realism.

While this type of art certainly existed throughout the forty-year history of the GDR, it reached its official apex in 1953 with works like Harald Hellmich and Klaus Weber's *The Youngest Fliers.*[2] In the wake of Stalin's death and the workers' revolt in June of that year, however, East German artistic policy loosened in the first of many thaws, and visual artists began experimenting in the styles of Picasso and Léger in the mid-1950s, as can be seen, for example, in Harald Metzkes's painting *Removal of the Six-Armed Goddess.*[3] In fact, there was a multi-issue discussion of Picasso as a possible role model for East German artists in *Bildende Kunst*, the GDR's main art magazine, in these years; Picasso seemed a particularly interesting figure because he combined a modernist aesthetic with a political commitment to Communism.

By the mid-1960s, artists in Leipzig—and, in particular, Bernhard Heisig, Wolfgang Mattheuer, and Werner Tübke, along with Willi Sitte from neighboring Halle—had developed a uniquely East German style of contemporary art that would come to represent the GDR in the more relaxed cultural atmosphere of the Honecker era in the 1970s and 1980s. And it is paintings like theirs—multivalent works that reflect a commitment to the modernist tradition—that would be exhibited in the West to great praise in the latter decades of the Cold War era.

In the Federal Republic of Germany, the development of art in East Germany after 1953 is better known, albeit problematic. Already in the late 1960s Eduard Beaucamp was writing about Heisig, Tübke, Mattheuer, and Sitte—the so-called Band of Four—in the *Frankfurter Allgemeine Zeitung*. A few years later, in 1977, these four artists were invited to exhibit works at the international art exhibition *documenta 6* in Kassel, West Germany. This event marks the emergence of contemporary East German art *en masse* onto the Western art scene. In the wake of this exhibition, these four artists became virtually synonymous with East German art in the minds of many West German curators, and it was these artists who were the most heavily praised, collected, and exhibited in West Germany throughout the 1980s. It was also they who were most frequently at the center of controversy in the wake of 1989/90 as the GDR's so-called Staatskünstler.

The controversy around these artists was not new to the *Mauerfall* but rather had already begun with their inclusion in *documenta 6*. Protestors delivered leaflets and conducted a sit-in; Georg Baselitz pulled his work from the show (Schirmer 2005). But these voices did not command the press's attention the way they would in the wake of November 1989. In large part this was because of the leftist leanings of West Germany in the 1970s and 1980s. With the sudden collapse of the GDR, however, the authority that leftist intellectuals had enjoyed since Willy Brandt's Ostpolitik was undermined, and conservative voices came to the fore in a wave of victor's glory (Brockmann 1999; Jarausch 1994).

The change in contemporary East German art's reception in the Federal Republic of Germany (FRG)—West Germany before 1990, unified Germany afterward—in the wake of the Mauerfall occurred almost immediately. Whereas Heisig's *Retrospective* had opened to positive reviews in October 1989, by the end of November it was being criticized. Similarly, Peter Ludwig, a major West German collector and exhibitor of East German art, commented on the virtual ban he was seeing on East German art in the FRG the following summer. It was a couple of years, however, before what has become known as the German-German Bilderstreit began in earnest.

The first clash took place in 1993 when eighteen prominent West Germans—including the GDR emigrants Georg Baselitz and Gerhard Richter—left the visual arts department of the West Berlin Academy in protest against the en-bloc acceptance of colleagues from its eastern counterpart.[4] The following year, the Neue Nationalgalerie in Berlin became the center of controversy for an exhibition of postwar German art from its permanent collection that placed masterpieces from the two Germanys side by side. The right-of-center Christian Democratic Party (CDU) in Berlin ignited the debate, likening the museum to a Parteischule (party school) because of its inclusion of Heisig, Sitte, Tübke, and Mattheuer.[5]

A third major Bilderstreit took place in 1998 when Heisig was invited—as one of only two East German artists—to contribute work to the Reichstag's permanent collection. Heisig was attacked for being a teenage soldier in the Waffen SS and for being a Staatskünstler. In fact, the two were conflated by Uwe Lehmann-Brauns of the CDU, who stated that Heisig had "loyally served two dictatorships."[6] In the end, however, it was Heisig's commitment to the GDR that was the real problem.

It is shortly after this debate that the *Aufstieg und Fall der Moderne* exhibition opened in Weimar, marking the climax of the Bilderstreit. In this exhibition, the West German curator's contempt for the East German works on display was obvious—the paintings were crowded together and hung up haphazardly against drop cloths in a space without climate control. Moreover, an exhibition of Nazi works elsewhere in the building suggested not only a connection between the two regimes but also that the Nazi works were more valuable, as they had been hung with more care.[7]

This debate was followed by another major Bilderstreit, that over the planned 2001 exhibition of Willi Sitte's work at the Germanisches Nationalmuseum in Nuremberg for his eightieth birthday. Ultimately, the furor in the press over Sitte's connections to the East German state—his position as Staatskünstler—led to Sitte cancelling the show.

State Artist

On its surface, the term *Staatskünstler* is not a negative one. It means, literally, "State artist." The history of art is filled with them, from the Romans to Jacques-Louis David: artists who fulfilled commissions for—and whose art came to represent—the State. From this perspective, Heisig was indeed a Staatskünstler, as were Tübke, Mattheuer, and Sitte. He fulfilled artistic commissions, and his work represented the GDR in major international exhibitions, including *documenta* 6 (1977) and the *Venice Biennale* (1984). But the term *Staatskünstler*, when used with East German art, has a number of negative connotations that upon closer examination do not apply to Heisig (or, for that matter, to Tübke or Mattheuer).

The first connotation is the idea that Staatskünstler forfeited artistic integrity in exchange for fame and power. In Heisig's case, however, it was just the opposite. First, he actually changed from an Adolf von Menzel-inspired realism in the 1950s to one inspired by Lovis Corinth, Oskar Kokoschka, Max Beckmann, and Otto Dix in the early to mid-1960s.[8] That is, he changed from an artistic style that was acceptable to political functionaries to one that was not (Eisman 2007, ch. 3).

Second, rather than Heisig changing his style to fit the regime, it was actually the regime that changed its stance on art. Until it did so in the early 1970s, Heisig was repeatedly at the center of controversy. In 1964, for example, he gave a speech at the Fifth Congress of the Union of Visual Artists in which he defended the use of modern artistic styles in East German art. As a result, he underwent a multiweek investigation into his loyalty to the party and was forced to deliver an official self-criticism to redeem himself in the eyes of the State.

Less than a year later, in 1965, he created a series of murals in Leipzig that were the focus of heated debate for months: Seen as a success by artists, these murals were criticized by political functionaries for their formalist qualities (Eisman 2011). Then, later that year, Heisig was the center of yet more criticism when he exhibited *The Paris Commune* at the *Seventh District Art Exhibition* in Leipzig. Political functionaries condemned the work for its formalist qualities and, worse still, for its pessimism.

What these examples show is that Heisig did not forfeit his artistic integrity for fame and power but rather stood up for his artistic beliefs even when those beliefs were unpopular. He was not afraid of creating controversy. These examples also show that artistic policy in the GDR was not as top down as is often thought.[9] If it were, the works would not have been created in the first place, not to mention exhibited and even praised in the press. Rather than consistent top-down repression, there was often an attempt to reconcile the two sides.

With the rise of Erich Honecker to power in 1971, artistic policy in the GDR relaxed considerably in an era of "breadth and variety" that lasted, by and large, until the GDR's collapse.[10] In a speech given shortly after becoming East German leader, Honecker stated, "for those artists who truly believe in Socialism, there can be no more taboos on their work, neither in content nor in style."[11] It is in the wake of this change that Heisig's meteoric rise to fame and power really began. Although Heisig may not have contributed directly to this change in policy, his repeated provocations in the 1960s and the discussions between functionaries and artists that ensued certainly contributed to the creation of the art style that would be praised in the 1970s and 1980s in both East and West. Without Heisig, in other words, the very art that was promoted once cultural policies loosened would probably not have come into existence, at least not in the form that it did.[12]

A second implication behind the term *Staatskünstler* is that these artists actively oppressed others. In Heisig's case, the implied accusation is that he, as professor at and rector of the Leipzig Academy, prevented those with a more radical view of art in terms of stylistic innovation from becoming artists. This is a complicated libel because it faults Heisig for doing his job, that is, for accepting and rejecting applications for the Leipzig Academy, and implies that his choices were merely politically or personally motivated rather than stemming from choices about an applicant's artistic worth.[13] It is exacerbated by the fact that it was more

difficult to become an artist in East Germany than in the West: one usually had to graduate from one of the four main art academies to be considered an artist, so if Heisig rejected an application, there were not a lot
of other options for the would-be student except to reapply the following
year or to apply to one of the other three schools. It argues in Heisig's
favor, however, that many of the major names in the East German art
world of the 1970s and 1980s were once his students. That they were
recognized on both sides of the Wall—and therefore in places beyond
Heisig's direct influence—further emphasizes their artistic merit.

As rector, Heisig also worked to make the Leipzig Academy more
modern. He hired Hartwig Ebersbach to create and teach a multimedia
class and ran interference with political functionaries in Berlin for years
before the class was ultimately shut down.[14] Similarly, as vice president
of the national Artists' Union he helped negotiate a compromise for the
controversial *Herbstsalon* in Leipzig in 1984, a so-called underground
exhibition of young artists who were able to display works not considered
acceptable by the government (Grundmann and Michael 2002, 32–33;
Lang 2002, 210–11). All of these facts—and more—suggest that Heisig
was open to the younger generation and worked to include them and
their broadening interests in the system, even if he was not interested in
creating such works himself.

In the end, however, the truth of whether or not Heisig and the
other so-called Staatskünstler had actually oppressed others—or sold out
their artistic integrity—did not really matter to those making the accusations. What mattered was these artists' high-profile association with the
GDR, a country that collapsed in 1989/90, which seemed to prove it
was an *Unrechtstaat*.[15] In the heavily charged political atmosphere of
Germany in the 1990s, the so-called Staatskünstler were seen by many
(West) Germans as having helped legitimate the East German regime—
and thus having contributed to its longevity—by the very fact that they
had not left it, thus tacitly, if not actively, supporting it. This subtly poi-
sonous accusation recalls the exiles-*Hierbleiber* debates from the Third
Reich, where exiles were castigated for abandoning the German people in
their time of greatest need and Hierbleiber for tacitly lending their support to the regime by not leaving. Artists like Heisig were thus castigated
for being Hierbleiber—for staying in the GDR and attempting to change
it from within.[16]

Not all of the criticism came from West Germans, however. There
were, in fact, at least three distinct groups of East Germans in the art
world whose condemnations of the so-called Staatskünstler were used
to buoy conservative (West) German criticisms. The first came from the
youngest generation of artists in the GDR, those whose radicalism in
terms of formal innovation had caused conflict with the government, and
for whom the Mauerfall had ended the GDR before such conflicts could

be worked out, or, in the case of those who had recently immigrated to the West, before they could dissociate themselves from their East German past. It is this group in particular that saw—and continues to see—the so-called *Staatskünstler* as having sold out their artistic integrity and misused their power to oppress younger, more formally radical artists. Archival evidence and interviews, however, suggest the issue at stake here was less one of aesthetic repression than of a generational conflict, one typical for Germany, where, as the Mitscherlichs (1967) observed, intergenerational conflicts were particularly strong owing to the horror of the German past.[17] These younger artists were rebelling against the hegemony of the Hitler Youth generation of artists—the so-called Staatskünstler—who were not only greatly praised in the GDR and internationally in the final decades of the Cold War but were also in control of the East German art academies and institutions and, as such, dictating policy.[18]

A second group of East German voices critical of the Staatskünstler came from artists who left the GDR and made an international name for themselves as "German" artists. The most notable example of this is Baselitz, who stated in a much-quoted interview in *Art* magazine in 1990: "There were no artists in the GDR, they all left . . . no artists, no painters. None of them ever painted a picture. . . . They are interpreters who fulfilled the program of the East German system . . . [they are] simply assholes" (Hecht, Welti, and Baselitz 1990, 70). Both he and Gerhard Richter left the GDR as adults for the West, where they became internationally famous. Their East German backgrounds—including artistic training—were glossed over.[19] And yet, this background presumably contributed to their positive reception, lending them an aura of Otherness that also confirmed the seeming superiority of the West by their choice to live there.

The third group of East German voices comprises artists, critics, and art historians from places other than Leipzig or Halle. These individuals have attempted to reconfigure—perhaps unconsciously—the history of East German art in recent years. In particular, they downplay the importance of the Leipzig School. This view was particularly apparent in the 2003 exhibition *Kunst in der DDR: Eine Retrospektive* at the Neue Nationalgalerie in Berlin, where the "Leipzig School" as such had only one small, artificially lit room, while artists from Berlin enjoyed three of the five rooms in the exhibition that were open to natural lighting. For those unfamiliar with the history of East German art, the "Leipzig School" would have seemed no more important than Hermann Glöckner—an artist who lived in obscurity for most of his life in the GDR—while Berlin enjoyed an importance it did not possess before the Mauerfall, at least not in the West.[20]

This antipathy toward Leipzig among some East German curators currently working in Germany had a direct bearing on an exhibition of

Heisig's work that took place in 2005, *Die Wut der Bilder*. It was intended to be held in and curated by the Neue Nationalgalerie, but the East German curators there refused to do the show. As a result, the exhibition was moved to the Martin-Gropius-Bau, and a (West) German art historian was brought in as curator. The resulting exhibition was clearly a West German production, one that—despite its claims to be a "comprehensive overview of Heisig's work"—focused almost exclusively on his history paintings and related portraiture (Gillen 2005, 10). Heisig appeared to be an artist obsessed by his past as a teenage soldier in World War II, rather than an intellectual artist engaged with important issues of the day. This view was further encouraged by the ahistorical approach taken toward his paintings; their development within his oeuvre and relationship to the Cold War context in which they were created were not explored. Instead, the emphasis was on trauma, and the works were praised as an invaluable contribution to Germany's *Vergangenheitsbewältigung*.

This interest in "coming to terms with the past," however, did not include the more recent past of the Cold War era. Any positive relationship Heisig had to the GDR was overlooked or dismissed in the exhibition and its catalog. In fact, Heisig was presented as a great German artist in spite of the East German context in which he lived and worked. It was, however, because of the East German context that he became the artist he did. The battles he fought affected not only those around him but also his own art and views, such as his commitment to figuration and tradition.

A closer examination of the 2005 exhibition suggests that it was, ultimately, an attempt—already successful with Tübke and Mattheuer—to free Heisig from the *Staatskünstler* label and thereby redeem him for a post-Wall German audience. While the recasting of Heisig's life and work appears to have been successful—the show was not canceled, and it was fairly well received in the press—it has left behind a distorted view of the artist and his work. Anyone who looks at the 2005 catalog rather than the one from 1989, for example, will presume that Heisig was an artist of limited repertoire; it seems that he painted only images of war and a few portraits.[21] In the earlier catalog, these works were just a small part of his total oeuvre, and he was portrayed as an artist actively engaged in the East German art world (Merkert and Pachnicke 1989).

This more comprehensive view of Heisig's work and life in the 1989 catalog was the result of the inclusion of a number of East German authors. Indeed, there was an almost fifty-fifty split between East German and West German writers, making it the high point of Heisig's reception to date and the one moment of balance between Eastern and Western views of his life and work. Before 1989, scholarship on Heisig was dominated by East German voices, and afterward, by West German ones.

Over the course of the past thirty years the reception of East German art in Germany has changed dramatically, most notably with the Wende. In

the 1980s the loudest voices speaking about East German art in the FRG
were those who praised it; in the 1990s, those who condemned it. Today,
there is a slow return to praise but at the expense of the art and artists'
relationship to the GDR.[22] For a country that has such an aversion to the
concepts of the nation and national pride, it is striking how nationalist the
FRG's reception of East German art is and has been, a reception that has
consistently buoyed the FRG's view of itself as the better Germany.[23]

Unwittingly, this politicized view of East German art is now becoming
the foundation for the nascent field of English-language scholarship on the
topic. In 2009 the Los Angeles County Museum of Art (LACMA) opened
a large traveling exhibition titled *Art of Two Germanys/Cold War Cultures*.
This exhibition marked the first time a major museum in the United States
had exhibited a large quantity of East German art.[24] According to the press
release, the intent was to examine "the art of the two Germanys without
reducing the works to familiar binaries of East versus West, national versus
international, and traditional and static mediums versus open and experimental art forms" (LACMA 2009).

The exhibition then traveled to Germany, where it was largely perceived to be an American—and thus more objective—view on the topic
than was possible in a German-made exhibition (Beaucamp 2009). In
reality, however, the LACMA exhibition was the result of a collaborative effort between an American curator and a German one, the same
(West) German curator who put together the 2005 Heisig exhibition. The results were similar: an exhibition and catalog that essentially
rewrote East German art history. Perhaps most surprisingly, the so-called
Staatskünstler were virtually absent from the LACMA exhibition, and the
striking comparison between the internationally famous West German
Neo-Expressionism of the 1980s and the Expressionist-inspired works
created in East Germany was not made.[25] Instead, official East German
painting after 1965 was largely nonexistent, and the main examples of
East German art for the 1980s were the *Autoperforationsartisten* (Self-
Perforating Artists), a small group of performance artists working largely
on the fringes of the official art world in Dresden. In the highly politicized atmosphere of the 1990s, however, this group became important
in German historiography because of its so-called dissident status and
unconventional performance-based art, both of which helped to support
a Western view of art and East Germany.[26]

Although the Bilderstreit may have quieted in the German press in
recent years, the effort to control the writing of this history nonetheless
continues and is now crossing into the English language and the global
landscape. Only by being aware of the tendentious nature of post-Wall
reception can a more nuanced view of East German art be written and
exhibited, one that includes East Germany's most significant painters: so-
called Staatskünstler like Heisig.

Notes

Parts of this article first appeared in "Whose East German Art Is This? The Politics of Reception after 1989," in *Imaginations: Journal of Cross-Cultural Image Studies* 8-1 (May 2017), doi:10.17742/IMAGE.GDR.8-1.6. Thanks to Sheena Wilson for permission to reproduce parts of that text here. Thanks also to Grant Arndt, Stephen Brockmann, Michael Dreyer, Franziska Lys, and Barbara McCloskey for comments on earlier versions of this article.

[1] The word *Bild* has a double meaning in this context; it can be "image" but also "picture" or "painting."

[2] An image of the artists standing in front of this large painting can be found online at the Deutsche Fotothek, http://www.deutschefotothek.de/documents/obj/90035138.

[3] This painting can be found online at http://kunstundfilm.de/wp-content/gallery/der-geteilte-himmel-neue-nationalgalerie/dergeteiltehimmelpressebilder10.jpg.

[4] Eckhart Gillen as quoted in Kaiser and Rehberg (1999, 589).

[5] For a reprint of some of the major press articles from the debate around the 1994 Neue National Galerie exhibition, see Kahlcke (1994). Thank you to Bettina Schaschke for providing me with this article.

[6] Uwe Lehmann-Brauns as quoted in Hecht (1998, 3).

[7] In the main rotunda East German paintings were hung, salon-style, upon walls draped with a gray plastic film used for trash bags. They were neither thematically nor chronologically arranged. Moreover, according to the anthropologist Barbara Wolbert (2001), "unlike Hitler's pictures [elsewhere in the exhibition], these canvases [from former East Germany] were deprived of their original trimming and framed in heavy strips of cheap, unfinished wood. The large paintings, some of them triptychs, [sat] on the concrete floor, leaning against the wall." The overall effect was that of a "painting depot" and, in the context of the other two parts of the exhibition, was "humiliating" (58, 59). See also Hohmeyer and Traub (1999).

[8] Compare Heisig's *Communards*, 1962 (http://www.deutschefotothek.de/documents/obj/30126977), as an example of his earlier realist style, with *Fortress Breslau*, 1973 (http://www.deutschefotothek.de/documents/obj/72042848), as an example of his later modernist style.

[9] Corey Ross (2000) was one of the first scholars to challenge the top-down approach to East German studies.

[10] A notable exception to this greater openness was in the immediate wake of Wolf Biermann's expatriation in 1976.

[11] Erich Honecker at the Fourth Conference of the Central Committee of the SED as reported in the Party's main newspaper, *Neues Deutschland* (December 18, 1971); quoted by Feist and Gillen (1990, 77).

[12] Heisig is also responsible for the creation of a painting class at the Leipzig Academy, which enabled students to study the medium officially (Guth 1990, 372).

[13] It should be noted that Heisig worked within a system in which political reliability was a prerequisite for studying at the university level. As such, he would necessarily have had to grade the political reliability of aspiring artists in his decisions as to who could attend the Leipzig Academy. Such decisions were standard at every level in the GDR, however, and were not specific to Heisig or the Leipzig Academy.

[14] At Heisig's request, Ebersbach taught a class in "experimental art" at the Leipzig Academy from 1979 to 1984 (Lang 2002, 275). For more about Ebersbach and this class, see Grundmann, Michael, and Seufert (2002, 10–11, 43–46, 48).

[15] While one might argue that from a legal or political point of view the GDR was an "Unrechtstaat" because of the curtailment of civil rights, the term itself is problematic because it has often been used to equate East Germany with the Third Reich, especially in the wake of unification, and thus to promote a specifically conservative political agenda (Sa'Adah 1998, 267).

[16] Two additional factors that contributed to the negative reception of East German artists in the new Germany were: (1) West German artists did not want the competition East German artists brought to the art market, and (2) after the Wende, Berlin lost the extra funding for the arts that it had had in the Cold War era, when it was a *Schauplatz* between East and West.

[17] In this book the Mitscherlichs were speaking about West Germany, but the concepts can also be applied to East Germany. The importance of generational differences in East Germany has been discussed by a number of scholars, including Stephen Brockmann (1999), Dorothee Wierling (2006), and Mary Fulbrook (2011).

[18] The members of the Hitler Youth generation were born between 1925 and 1935. See Brockmann (1999, 139). This generation of artists held most of the jobs in the GDR in the 1980s, thus inadvertently blocking the upward mobility of younger generations. This was the result of historical circumstances: in the wake of the Second World War, there were plenty of openings in the art world that needed to be filled. By the 1980s, the generation who had taken these jobs was only just getting to retirement age. Had the GDR survived another ten years, there would have been a significant change in the artistic guard that presumably would have alleviated some of the tension between this generation and the ones that followed.

[19] This is beginning to change. In 2005, for example, Jeanne Nugent completed a dissertation on Gerhard Richter that includes a discussion of his East German work and training. See also Belting (1992, ch. 7) and Barron and Eckmann (2009).

[20] Officially, (East) Berlin was one of two official centers for painting in East Germany. It did not attract the same level of interest in the West as Leipzig did.

[21] Several authors called the 2005 exhibition the most comprehensive show of Heisig's work to date. See Ruthe (2005) and Höhn (2005).

[22] (N)Ostalgia has certainly contributed to the improved reception of East German art, most notably with the Neue Nationalgalerie's award-winning *Kunst in*

der DDR (Art in the Deutsche Demokratische Republik) exhibition in 2003. Although public controversies with regard to the Staatskünstler have largely quieted in the new millenium, the Bilderstreit are not over. In 2009, for example, a major exhibition celebrating the FRG's sixtieth anniversary was criticized for excluding the GDR. While the title of the exhibition, *60 Jahre BRD* (60 Years Bundesrepublik Deutschland), explains the exclusion, people questioned the appropriateness of having a triumphalist exhibition in light of Germany's past and the fragile relationship between East and West since reunification (Rauterberg 2009).

23 Whether or not the latter is true, such thinking prevents us from understanding East German art and artists. Heisig's paintings of war, for example, are not simply Vergangenheitsbewältigung but also a critique of militarism and its continuation into the present.

24 Previously, only two small exhibitions of East German art had taken place in the United States: *Twelve Artists of the GDR* at the Busch-Reisinger Museum in Cambridge, Massachusetts, in 1989 and *New Territory: Art from East Germany* at the School of the Museum of Fine Arts Boston in 1990.

25 For a German audience familiar with the Staatskünstler as a result of the many exhibitions of their work and the vehement debates in the press, the handful of works by Tübke, Mattheuer, and Heisig function as a metonym for a larger body of works. For an American audience unfamiliar with East German art, however, and largely expectant that none existed, such a minimal presentation essentially negates their importance.

26 For a more detailed look at the problematic nature of the portrayal of East German art in this exhibition, see my review of its catalog (Eisman 2009).

Works Cited

Barron, Stephanie, and Sabine Eckmann, eds. 2009. *Art of Two Germanys/ Cold War Cultures.* New York: Abrams.

Beaucamp, Eduard. 2009. "The Cold War May Be Over, but It Is Still Being Fought in Terms of Its Artists. Must the Americans Once Again Show Germans How to Handle a Dual Heritage?" *Art Newspaper*, January 21.

Belting, Hans. 1992. *Die Deutschen und ihre Kunst: Ein schwieriges Erbe.* Munich: Verlag C. H. Beck.

Brockmann, Stephen. 1999. *Literature and German Reunification.* Cambridge: Cambridge University Press.

Eisman, April. 2007. "Bernhard Heisig and the Cultural Politics of East German Art." Diss., University of Pittsburgh.

———. 2009. "Art of Two Germanys/Cold War Cultures." *German History* 27 (4): 628–30.

———. 2011. "In the Crucible: Bernhard Heisig and the Hotel Deutschland Murals." In *Art Outside the Lines: New Perspectives on GDR Art & Culture*, edited by Amy Wlodarski and Elaine Kelly, 21–39. Amsterdam: Rodopi.

Feist, Günter, and Eckhart Gillen, eds. 1990. *Kunstkombinat DDR: Daten und Zitate zur Kunst und Kunstpolitik der DDR 1945–1990*. Berlin: Museumspädagogischer Dienst.

Fullbrook, Mary. 2011. "Living through the GDR: History, Life Stories, and Generations in East Germany." In *The GDR Remembered: Representations of the East German State since 1989*, edited by Nick Hodgin & Caroline Pearce, 201–220. Rochester, NY: Camden House.

Gillen, Eckhart, ed. 2005. *Bernhard Heisig: Die Wut der Bilder*. Cologne: Dumont.

Grundmann, Uta, Klaus Michael, and Susanna Seufert, eds. 2002. *Revolution im Geschlossenen Raum: Die Andere Kultur in Leipzig, 1970–1990*. Leipzig: Faber & Faber.

Guth, Peter. 1990. "Phänomen oder Mißverständnis? Die Leipziger Kunsthochschule." In *Kunst in der DDR: Künstler/Galerien/Museen/Kulturpolitik/Adresse*, edited by Eckhart Gillen and Rainer Haarmann. Cologne: Verlag Kiepenheuer & Witsch.

Hecht, Axel. 1998. "Editorial." *Art: Das Kunstmagazin* 5: 3.

Hecht, Axel, Alfred Welti, and Georg Baselitz. 1990. "Ein Meister, der Talent verschmäht." *Art: Das Kunstmagazin* 6: 54–72.

Hohmeyer, Jürgen, and Rainer Traub. 1999. "Wut über den Wessi." *Der Spiegel* 22: 208–10.

Höhn, Tobias D. 2005. "K20: Die Wut der Bilder." *Westdeutsche Zeitung*, March 22.

Jarausch, Konrad. 1994. *The Rush to German Unity*. New York: Oxford University Press.

Kahlcke, Wolfgang. 1994. "Pressedokumentation zu einem durch die Neue Nationalgalerie ausgelösten 'deutschen Bilderstreit.'" *Jahrbuch Preußischer Kulturbesitz* 31: 365–408.

Kaiser, Paul, and Karl-Siegbert Rehberg, eds. 1999. *Enge und Vielfalt—Auftragskunst und Kunstförderung in der DDR: Analysen und Meinungen*. Hamburg: Junius.

Lang, Lothar. 2002. *Malerei und Grafik in Ostdeutschland*. Leipzig: Faber & Faber.

Los Angeles County Museum of Art. 2009. LACMA Features First U.S. Exhibition to Examine Complexity of Art Developed During the Cold War in East and West Germany. Los Angeles: LACMA Print.

Merkert, Jörn, and Peter Pachnicke, eds. 1989. *Bernhard Heisig: Retrospektive*. Munich: Prestel.

Mitscherlich, Alexander, and Margarete Mitscherlich. 1967. *Die Unfähigkeit zu Trauern: Grundlagen kollektiven Verhaltens*. Munich: Piper.

Nugent, Jeanne. 2005. "Family Album and Shadow Archive: Gerhard Richter's East, West and All German Painting, 1949–1966." Diss., University of Pennsylvania.

Rauterberg, Hanno. 2009. "So sehen Sieger aus: Die Bundeskanzlerin eröffnet eine Ausstellung, in der die Künstler der DDR gedemütigt werden." *Zeit Online*, April 30. www.zeit.de/2009/19/Meinung-Kunst.

Ross, Corey. 2000. *Constructing Socialism at the Grass-Roots.* New York: St. Martin's Press.

Ruthe, Ingeborg. 2005. "Malen am offenen Nerv." *Berliner Zeitung*, October 22.

Sa'Adah, Anne. 1998. *Germany's Second Chance: Trust, Justice and Democratization.* Cambridge, MA: Harvard University Press.

Schirmer, Gisela. 2005. *DDR und documenta: Kunst im deutsch-deutschen Widerspruch.* Berlin: Reimer.

Wierling, Dorothee. 2006. "The Hitler Youth Generation in the GDR: Insecurities, Ambitions and Dilemmas." In *Dictatorship as Experience: Towards a Socio-Cultural History of the GDR*, edited by Konrad Jarausch, 307–24. New York & Oxford: Berghahn Books.

Wolbert, Barbara. 2001. "De-arranged Places: East German Art in the Museums of Unified Germany." *Anthropology of East Europe Review* 19 (Spring): 57–64.

7: East German Orchestras and Theaters: The Transformation since the Wende

Daniel Ortuno-Stühring

A Unique Heritage

THE THEATRICAL AND ORCHESTRAL landscape in Germany is unique.[1] There are 131 professional, permanently staffed, publicly financed orchestras: 83 theater orchestras for operas, operettas, and musicals playing in state and municipal theaters; 29 concert orchestras performing in concert halls; 7 publicly funded chamber orchestras; as well as 12 radio or radio symphony orchestras (Mertens 2014). This listing does not include the many professional chamber orchestras and ensembles in Germany, which play on a project-to-project basis, often employing freelance musicians. Germany has—relative to its population and compared to other countries worldwide—the highest density and diversity of symphony and chamber orchestras. Every year, around 35 million people attend more than 120,000 performances of plays and operas, as well as 9,000 concerts. The uniqueness of Germany's theatrical and orchestral landscape was officially recognized in December 2014 by UNESCO as an "intangible cultural heritage of humanity" ("Germany's 'Orchestral Landscape'" 2014). Yet this cultural treasure is in danger.

Shortly after the Wende, Germany had 168 publicly financed concert, opera, chamber, and radio orchestras ("Germany's 'Orchestral Landscape'" 2014). Since then, following a period of economic readjustment primarily in the former Eastern parts, 37 ensembles have been dissolved or have merged with other orchestras. This trend is still continuing. For example, in 2016–17 the Stuttgart Radio Symphony Orchestra merged with the Freiburg Symphony Orchestra, with the new orchestra residing in Stuttgart. Some eighty positions were lost through the merger (Mertens 2014b).[2]

Music, as performed by orchestras and opera companies, is different from art and literature. A painting just needs a wall to hang on. For a book, even less is required: just a bit of space on a shelf. But classical music is expensive; it requires a large number of musicians and technical personnel to perform it. Costs are rising, while audiences are dwindling, especially in the east German states. The Cologne musicologist Arnold Jacobshagen (2000, 13–24) published a study on the "structural change in the orchestral landscape," and I will update that study, following his methodological assumptions. Unlike Jacobshagen, however, I will focus exclusively on East Germany—by now, of course, a geographical and no longer a political designation. This article deals, therefore, with the legacy and the current situation of opera houses and classical orchestras in East Germany, but not with the legacy of classical music which was created by East German composers during the lifetime of that country.[3]

Structures and Financing
of Orchestras and Theaters

In contrast to the United States, most of Germany's professional orchestras are publicly financed. They have permanent year-round staffs, and the musicians are paid for twelve months. Their performance schedule focuses primarily on the "classical repertoire." The pay scale for musicians is roughly based on the number of permanent positions in the given orchestra: the bigger the orchestra, the higher the salary. This means that large orchestras are able not only to play a more cost-intensive repertoire but also to attract more skilled musicians because of the higher salaries. As a result, larger ensembles generally offer higher-caliber performances than smaller ones.

The typical theater in Germany is municipally administered and city owned and includes its own opera company. Most municipal theaters are so-called *Dreispartenhäuser*, which means that they unite theater, opera, and a dance company under a single roof and management. The repertoire principle and ensemble principle form another specific feature and a unique cultural heritage and allow for significantly more variety in repertoires and for well-functioning ensembles. The costs to taxpayers for orchestras and theaters that apply the repertoire and ensemble principles are quite considerable, however. Every opera ticket in Germany is subsidized by the government to the tune of about EUR 100. Box-office returns and private resources can vary widely from ensemble to ensemble. In 2007, however, Germany's orchestras and theaters recouped on average only about 19 percent of their total costs in revenues.[4]

The alternative to the repertoire and ensemble principles is the so-called *stagione* principle, which was originally developed in Italy and is common practice in the United States. With the stagione principle, a production is repeated as long as there is enough interest in the performance. If audience attendance falls too low, the production closes. The ad hoc ensemble performing in these cases consists of guest singers and actors brought together for each particular production. As a result, costs are much lower, but repertoires are also more monotonous.

Another feature specific to the German orchestra and opera world is its decentralized structure. In contrast to the United States, concert halls and theaters are distributed more or less evenly around the whole country. Accordingly, about 30 percent of all professional orchestras are located in towns of fewer than one hundred thousand inhabitants, with another 22 percent in cities of up to two hundred thousand (Schulmeistrat 2006, 263). As a result, cultural events staged by symphony orchestras and theaters shine important spotlights on locations that would otherwise be considered provincial. The decentralized structure of German orchestras and theaters is also reflected in their financing, which is almost exclusively provided by the individual states and municipalities. In total, Germany currently spends about two billion euros annually on public theaters and orchestras. This corresponds to roughly 0.2 percent of total public expenditures at the federal, state, and local levels (Deutscher Bühnenverein 2015).

Historical Overview

One reason for the unique density of orchestras and theaters in Germany today is the former fragmentation of the country into many independent states. Thuringia, for example, was subdivided in the fifteenth century into a number of smaller states called the "Saxon duchies," each developing its own court theater and orchestra. Initially financed by wealthy people to bolster their political ambitions, these court theaters and orchestras later became state or municipal institutions of the bourgeoisie.

Today, Thuringia still boasts, among other institutions, the German National Theater in Weimar—the theater of Goethe and Schiller—and the Theater of Meiningen, which was already known around the world in the nineteenth century. There is also the Ekhof Theater in Gotha, one of the most impressive examples of theater culture on the sites of princely residences. It was founded in 1683 and is the oldest palace theater in the world to be completely preserved, its stage machinery and equipment included. Responsibility—and funding—for these numerous court theaters and their corresponding court orchestras was assumed by the newly formed democratic states after World War I, and many theaters thus boast long and often distinguished traditions that persevered throughout Germany's tumultuous twentieth century.

Nevertheless, Germany's unique cultural landscape is only partly the result of the plethora of smaller principalities of its past. The majority of today's orchestras and theaters are, in fact, the product of private civic foundations (Private Bürgerstiftungen) established in the nineteenth century. One of the oldest of these orchestras is the Leipzig Gewandhaus Orchestra, whose roots go back as far as the fifteenth century. Another example is the Berlin Philharmonic, founded in 1882.

Most of the 52 municipal theaters existing in Germany today were founded in the nineteenth century through private initiatives and were initially run as private enterprises, featuring plays, operas, and ballets under a single roof. They mostly included a professional orchestra, since even the plays were usually accompanied by more or less extensive incidental music. The oldest public stages include the National Theater of Mannheim (1838) and the Municipal Theater Freiburg (1868). Before the fall of the German Empire in 1918, however, there were only 16 municipal theaters under communal management, in contrast to more than 360 private theaters. Most of these, private and public alike, were taken over by the newly created democratic local governments after the war. Taking all of these diverse origins together, only one-sixth of Germany's cultural orchestras have their roots in former court orchestras. These numbers contradict the conventional wisdom that the variety and density of Germany's contemporary cultural landscape are based primarily on earlier support for the arts by aristocratic sponsors.

Orchestras and Theaters in East Germany and the Cultural Erbe

After World War II, West Germany reestablished the connection between bourgeois cultural and political traditions that had been ruptured by the Nazi regime in 1933. A different approach was taken in East Germany, where after 1949 the blending of culture with politics drew upon the cultural ideals of the second half of the nineteenth century aimed at culturally educating the working class. The national official goal was to appropriate the "great humanistic educational traditions and cultural traditions" for that class. Accordingly, a report issued by the Central Committee of the SED stated in 1960: "It is part of the education of the socialist person that he gets to know, understand and love the best works of world art and national culture."[5] Low ticket prices subsidized by the state were intended to make theatergoing affordable for everyone. Nevertheless, the primary purpose of East Germany's numerous orchestras and theaters was to aesthetically legitimize the "state of workers and peasants [Arbeiter- und Bauernstaat]." To achieve this goal, thirty-three ensembles were founded in East Germany by 1966, including a number of youth theaters and puppet theaters. All in all, this meant an increase in the number of orchestras and theaters of roughly 70 percent compared to the prewar years. Permanent positions for orchestra musicians increased accordingly, from 2,000 to 4,500, an enormous rise. By comparison, orchestra positions in West Germany during the same period went up by only 13 percent, new ensembles by about 16 percent (Schulmeistrat 2006, 259).

These cultural policies gave rise to the densest cultural infrastructure in the world. In 1988, there were 213 theaters in East Germany (including 49 opera companies) and 79 orchestras—all serving a population of only eighteen million people. Per capita, the GDR boasted more than twice as many orchestras as West Germany.

This ambitious cultural program entailed various problems above and beyond the obviously immense financial burden. One issue was the politicocultural doctrine of the so-called *Erbetheorie*, a doctrine of cultural heritage that can be traced back to Ernst Hermann Meyer, one of the state composers of the GDR. This policy forced even smaller houses to offer the core classical repertoire of Wagner, Verdi, and others, despite the fact that these works were in many cases too difficult for their smaller companies to perform. Another problem were the so-called tombstone contracts (*Grabsteinverträge*), which guaranteed lifetime employment for East German artists in the 1970s. Neither dancers, singers, nor orchestra musicians could be dismissed prior to retirement, and artistic quality often declined accordingly. The playwright Heiner Müller claimed that these contract rules meant the beginning of the end for musical theater on the small stage (Spahn 1990). By 1990, many East German performers longed for deregulation, liberalization, and basic reform in the hope that such measures would bring about greater artistic freedom and higher quality. Yet in the harsh realities of unified Germany, cultural policy reform meant, above all, difficult and sometimes necessary restructuring and downsizing.

The Wende and Its Consequences

The unification treaty of the Federal Republic of Germany of September 6, 1990, stipulated in §35 (2) that "the cultural substance of the new federal states may not be damaged in any way." But it soon became clear that this was not so easy to guarantee. A 1993 study by Jutta Allmendinger counted a total of 165 East German orchestras. One illustration of the high levels of state support this cultural cornucopia required can be found in the aforementioned state of Thuringia, which faced obligations to fund eight full-fledged theaters and nineteen state or municipal orchestras performing in thirty different locations. After unification, the financially weak former East Germany, now referred to as the "five new states," simply had too many cultural institutions requiring ongoing funding. Drastic changes, including the merging or closing of entire venues, were inevitable. The following three case studies will demonstrate that during this process, artistic needs and quality quite often played a smaller role than tradition and political interests.

First Case Study: Thüringer Landestheater GmbH Eisenach-Rudolstadt-Saalfeld

As a first step in Thuringia, the orchestras in Rudolstadt and Saalfeld, only ten miles apart from each other, were merged. The restructuring of these two ensembles was emblematic of the changes to the German orchestra landscape. The Rudolstadt orchestra, founded as a court orchestra by a princess of Rudolstadt-Schwarzburg in the mid-seventeenth century, was one of the oldest continuously active orchestras in the world. By contrast, the Saalfeld Philharmonic was an East German institution founded in the 1950s. The resulting merged orchestra at first retained all the musicians from both former orchestras. It began losing positions owing to financial cuts, however, and it now operates at about two-thirds of the personnel capacity previously attained by each of the individual orchestras. It employs only forty-two musicians and is, in terms of quantity and quality, far removed from what the two original orchestras had been able to perform both before and immediately after the merger.

In 1993, the theater in Eisenach, sixty miles to the west, was closed. As as result, in 1995, the Rudolfstadt-Saalfeld orchestra also had to merge with the orchestra in Eisenach and had to provide musical sustenance to Eisenach, with the musicians forced to commute hundreds of miles every month. This incurred considerable costs and logistical expenses. The forced collaboration was abandoned in 2003, and the orchestra began cooperating with the conservatories of Mainz and Weimar, as well as with the opera house in Nordhausen. To set itself apart, the Rudolstadt orchestra increasingly concentrated on a repertoire of rarely played music, such as the operas of Siegfried Wagner or the works of minor Rudolstadt masters.

Second Case Study: Thüringen Philharmonie Gotha-Suhl

In 1998, the Thuringia Philharmonic Orchestra Gotha-Suhl was founded as a result of considerable financial and political pressure. It arose as the merger of two orchestras: the Landessinfonieorchester Thüringen-Gotha, which included the Gotha court orchestra founded by Duke Ernst the Devout, a tradition going back more than 350 years, and the Thüringen Philharmonie Suhl, which was established in 1953 and quickly became one of the more artistically renowned orchestras in Thuringia. Yet with the merger of the Gotha and Suhl orchestras, the number of musical positions decreased from 147 overall (81 in Suhl and 66 in Gotha) to just 51. When the State of Thuringia again reduced its subsidies for theaters and orchestras for the year 2009, the city of Suhl chose to discontinue its sponsorship and funding of the Gotha-Suhl orchestra beginning on January 1, 2009. It was decided to relocate the merged orchestra from

Suhl to Gotha, as Gotha had a longer orchestra tradition. Today, an ensemble still exists in Gotha, just twelve miles from the state capital, Erfurt. With permanent financial reductions and the orchestra's uncertain future, artistic quality has clearly suffered. Meanwhile, the city of Suhl, situated on the underdeveloped periphery of the state, can no longer boast its own orchestra.

Third Case Study: Symphonieorchester Pirna—Riesaer Elbland Philharmonie

The third case study demonstrates that under certain circumstances a merger can actually make artistic sense and not simply be the result of financial necessity. The orchestras in Riesa and Pirna, two smaller towns near Dresden, were founded in the 1950s. The idea was to promote classical music in these rural regions, and both orchestras provided the musical accompaniment for numerous public festivities. Because of their small sizes of thirty-six musicians in Riesa's orchestra and thirty-five in Pirna's, neither one was able to perform even a Beethoven symphony without hiring expensive freelance musicians. In 1997 a merger was initiated. Today the orchestra maintains fifty permanent posts, significantly more than either of the independent orchestras before the merger. In this case, therefore, artistic capacities actually improved. The legal basis for the merger was the so-called *Kulturraumgesetz* (cultural areas law) passed by the state of Saxony in 1993, which established a smaller number of larger, more efficient orchestras where there had previously been a large number of smaller ones. Some orchestra locations were shut down, but those remaining have been stabilized, at least for the time being. The law increased overall support for cultural institutions and allowed for a fairer distribution of expenses among the state's regional subdivisions. The law's success has led the states of Mecklenburg-Western Pomerania and Thuringia to express interest in introducing similar legislation.

Summary and Outlook

The changes in the German orchestral landscape since unification defy easy classification. Simply preserving the 1990 status quo would have been neither possible nor reasonable, for financial as well as artistic reasons. As of today, 35 ensembles out of a previous grand total of 168 publicly funded concert, opera, chamber, and radio orchestras have been either dissolved or merged. It was not only small orchestras in a handful of rural areas or in former East Berlin that met with this fate. Larger orchestras in the former regional capitals of East German districts—including Schwerin, Erfurt, Potsdam, and Suhl—were also affected, as were individual radio orchestras in Berlin and Leipzig. All told, some seven thousand theater and orchestra jobs have been lost since reunification.

There have also been fundamental changes to the terms of employment within the remaining institutions. On the one hand, the traditional German ensemble and repertoire company is moving more and more in the direction of a quasi-stagione company, hiring a significant number of guest artists for specific productions. The number of guest contracts, which sometimes cover the artists for only a few days, rose from 8,500 in 2001 to 14,000 in 2011 (Jacobshagen 2013). On the other hand, it is now possible for smaller houses to stage more-demanding operas that would have been beyond their artistic reach with the original (smaller) cast of ensemble members. Yet as many of these cases demonstrate, systematically reducing the number of orchestra positions, particularly under the German Orchestra Law that links funding to size, often leads to the slow decline of orchestras, many of which are ultimately left as shadows of their former selves. Still, an orchestra and opera scene following the American model and predominantly funded by the private sector would not be acceptable in Germany. Even apart from considerations of cultural heritage, tradition, and civic engagement on behalf of traditional municipal multifunctional theaters, German tax and endowment laws would hinder such a development. Nevertheless, many theaters and orchestras in Germany are now trying to attract sponsors in the corporate world to supplement their public funding. Yet corporate sponsorship currently generates only 1 percent of their funds. Moreover, corporate sponsors tend to focus on promoting prestigious projects and highly visible "events," such as performances of Wagner's Ring cycle. Another problem to be taken into account is the fact that there is very little room for cutting overall costs: personnel expenditures make up about 75 percent of a given theater's permanent costs, but eliminating artistic or support staff could seriously jeopardize the quality of the performances. It should also be borne in mind that public funding of theaters protects the constitutionally guaranteed freedom of the arts and ensures that everyone, regardless of social and financial status, has the opportunity to participate in the cultural life of his or her town.

The withdrawal of state and municipal funding from opera houses and orchestras would inevitably lead to the closure of a great number of theaters. In addition, in the absence of guaranteed subsidies, ticket prices would have to be raised considerably in order to cover the costs of the performance.[6] Overall, the withdrawal of funding would lead to drastic changes in the cultural life of Germany, not to mention the public outcry such a plan would elicit. Even if the complete withdrawal of government funding for classical musical events will not occur in the foreseeable future, however, Germany's unique cultural heritage will still face huge challenges in the coming years. For example, the *Solidarpakt II*, with its massive transfer of money from West to East Germany, will end in 2019, to be followed in 2020 by the taking effect of the so-called debt brake, which prohibits state and local governments from incurring new debts. This could lead to further debates on whether to shut down additional theaters and orchestras, probably mostly in the new German states, which for the most part are still plagued by weak infrastructure and finances.[7] Orchestras and theaters will have to continually think about how to deal with these threats, not just financially but also in terms of adapting their artistic mission.[8] Can we really be certain, for example, that the German ensemble principle will make sense for all theaters in the future? Is it really necessary for even small theaters to repeatedly stage standard works that they are barely able to master even in purely artistic terms, given their size? Even if the local experience of live opera, theater, and concert performance is invaluable, competition from world-class artists on CDs and DVDs is formidable. Can a municipal theater offer a production of *Carmen, Tosca,* or *Aida* that can truly compete against the global broadcasts of the Met or the Vienna State Opera? Is there any reason for *The Magic Flute* to be performed in all three of a city's opera houses several times in the same month, as happened recently in Berlin? Would it not be better for them to revive lost treasures that have not been performed for decades, many of which are absolutely worth seeing? Some opera houses are already pursuing this path. The Chemnitz Opera has presented productions of Hans Pfitzner's almost completely forgotten opera *Der Liebesgarten* (*The Garden of Love*) and Otto Nicolai's 1842 Italian smash hit *Templario*, while Erfurt has revived Carl Martin Reinthaler's 1881 opera *Käthchen von Heilbronn*, and Gera has staged Jaromir Weinberger's 1937 opera *Wallenstein*.

Another aspect to consider is the prevalence of *Regietheater* (director's theaters) in Germany.[9] On the one hand, Regietheater, which allow the director of an opera to make some liberal changes in staging, sometimes even at the expense of the music, help "modernize" works whose average year of origin is 1846. On the other hand, the sometimes absurd stagings are not necessarily very popular with regular theater audiences, which in turn results in many empty seats. Nevertheless, the variety and density of the theatrical scenery not only offers a broader spectrum within the repertoire but also represents the kind of stagings that might appeal to a new society or win back lost audiences. In addition, it is gratifying to see that since the Wende, one mainstay of East German cultural policy has also emerged in the western parts of the country: the diverse offerings of children's and youth theaters. Even solely in terms of promoting the 2,500-year-old art form of theater in the future, such youth-oriented programs represent a cultural obligation, not a superfluous luxury.

Monument Conservation for Culture?

Did it really make sense, given the circumstances described above, to add the historical cultural inheritance of the German orchestra and theater landscape to the UNESCO World Heritage List? Inclusion on the list of the world's protected cultural heritage is not connected to any form of financial support. What then does it accomplish? Does it hinder theater from examining itself as a process and art form in constant transformation? Does it encourage a stifling canonization or the transformation of stagecraft into a kind of museum? No, it doesn't; instead, it serves as a kind of structural protection. While not affecting questions of artistry or content, it designates Germany's theatrical scene and the principle of the repertoire theater company, with its combination of plays, opera, and ballet, as worthy of being protected. The statement creates a new public consciousness of the fact that this centuries-old inheritance is a unique achievement of the former particularistic political structure of Germany; of its princely, aristocratic, and bourgeois traditions; of civic and state support for the arts in both East and West. And most importantly, it is a strong reminder that this heritage is not a burden but a gift, for which Germany is envied by music lovers around the world.

Notes

[1] A "theater" in Germany is a usually a municipal- or state-financed enterprise that stages both plays and operas, often also ballet or puppet theater, and it usually employs a full-time professional orchestra. The term is used in this way throughout the article.

[2] For a map of the current state of orchestras in Germany, including mergers and closings, see Schulmeistrat (2009).

[3] There are several comprehensive studies covering that time period; most recently, the book by Frackmann and Powell (2015). Compare also Berg, Holtsträter, and von Massow (2007) and Berg, von Massow, and Noeske (2004), where the New Music scene in East Germany as well as the politics of avant-garde music are discussed.

[4] Owing to the variety of the German landscape of theaters and orchestras as well as to their communal and state sponsorship, federal numbers are hard to come by. In 2007 the German Bundestag published the report of a commission on "Kultur in Deutschland." Cf. also Jacobshagen (2005, 3). Later data seem to confirm the numbers; according to Jacobshagen (2013), in 2010–11 German opera houses earned about 18 percent of their operating costs on their own.

[5] From the resolution of the 1960 Cultural Conference of the Central Committee of the Ministry of Culture and the German Cultural Alliance (*Neues Deutschland*, July 8, 1960).

[6] Compare, for example, the Berlin Philharmonic, which recoups about 28 percent of its total costs through ticket revenues, with the New York Philharmonic

Orchestra, which recoups about 50 percent. The cheapest ticket in Berlin during the 2015–16 season cost just EUR 24, while tickets in New York were at least USD 45 for some concerts. The range was USD 45–USD 130 in New York vs. EUR 24–EUR 132 in Berlin. At the Staatsoper Berlin, the cheapest tickets start at EUR 14, while at the Metropolitan Opera they are available starting at USD 25. The most expensive tickets for a regular performance in Berlin are most often EUR 88, in New York USD 300. These data are difficult to compare, since they change with the day and the program, depending on the perceived popularity of the event. The general trend, however, is clear: tickets in Germany, where culture is heavily subsidized, are cheaper than in the United States (for comparison purposes, on July 24, 2017, EUR 1.00 = USD 1.17).

[7] A debate on a possible fusion of the Jena Orchestra with the Altenburg/Gera Opera House as well as a fusion between the opera houses in Weimar and Erfurt was initiated by the newly elected Thuringian administration in 2015. After significant resistance in all places the plan went nowhere ("Orchesterfusion für Thüringen angeregt" 2015).

[8] The possible consequences of the withdrawal of financial support are being demonstrated in Mecklenburg-Western Pomerania, the first federal state in the country to develop a long-range plan for its theater and orchestra infrastructure for the years 2010 to 2020. In accordance with this plan, from 2010 only larger theaters will be supported by the state. All smaller theaters will have to either merge or close entirely.

[9] In a Regietheater the director has the freedom to change the staging, geographical location, and chronology of events, as well as the casting and plot of a musical work in order to make a political point or update a cultural interpretation.

Works Cited

Allmendinger, Jutta. 1993. "Staatskultur und Marktkultur: Ostdeutsche Orchester im Vergleich." In *Kultur und Kulturträger in der DDR: Analysen*, 215–81. Bonn, Berlin: Stiftung Mitteldeutscher Kulturrat.

Berg, Michael, Knut Holtsträter, and Albrecht von Massow, eds. 2007. *Die unterträgliche Leichtigkeit der Kunst: Ästhetisches und politisches Handeln in der DDR*. Cologne: Böhlau.

Berg, Michael, Albrecht von Massow, and Nina Noeske, eds. 2004. *Zwischen Macht und Freiheit: Neue Musik in der DDR*. Cologne: Böhlau.

Deutscher Bühnenverein. 2015. *Theater- und Orchesterlandschaft*. http://www.buehnenverein.de/de/theater-und-orchester/19.html.

Deutscher Bundestag. 2007. 16. Wahlperiode, Drucksache 16/7000, 11.12.

"Germany's 'Orchestral Landscape' Recognised by UNESCO as 'Intangible Cultural hHeritage.'" 2014. *Strad*, December 16. Frackman, Kyle, and Larson Powell. 2015. *Classical Music in the German Democratic Republic: Production and Reception*. Studies in German Literature Linguistics and Culture. Rochester, NY: Camden House.

Jacobshagen, Arnold. 2000. *Strukturwandel der Orchesterlandschaft: Die Kulturorchester im wiedervereinigten Deutschland*. Cologne: Dohr.

——. 2010. *Musiktheater*. http://www.miz.org/static_de/themenportale/einfuehrungstexte_pdf/archiv/jacobshagen_musiktheater_2005.pdf.

——. 2013. *Music Theatre*. http://www.miz.org/musical-life-in-germany/.

Mertens, Gerald. 2014a. "Kulturorchester, Rundfunkensembles und Opernchöre." In *Deutsches Musikinformationszentrum*, edited by Themenportal Konzerte and Musiktheater. http://www.miz.org/artikel_themenportale_vorbemerkungen_tpkmkonzertemuziktheater.html.

——. 2014b. "A United Front against Orchestral Mergers." *Strad*, March 3.

"Orchesterfusion für Thüringen angeregt: Kulturminister will Staatstheater Weimar-Erfurt." 2015. *Thüringer Allgemeine* (November 5). http://www.thueringer-allgemeine.de/web/zgt/kultur/detail/-/specific/Orchesterfusion-fuer-Ostthueringen-angeregt-Kulturminister-will-Staatstheater-W-450098480.

Schulmeistrat, Stephan. 2006. "Die Orchesterlandschaft in Deutschland—ein 'Weltkulturerbe'?" In *Musik und Kulturbetrieb: Medien, Märkte, Institutionen. Handbuch der Musik im 20. Jahrhundert*, edited by Arnold Jacobshagen and Frieder Reininghaus, vol. 10: 253–64. Laaber: Laaber-Verlag.

——. 2009. "Kulturorchester in Deutschland." In *Nationalatlas aktuell* 3 (30 July). Leipzig: Leibniz-Institut für Länderkunde (IfL). http://aktuell.nationalatlas.de/Orchester.7_07-2009.0.html.

Spahn, Claus. 1990. "Stunden wie damals." *Die Zeit*, February 3.

UNESCO. 2016. "Deutsche Theater- und Orchesterlandschaft für UNESCO-Liste des Immateriellen Kulturerbes nominiert." https://www.unesco.de/kultur/2016/deutsche-theater-und-orchesterlandschaft-fuer-unesco-liste-des-immateriellen-kulturerbes-nominiert.html..

Part IV.

A Virtual Wall?
Education and Society

8: What Do German High School Students Think about the GDR? Memory Culture between Glorification and Evaluation

Andreas Eis

Introduction

THE GERMAN CARTOONIST Felix Görmann, known as Flix, published a book in 2009 combining a two-year-long series of weekly recollections in the Berlin daily newspaper *Tagesspiegel*. The subject matter of these reflections involves personal experiences—Görmann's own and those of friends—regarding the German Democratic Republic (GDR) before 1989. Unlike many movies and TV shows about daily life in the former GDR, the stories presented in Flix's cartoons neither romanticize nor condemn the Communist regime, nor do they overemphasize the Stasi secret police. The authentic episodes illustrate people's ambivalent experiences with the GDR from *both sides* of the Iron Curtain.

These cartoons can be seen as part of a new culture of remembrance that stands in opposition to lingering ideological positions that either glorify or totally renounce the political system and social aspects of the former GDR. Surrounding the twentieth anniversary of the fall of the Berlin Wall, a lively debate about memory culture surfaced in German public discourse. The main points discussed by prominent politicians and intellectuals as well as in the media centered around the question of whether the GDR was a totalitarian dictatorship, terrorized to the end by secret police, or rather a more liberal dictatorship, given its investments in public health care and preschool education, to name two examples. A considerable part of the population of the former GDR is unwilling to regard itself as having belonged to a totalitarian society. More than twenty-five years after the fall of the Wall, they still recall happy memories of everyday life in the GDR, which they then conflate with a nostalgic view of the old political system.

Fig. 8.1. Front cover of *Da war mal was: Erinnerungen an hier und drüben* (Once, there used to be something: Memories of here and on the other side). © Flix 2014. Reproduced by permission of the illustrator.

The different sides of this debate will be summarized here from three perspectives. First, I will identify the key points of the ongoing discussion regarding the political and social system of the GDR. This debate not only highlights the various ambivalent evaluations of East German society but also raises the question of how to present this topic in history and political-science classes in schools. Second, I will discuss the most important results of two empirical studies demonstrating what current middle and high-school students in Germany know about the GDR and what their political opinions are. The results of these studies are interesting for two reasons: first, they reveal the perceptions of a generation that did not experience the GDR firsthand, and second, they raise important questions about the impact of educational policies regarding history and political-science instruction in Germany. The final part of the chapter will discuss the methodological problems and didactic consequences of the present discussion with respect to teacher training.

The Debate about the Totalitarian Character of the GDR and Its Impact on Educational Policies

Prominent politicians and academics have participated in the recent discourse on memory culture, which has highlighted a variety of issues. This discussion attracted much public attention in light of the quest for East German votes in the 2009 electoral campaign. At the heart of the debate were the results of two empirical studies, which showed that German students (particularly those from the former East) knew very little about the social and political reality of the former GDR and even held the former regime in high regard (Arnswald 2006; Deutz-Schroeder 2008; Deutz-Schroeder et al. 2012). Many of the students who participated in the study did not classify the GDR as a dictatorship. The ensuing discussion concerned not only the apparent lack of a balanced view of history and politics being taught in schools but also general assessments of the political system of the GDR that did not seem to take into account the reality of East German citizens' daily lives.

The debate in 2009 deviated from the debates of the 1990s. Topics such as involvement of the general population with the Stasi, the denunciation of politically suspicious or socially undesirable fellow citizens, the moral and legal justifications of *Mauerschützen* (border guards who killed individuals trying to escape the GDR), or the passing of judgment on *Mitläufer* (the millions of passive supporters of the regime who were members of state-run organizations or the Sozialistische Einheitspartei Deutschlands [SED]) were no longer part of the discussion. The new issue at stake was the classification of the SED dictatorship as an illegitimate and inhumane system. A number of politicians and intellectuals pointed out that certain policies of the German Democratic Republic had been carried out according to the rule of law, and that before 1990, social justice had in some respects been achieved to a greater extent in East Germany than in the West. Was the GDR an illegitimate totalitarian state, an authoritarian dictatorship, or a failed social utopia? Are historical comparisons of the GDR and National Socialism as two kinds of dictatorships appropriate and useful, or is it not justified to compare the GDR to the unparalleled crimes and genocide of the Nazis? A reevaluation of the GDR also leads to the question of whether some of the GDR's social policies merit comparison with the welfare state of the Federal Republic of Germany (FRG)—for instance, in terms of educational outcomes or the benefits of health, family, and gender policies—or whether focusing on these isolated aberrations and "socialist achievements" trivializes the political ideology and systematic human rights abuses of East Germany by casting them as mere "side effects" of a "classless society."

The debate about the appropriate interpretation of the GDR's history became increasingly controversial and emotional. One perspective represented the everyday perceptions of John Q. Public—"Otto Normalverbraucher" in German—in East German society by pointing to the East German people's experiences of daily life, while another perspective related those daily life experiences to theoretical (or ideological) positions based on a classification of the GDR according to the academic concepts and methodical categories of comparative politics. The controversy began with an interview with Erwin Sellering (2009), a member of the Social Democratic Party (SPD) and prime minister of Mecklenburg-Vorpommern, one of the five new Länder (states in East Germany). Sellering, born and raised in the West, protested against fundamental denunciations of the GDR "as a totally illegitimate state in which no good whatsoever existed." He lamented that the discussion had revolved exclusively around the history of the former GDR, whereas a truly critical evaluation should involve research into the political and social systems of both East and West Germany. He argued against historical representations that depicted a condemnable illegitimate dictatorship being replaced by an ideal Western democratic welfare state: "The old Federal Republic also had weaknesses. The GDR also had strengths."[1] In particular, his bold remark that the GDR system had, of course, always included "a bit of despotism" was the cause of considerable outrage, and protests were launched by various victims' organizations as well as by both liberal and conservative politicians. Sellering's statements were criticized sharply both as an insult to the victims of East German political oppression and prosecution and as an attempt to trivialize and romanticize the SED dictatorship.

Sellering's fellow party member, Wolfgang Thierse (2009), then vice president of the German Bundestag, tried to temper the emotionally intense debate with his plain statement that the evaluation of a political system must always be distinguished from the achievements of individual persons: "The system has failed, the people have not." Thierse further stated that as a political system, the GDR "was not a constitutional state. It was a dictatorship." He added, however, that East German history before 1990 cannot be reduced to a "scandalous history of cowardice and treason [Skandalgeschichte von Feigheit und Verrat]." Thierse further criticized an absurd present situation in which "any attempt to judge GDR history more precisely and distinctly immediately leads to an outpouring of condemnation [Bannflucht]." For Thierse and many other participants in the debate, their judgment of the GDR was final with regard to its political classification as a dictatorship: democratic law was systematically violated, and human rights were abused. They also asserted, however, that a full assessment of the GDR cannot be reduced to its political dimension alone but must also take into account social living standards and recognize individual life achievements. Thierse not only argued for a just distinction between political system and everyday life experiences but also campaigned for an open discussion and the legitimacy of thinking about "the idea of democratic socialism," a term that previously had been used primarily by dissidents as a discursive weapon against the Communist dictatorship and the "real socialism" of the SED system. In Thierse's view, it is necessary to create an opportunity for debates about democratic and economic alternatives in which supporters of such alternatives are not immediately denounced as left-wing extremists or manipulators of history.[2]

Like Thierse, Gesine Schwan (2009, 13), former president of Viadrina University in Frankfurt an der Oder (Brandenburg) and SPD candidate in the presidential elections of 2004 and 2009, has left no doubt that the GDR should be classified as a dictatorship. Schwan, however, regards it as highly problematic to call the GDR an "illegitimate state" (Unrechtsstaat), as in her view this term carries totalitarian implications and casts "general moral suspicion" on the whole of East German social reality.[3] Schwan instead proposes drawing on Ernst Fraenkel's (1941) distinction between a "normative state" (*Normenstaat*) and a "prerogative state" (*Maßnahmenstaat*), originally an analytical instrument for understanding the totalitarian character and bureaucratic structures of National Socialism. Referring to the "normative state," Schwan emphasizes that there were certain "areas within the GDR state in which people strived for justice" and attempted to organize social life in accordance with the rule of law. At the same time, GDR citizens lived in constant fear of "the sword of Damocles of SED despotism" and could never trust in the stability of those policy areas that seemed to be operating within the rule of law. At no point, however, has Schwan denied the totalitarian alignment of the SED regime, as one of her critics, Marianne Birthler (2009, 11), forcefully accused her of doing. Birthler, federal commissioner for the Records of State Security of the former GDR,[4] has argued vehemently that Schwan, like other *Ossiversteher* (a patronizing term for those Westerners who seemingly thoughtfully consider the feelings, experiences, and interests of East Germans), refuses to call the GDR reality what it actually was, namely an illegitimate totalitarian state. Schwan's strategy, Birthler claims, cultivates nostalgic glorification, offends the victims of the SED regime, and turns former GDR citizens into "unaccountable recipients of political and pedagogical welfare."[5] Birthler's statement may have been justifiably applicable to some participants in this debate, but she was wrong to apply it to Gesine Schwan, who was arguing from a completely different analytical level. In particular, Schwan claimed that "spheres of legal justice in the

GDR state were not established voluntarily or out of any appreciation of constitutionality, but rather had to be conceded in the face of society's resistance against outright, politicized despotism and injustice."[6]

What Does Today's Generation Know? Empirical Results

The debate about how to normatively assess and categorically classify the GDR system reveals West Germans' diverse and often ambivalent perceptions of East German society. It also illustrates the problem of how the topic ought to be presented in history and politics classrooms. The interpretation of GDR society should be presented in schools as an open question as long as public evaluation of East German history remains controversial. The academic community has fueled the recent debate on the culture of remembrance through a number of studies on the effectiveness of political-historical education among middle-school and high-school students.

Empirical studies show that German students, particularly those from the former East, have only very limited knowledge of the social and political reality of the GDR and the peaceful revolution that brought about its end. The question of what the social and political reality of the GDR actually *was*, however, remains a highly controversial issue. Hence, it is not easy to conduct a study that not only tests reproducible knowledge, such as isolated dates and facts, but at the same time also explores individuals' historical and political understanding of basic concepts as well as how individuals' perceptions of historical meaning influence the construction of their identities.

The two studies discussed below did not involve standardized proficiency tests based on diagnostic methodical procedures like the Civic Education Study of the IEA[7] (Schulz 2010; Kerr 2010). As of yet, tests measuring students' knowledge of GDR politics and history have not been conducted. Rather, the data presented in both studies were derived from polls of students ages fifteen to eighteen that involved factual questions, expressions of opinion, and statements about their perceptions of the GDR. In particular, the study conducted by the Forschungsverbund SED-Staat (Research Center SED State) at the Free University (FU) of Berlin under the direction of political scientist Klaus Schroeder (Deutz-Schroeder and Schroeder 2008; Deutz-Schroeder et al. 2012) has attracted considerable public attention. The Berlin-based research group not only confirmed the prevalence of exceedingly low levels of historical knowledge, especially among East German students, but also documented that many young people have inappropriate, glorified perceptions of the GDR as a "social paradise." A majority of East German students did not classify the GDR as a dictatorship (Deutz-Schroeder and Schroeder 2008,

715). Students in the Western federal states, for example, in Bavaria, scored significantly higher on knowledge-based questions, while judging the GDR political system more critically. In its interpretation of the data, the FU study found the taboo nature of the topic of the GDR in politics and history classrooms in the new federal states to be the main reason for East German students' weak knowledge and poor understanding of history. Many teachers in eastern Germany today were socialized in the former GDR and had to adapt to its ideological pedagogical system. Accordingly, it should not come as a surprise that some East German teachers still interpret GDR history from the perspective of their own, largely privileged experiences and therefore may not wish to discuss the topic openly in class, or that such teachers may pass on nostalgic misinterpretations of the GDR to their students.

Regarding the acquired knowledge of East and West German students, the FU study contradicts in several important ways another study conducted two years earlier by the historian Ulrich Arnswald (2006) on behalf of the Association of German History Teachers (Verband der Geschichtslehrer) and the government-funded Organization for the Examination and Reappraisal of the Communist Dictatorship (Stiftung zur Aufarbeitung der SED-Diktatur). On the one hand, Arnswald's study, like that conducted by the FU, documents large deficits in the historical and political knowledge of German high-school students overall. Contrary to the findings of the Schroeder survey, however, Arnswald finds that students in the new federal states and in Berlin scored far higher in response to certain factual questions than did students in the West German states. Consequently, researchers relying on Arnswald interpret the success levels of historical and political education far more optimistically. Indeed, according to Arnswald, the comparative results for the Eastern and Western federal states do not verify the continued existence of distinct Eastern and Western historical identities, as the FU study implies. In contrast, his results demonstrate that differing experiences have been integrated into a common German-German history; they provide "a real indication of growing closer" (175). Our discussion below of these two studies will attempt to answer the following controversial questions:

- What kind of knowledge and understanding were tested in the two studies?
- Did the researchers clearly distinguish between (indisputable historical) knowledge, on the one hand, and political opinions and value-based judgments, on the other?
- How "concerning" or "frightening" are results claiming that a significant number of students overestimate the "welfare-state aspects" of the GDR and are unwilling to classify the Communist SED regime as a dictatorship as opposed to a social utopia?

- Should we conclude from these studies that current teaching methods and curriculum guidelines are ineffective and of poor quality? In this regard, we also have to ask:
- How much influence does historical and political education have on an individual's personal understanding of historical meaning and his or her development of democratic awareness?

Schroeder's and Arnswald's studies are based on standardized questionnaires similar to Gallup polls. In both studies around five thousand students were asked to answer questions about facts and dates pertaining to the GDR and reunification and to give their opinions in response to a list of statements.[8] According to the students' self-assessments, 80 percent of German middle- and high-school students claim to know very little or nothing at all about the GDR. Nearly 60 percent, however, state that they are interested in and would like to learn more about the conditions of daily life in the former East Germany (Deutz-Schroeder and Schroeder 2008, 653–55). In the new federal states in particular, students claim that the topic is not sufficiently taught in school (East 52 percent; West 43 percent) or even not taught at all (East 20 percent; West 21 percent; Deutz-Schroeder & Schroeder 2008, 652), although the history of the GDR certainly is part of the curriculum in all federal states.[9] Even if the topic is actually taught extensively in schools, however, the extent to which such instruction is able to actually change students' opinions and transform their day-to-day attitudes and perceptions into empirical knowledge remains an open question. There are indications that students develop their perceptions about the history and society of the GDR more through movies and TV shows than via formal schooling. They also learn about German history through conversations with their families and friends, as well as at museums, and sometimes from literature (see fig. 8.2).

The Schroeder study includes similar figures showing the heavy influence of movies, families, and contemporary witnesses on perceptions of the GDR and its social and political structure. According to Schroeder, many students talk at home about German history and, especially in East Germany, about the former GDR (Deutz-Schroeder 2008, 656–59). This daily-life experience is, however, not sufficiently exploited in the classroom, where teaching factual historical knowledge is emphasized. Students' interests and preconceptions are rarely taken into consideration, thus missing an opportunity to help students form an opinion based on facts rather than on beliefs, views, or personal sentiments.

What kind of knowledge-based questions were students asked in these studies? Did the researchers clearly distinguish these questions from those meant to elicit individual opinions? Both studies included several multiple-choice questions about important dates, such as "When did

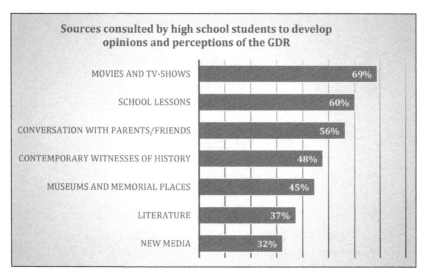

Fig. 8.2. Data from Arnswald (2006, 142).

World War II end?" and "In which year was the Berlin Wall built?" as well as about historical facts, such as "Which two parties merged to form the SED in 1946?" and "Who built the Berlin Wall?" Possible answers to this last question included "West Germany," "the Allies," "the Soviet Union" (chosen by 45.7 percent of students), "the USA," "the GDR," and "both the GDR and the Soviet Union" (fig. 8.3).

This last option was considered a wrong answer, which is both misleading and historically debatable. Although the GDR built the Wall with neither active participation on the part of Russian troops nor direct orders from Moscow, it is unlikely that East German authorities acted without the Soviet Union's support and tacit approval (Uhl and Wagner 2003; Borries 2011, 223).

Overall, a large majority (sometimes up to two-thirds) of students did not know the correct answers to knowledge-based questions in either study. There were significant differences between East and West German students with respect to comparative questions about social conditions in the former GDR and the Federal Republic before unification (fig. 8.4). It seems that students did not know the answers and merely guessed according to their sympathies and regional allegiances.

About twice as many East German students (43 percent in all) believed that the environment was less polluted in the East than in the Federal Republic—a result that is surprising to anyone who ever visited the former GDR. These kinds of factual questions, however, likely reveal more about East and West German patterns of regional identity construction than about what students have learned in school.

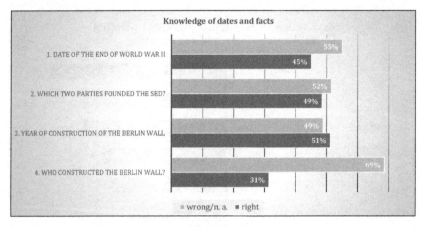

Fig. 8.3. Questions 1 and 2 from Arnswald (2006, 116); questions 3 and 4 from Deutz-Schroeder and Schroeder (2008, 733, 736).

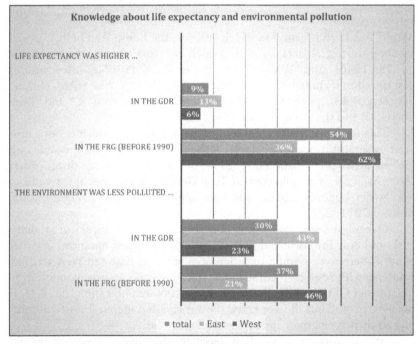

Fig. 8.4. Data from Deutz-Schroeder and Schroeder (2008, 731–32).

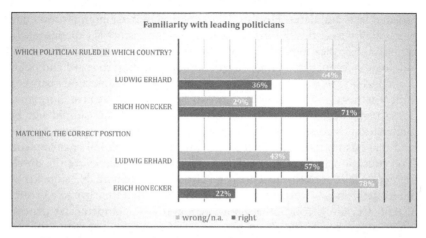

Fig. 8.5. Question 1 from Deutz-Schroeder and Schroeder (2008, 739, 745); question 2 from Arnswald (2006, 125).

Students' knowledge of isolated facts and their familiarity with historical dates or leading politicians do not give a reliable picture of their deeper understanding of history. In both studies, students were presented with the names of several East and West German politicians. While in the FU study students simply had to match each politician to his or her proper country (GDR or FRG), in Arnswald's study they had to match names with their corresponding positions in government. Figure 8.5 shows the limited information value of these questions.

Many students (over 60 percent) were apparently familiar with Erich Honecker but did not know his position as the "*last* long-term general secretary of the SED" (more students thought that he was the *first* and only president of the GDR). The example of Ludwig Erhard seems even more astonishing. According to the Arnswald study, 57 percent of high school students were able to correctly give Erhard's position as the "second chancellor of the FRG and founder of the *Wirtschaftswunder*" (West Germany's economic boom in the 1950s and 1960s), whereas in the Schroeder study, only 36 percent even knew in which country he had been elected.

How Do Students Develop Their Political-Historical Understanding? Methodological Problems of Testing Students' Knowledge and Judgments

Empirical studies would not be very valuable for the purpose of teaching history and politics if they tested only reproducible knowledge about isolated facts and dates. Historical and political understanding is rooted in one's ability to critically *interpret* data, facts, and historical experiences. In addition, historical-political knowledge includes the ability to make methodological comparisons and analyze sources according to social and political concepts, to examine meaningful and coherent connections between different historical experiences, and to argue for or against normative assessments according to defined categories. Knowledge should not be understood as passively acquired information that students learn by rote and that has no meaning for their personal lives or cultural environment. The educational objectives of classes in history and politics are the development of the core competences and civic literacy that enable students to understand themselves and the social reality in which they live to a greater extent. Certainly, conceptual knowledge and civic competencies depend on reliable information about historical facts, and the acquisition of this kind of reproducible knowledge can easily be tested in empirical (quantitative) knowledge surveys. But there is almost no way for such standardized tests to examine whether the participants understand analytical models and theoretical approaches (e.g., the classification of differences among various forms of democracy and dictatorship) or are able to contextualize them in order to analyze political-historical reality according to appropriate normative categories.

Both of the studies discussed also contain greater methodological issues, particularly the later and highly controversial FU study by Deutz-Schroeder and Schroeder, in which several items do not clearly distinguish knowledge-based questions from statements of opinion. For example, it classifies an affirmation of the statement "In the GDR everyone had about the same income and wealth" as a clearly wrong answer to a knowledge-based question. Its major argument in doing so refers to income differences between occupational groups of about 20–30 percent, as well as to high incomes for leading managers and politicians, which were double or even triple that of blue-collar workers in the former GDR (Deutz-Schroeder and Schroeder 2008, 414–15.). One can easily assume that students obviously answered this question in comparison with today's income gaps, with top executives sometimes earning two or three hundred times as much as their average employee. Accordingly, the question of whether everyone had *about* the same income in the GDR should be treated as a debatable statement of opinion rather than as a knowledge-based question (see Borries 2008, 29).

One academic critic of the FU study, the historian Bodo von Borries, has argued that the study consistently claims to know what is right and what is wrong. He criticizes the cultural-historical approach of Schroeder and his colleagues: "In a naively progressive and even somewhat bigoted way, they demand an intellectually and morally correct model image of the past"[10] that ought to be taught in schools (Borries

2008, 31; Borries 2011). Borries, who has written an assessment of both studies, emphasizes that they include very few questions about the personal experiences and perceptions students have gleaned from "family and neighborhood narratives." According to Borries (2011, 19), "history is not made by simply piling up facts . . ., but is an interpretative affair [*Deutungsgeschäft*]." Empirical knowledge about students' personal perspectives and concepts of German-German history would be a valuable resource for pedagogical theories and practices. Unfortunately, the studies give only isolated pieces of information on individual students' conceptions of German history, which could be better verified through qualitative research on classroom teaching.

There are, however, several interesting, helpful, and even alarming statements of opinion that paint a rather unrealistic and nostalgic picture of the GDR, especially among East German students but also among many in the West (figs. 8.6[11] and 8.7). Generally, students in West Germany view the political system of the GDR more critically than do students in the new federal states and in Berlin. In the old federal states, a vast majority "recognize the dictatorial character" of the Communist regime, while a majority in East Germany "praise the social benefits of the SED state" (Deutz-Schroeder and Schroeder 2008, 607).[12]

The interpretation of data in this sort of presentation (as in figs. 8.6 and 8.7) may be misleading and somewhat suggestive where affirmative and neutral positions are combined. It is not true that more than 50 percent of East German students think the GDR *was not* a dictatorship. In fact, many of the students did not state an opinion at all (in this case 20.2 percent overall, 24.4 percent in the East). These charts are indicative of how Schroeder presented his results in the media and illustrate very clearly the reasons behind the heated public discussion. The "alarming" results were often presented so as to suggest that more than 60 percent of East German students agreed with the statement that the government of the GDR had been legitimated through free elections. In fact, the percentage of students who thought that the SED regime had been democratically elected was no more than 17.1 percent in the East and 11.5 percent in the West. More than 40 percent simply could not decide whether to agree or to disagree. In the third item of figure 8.6, however, we can see that a clear majority of all respondents recognized that the GDR was not a state that abided by the rule of law (*Rechtsstaat*).

According to the FU survey, students most obviously tended to idealize the GDR when asked to respond to a long list of sociopolitical terms with rather vague definitions. Respondents were asked to decide whether the GDR or FRG was better or if they shared equal achievements in the areas of education, health care, child care, and emancipation, as well as whether one state had a better record with regard to freedom of the press, law and order, and social justice (Deutz-Schroeder and Schroeder 2008,

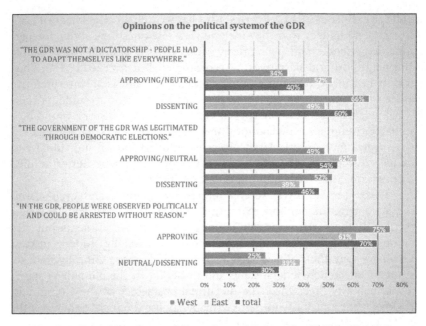

Fig. 8.6. Data from Deutz-Schroeder and Schroeder (2008, 714–16).

662ff.). It seems the researchers were uninterested in what meaning the respondents ascribed to each individual term, and the basis of knowledge for their answers was not defined. The study's authors nonetheless demonstrate a direct correlation between the respondents' levels of knowledge and their willingness to downplay dictatorship or claim parity with the West[13] in their overall evaluations of the GDR.

Criticism of both studies has gone beyond methodological problems such as sampling processes and the suggestive formulations of various questions. Professional teachers in the fields of history and politics were not surprised by the results of the studies, nor were these findings new to them. Instead, they saw the studies' primary shortcoming in their apparent indifference toward the interrelation between students' historical and political conceptions and the *methods they apply to processing* historical experience and political knowledge. Researchers did not succeed in disclosing the way students *incorporate oral history and communicative-cultural memory* into individual identity construction. "Most of the questions have nothing at all to do with a modern, reflective approach to teaching history aimed at enabling young people to independently and responsibly 'learn to think historically'" (Borries 2011, 223).[14] Borries also advises against unduly high expectations of what classroom teaching can accomplish. In particular, superficially science-oriented, positivistic approaches offer no pedagogical opportunities for supplanting the myths

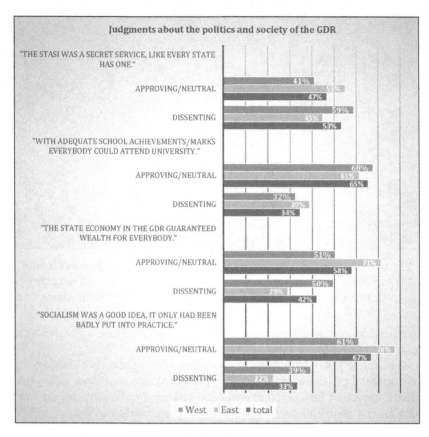

Fig. 8.7. Data from Deutz-Schroeder and Schroeder
(2008, 717, 707, 701, 724).

and legends students have acquired in their daily lives with historically confirmed knowledge, and such approaches thus exert little sustainable influence on the public culture of memory. Generally, Borries (2008, 44; 2011) considers the potential of classroom teaching for shaping awareness and helping construct political-historical identities to be extremely limited and normatively debatable.

New approaches to teaching history and politics attempt to identify students' (and teachers') political and historical preconceptions and misconceptions and focus on their everyday experiences as the cognitive basis for developing interpretive knowledge and historical understanding. Students' preconceptions and mental models need to be activated and motivated toward self-critical thinking, for example, through a personal or "everyday" approach. By analyzing the political and socioeconomic system that shaped the everyday life of GDR citizens differently, students

Fig. 8.8. Cartoon from *Da war mal was: Erinnerungen an hier und drüben* (Once, there used to be something: Memories of here and on the other side). © Flix 2014, 71. Reproduced by permission of the illustrator.

acquire different kinds of interpretive knowledge. To give a first practical example, we return to Flix (2014).

I certainly would not argue for using only comics like this one as history textbooks. The episodes thus presented may, however, guide students' capacities for critical analysis and historical judgment toward various crucial problems of German history, particularly the connection of authentic everyday experiences with the pervasion of politics and ideology in East German society (Handro and Schaarschmidt 2011). Flix's cartoons are a valuable resource for classroom teaching not only because students may prefer cartoons to other kinds of literature but also because the short episodes, based on real-life experiences and told from both Eastern and Western perspectives, demonstrate several didactic dimensions:

- They are based on a very personal approach to the impact of the political system on daily life in both German states.
- The episodes are often told from the perspectives of children and young adults.
- Various contemporary witnesses reflect on their own methods of coping with their personal experiences and historical interpretations.
- Several of the comics document changes in individuals' perceptions of both the East and West before and after 1989.
- Some stories even treat the European and global dimensions of the East-West conflict.

Fig. 8.9. Cartoon from *Da war mal was: Erinnerungen an hier und drüben* (Once, there used to be something: Memories of here and on the other side). © Flix 2014, 72. Reproduced by permission of the illustrator.

Analyzing these episodes of reflective memory may offer a motivational and problem-centered approach to various fields of interrelation in German-German history. Simultaneously, personal perspectives on how individuals process their own life experiences within a specific politically and socially structured context are well reflected. The oppressive political character of the GDR is not minimized, nor is the "winner's perspective" of West Germany given priority. Further study of similar yet more detailed biographies (see, for example, Gedenkstätte 2004; Bundeszentrale 2006; Klier 2007; Wolle 2009; Apelt, Grünbaum, and Gutzeit 2013) would foster an environment in which students could learn to analyze and judge historically and politically without indoctrination.

Notes

[1] "Ich verwahre mich dagegen, die DDR als totalen Unrechtsstaat zu verdammen, in dem es nicht das kleinste bisschen Gutes gab. . . . Deswegen habe ich Bedenken vor Diskussionen, die sich nur auf die DDR beziehen. Es ist ja nicht so, dass ein idealer Staat auf einen verdammenswerten Unrechtsstaat stieß. Die alte Bundesrepublik hatte auch Schwächen, die DDR auch Stärken" (*Frankfurter Allgemeine Zeitung* 2009, March 22).

[2] Friedrich Schorlemmer, a former civil rights campaigner and theologian, also argues for a differentiated and unprejudiced discussion of the GDR's history. He criticizes the tendency toward a "general delegitimation of the GDR" which itself demonstrates a kind of "totalitarian attitude" (*Frankfurter Allgemeine Zeitung*, 2009, March 23).

[3] Originally cited as: Es gab "Bereiche im Staat der DDR . . ., in denen es trotz des Damoklesschwerts der SED-Willkür faktisch, wenn auch nie gesichert, auch rechtlich zuging. In denen die Menschen sich auch um Rechtlichkeit bemühten" (*Die Zeit*, 2009, June 25: 13).

[4] Bundesbeauftragte für die Unterlagen des Staatssicherheitsdienstes der ehemaligen Deutschen Demokratischen Republik, http://www.bstu.bund.de.

[5] "Einen Staat, dessen unrechtmäßiges Zustandekommen und dessen unrechtmäßige Praxis unbestritten sind, nicht Unrechtsstaat nennen zu dürfen oder zu sollen beleidigt den wachen, auch den ostdeutschen Verstand. Wer den Ostdeutschen aus Zartgefühl nicht sagen will, was nun mal über das politische System, in dem sie gelebt und gelitten haben, zu sagen ist, macht sie—wieder einmal—zu unmündigen Empfängern politischer oder auch pädagogischer Fürsorge" (*Die Zeit*, 2009, July 2: 11). For a similar argument, see Schroeder and Deutz-Schroeder 2012.

[6] "Die Rechtsbereiche im Staat der DDR hat sie nicht freiwillig oder aus rechtsstaatlichem Bewusstsein geschaffen, sondern infolge der Widerständigkeit der Gesellschaft gegen einen totalen politisierenden Willkür- und Unrechtsanspruch konzedieren müssen" (Schwan 2009, 13).

[7] International Association for the Evaluation of Educational Achievement.

[8] The two studies can only be compared with reservations. Although both claim that their surveys are representative, this is debatable from multiple standpoints (see the assessment by the historian Bodo von Borries 2008). Although Arnswald's study polled students in all federal states, its sampling method was still not representative. As it only surveyed students attending a Gymnasium (that is, an academic, as opposed to a vocational high school), more than half of students aged between fifteen and eighteen years were not represented at all. Moreover, the questionnaires were sent to schools by mail and were not filled out under the supervision of a trained staff. Meanwhile, the FU study did poll students attending other types of high schools (Hauptschule, Realschule, Gemeinschaftsschule),

but it only collected data in five federal states, and Gymnasium students were still disproportionately represented, as were certain federal states and age groups. Hence, absolute comparisons between different regions (e.g., East, West, or different federal states) or between the two studies in general may be considered methodologically dubious. In addition, only a few of the questions asked in both studies are directly comparable in terms of content.

[9] According to the Arnswald (2006, 115) study, about three-fourths of students polled responded that the GDR had actually been a topic addressed in school.

[10] "In naiv-aufklärerischer und auch etwas eifernder Weise wird ein intellektuell und moralisch korrektes Modell-Abbild der Vergangenheit verlangt" (Borries 2008, 31).

[11] Answers to these statements were given on a scale of 1 to 5. A closer look at the distribution of "partly" agreeing or disagreeing and especially neutral answers would give a much less drastic (much less "shocking") picture. Separate figures for the responses "fully agree" and "partly agree" are not listed in the FU study.

[12] "Ostdeutsche Schüler loben mit breiter Mehrheit die sozialen Seiten des SED-Staates und gleichzeitig neigt eine beträchtliche Minderheit unter ihnen zur Ausblendung diktatorischer und repressiver Aspekte." Many West German students value the social dimensions of the GDR as well as "erkennen aber mit sehr breiter Mehrheit den Diktaturcharakter dieses Staates" (Deutz-Schroeder and Schroeder 2008, 607).

[13] Various items were combined that support the attitude that while the two German states were different, neither was better.

[14] "Mit einem modernen, reflexiven Geschichtsunterricht, in dem die Jugendlichen selbständig und verantwortlich 'historisch denken lernen' sollen, haben die allermeisten Fragen nicht das Geringste zu tun" (Borries 2011, 223).

Works Cited

Apelt, Andreas H., Robert Grünbaum, and Martin Gutzeit. 2013. *Schöner Schein und Wirklichkeit: Die SED-Diktatur zwischen Repression, Anpassung und Widerstand.* Berlin: Metropol.

Arnswald, Ulrich. 2006. "Schülerbefragung 2005 zur DDR-Geschichte." In *DDR-Geschichte im Unterricht. Schulbuchanalyse—Schülerbefragung—Modellcurriculum*, edited by Ultrich Arnswald, Ulrich Bongertmann, and Ulrich Mählert, 107–77. Berlin: Metropol.

Birthler, Marianne. 2009. "Liebe Ossiversteher! Die DDR keinen Unrechtsstaat nennen zu dürfen beleidigt den wachen Verstand. Eine Entgegnung auf Gesine Schwan." *Die Zeit*, July 2: 11.

Borries, Bodo von. 2008. *Vergleichendes Gutachten zu zwei empirischen Studien über Kenntnisse und Einstellungen von Jugendlichen zur DDR-Geschichte.* http://www.berlin.de/imperia/md/content/sen-bildung/politische_bildung/kenntnisse_ddr_geschichte.pdf.

———. 2011. "Zwischen Katastrophenmeldungen und Alltagsernüchterungen? Empirische Studien und pragmatische Überlegungen zur

Verarbeitung der DDR-(BRD)Geschichte." In *Aufarbeitung der Aufarbeitung. Die DDR im geschichtskulturellen Diskurs*, edited by Saskio Handro und Thomas Schaarschmidt, 121–39. Schwalbach: Wochenschau.

Bundeszentrale für politische Bildung. 2006. *Damals in der DDR: Zeitzeugen erzählen ihre Geschichten.* DVD. Bonn: BpB.

Deutz-Schroeder, Monika, and Klaus Schroeder. 2008. *Soziales Paradies oder Stasi-Staat? —Das DDR-Bild von Schülern—ein Ost-West-Vergleich.* Munich: Ernst Vögel.

Flix. 2014. *Da war mal was: Erinnerungen an hier und drüben.* 3rd ed. Hamburg: Carlsen.

Fraenkel, Ernst. 1941. *The Dual State: A Contribution to the Theory of Dictatorship.* Translated by E. A. Shils, in collaboration with Edith Lowenstein and Klaus Knorr. New York: Oxford University Press. Retranslated into German by Manuela Schöps in collaboration with the author as *Der Doppelstaat: Recht und Justiz im "Dritten Reich."* 1974. Frankfurt am Main: Europäische Verlagsanstalt.

Gedenkstätte Berlin-Hohenschönhausen and Berliner Landesinstitut für Schule und Medien, eds. 2004. *Politische Verfolgung in der DDR: Die zentrale Untersuchungshaftanstalt Berlin-Hohenschönhausen—das Gefängnis der Staatssicherheit. Materialien für den Unterricht.* Berlin: Gedenkstätte Berlin-Hohenschönhausen (LISUM).

Handro, Saskia, and Thomas Schaarschmidt, eds. 2011. *Aufarbeitung der Aufarbeitung: Die DDR im geschichtskulturellen Diskurs.* Schwalbach: Wochenschau.

Kerr, David, Linda Sturman, Wolfram Schulz, and Bethan Burge. 2010. *ICCS 2009 European Report: Civic Knowledge, Attitudes, and Engagement among Lower-Secondary Students in 24 European Countries.* Amsterdam: IEA.

Klier, Freya. 2007. *Matthias Domaschk und der Jenaer Widerstand.* Berlin: Bürgerbüro Berlin e.V.

Schroeder, Klaus, and Monika Deutz-Schroeder. 2012. "Diffuses Geschichtsbild: Bei vielen Jugendlichen verschwimmen die Trennlinien zwischen Demokratie und Diktatur." *MUT* 538 (October): 8–25.

Schroeder, Klaus, Monika Deutz-Schroeder, Rita Quasten, and Dagmar Schulze Heuling. 2012. *Später Sieg der Diktaturen? Zeitgeschichtliche Kenntnisse und Urteile von Jugendlichen.* Frankfurt am Main: Lang.

Schulz, Wolfram, John Ainley, Julian Fraillon, David Kerr, and Bruno Losito. 2010. *ICCS 2009 International Report: Civic Knowledge, Attitudes, and Engagement among Lower-Secondary School Students in 38 Countries.* Amsterdam: IEA.

Schwan, Gesine. 2009. "In der Falle des Totalitarismus: Wer die DDR einen 'Unrechtsstaat' nennt, stellt ihre ehemaligen Bürger unter einen moralischen Generalverdacht." *Die Zeit*, June 25: 13.

Sellering, Erwin. 2009. "Die DDR war kein totaler Unrechtsstaat." *Frankfurter Allgemeine Zeitung*, March 22.

Thierse, Wolfgang. 2009. "Das System ist gescheitert, nicht die Menschen." *Berliner Zeitung*, April 6.

Uhl, Matthias, and Armin Wagner, eds. 2003. *Ulbricht, Chruschtschow und die Mauer: Eine Dokumentation*. Munich: Oldenbourg.

Wolle, Stephan. 2009: *Die heile Welt der Diktatur: Alltag und Herrschaft in der DDR 1971–1989*. Dritte aktualisierte und überarbeitete Auflage. Berlin: Links.

9: The Ongoing Significance of East Germany and the Wende Narrative in Public Discourse

Michael Dreyer

Images of Unification

IMPORTANT EVENTS EVOKE important images, images that can shape the public's imagination for a long time and that can in turn influence the way political theory thinks about these events.[1] The fall of the Wall and the events leading to it, as well as the events emanating from it, are no exception to this rule. They are truly historical events that are deeply ingrained in the consciousness of everyone who personally experienced that moment, and even in the consciousnesses of many who were not yet born. The pictorial evidence is there to document these events: The pictures of the mass demonstrations all over East Germany, the actual fall of the Wall and the people hacking away at its sturdy concrete are ubiquitous. They are on par with pictures of the John F. Kennedy assassination, the first man on the moon, the last helicopter out of Saigon, or, of course, 9/11.

Alongside these images, which have captured the imagination of the entire world, there are many images that were equally important to the immediate participants yet not equally well preserved in collective memory. The photos of Chancellor Kohl and General Secretary Gorbachev during their pivotal negotiations might be one example of this second order of images, with Kohl's roomy cardigan providing proof of the friendly and remarkably informal atmosphere of these high-level and high-stakes negotiations. And then there is "Zonen-Gaby (17)," who graced the cover of Germany's leading satirical magazine, *Titanic*, at the time of unification. "Gaby," with a "typical" East German hairdo and outfit, happily showed a peeled cucumber, with the headline reading "Zonen-Gaby (17) in Bliss (FRG): My First Banana." The image quickly became an icon,[2] and even today, twenty-five years later, it is still by far the best-known satirical pictorial comment on unification from inside Germany.

There is just one problem with the icon: "Zonen-Gaby" was actually Dagmar from Worms in West Germany. The fact that she was thirty years

old instead of seventeen is a minor issue; more importantly, the quintessential East German look was achieved by outfitting a West German
woman with appropriate clothing. This has some symbolic meaning for
the entire process of unification, as even making fun of East Germans
worked perfectly well for a West German magazine without any involvement of a real East German at all. It is only fitting that twenty years later,
the erstwhile model for "Zonen-Gaby" gave an interview in which she
revealed that she had never been to former East Germany since unification (Zips 2010).

Her lack of interest in East Germany is a bit unusual, but not
unheard-of among West Germans. And as the image of "Zonen-Gaby"
has stayed with Germany for more than two decades, so has the process
of unification shaped the current (and seemingly never-ending) German
discourses on what it means to be German. This is certainly true for very
practical measures,[3] but just as much for symbolic discourses. This chapter will have a look at both of them.

Facts and Figures

In many respects the success of German unification is undeniable. The
economic facts demonstrate that although there is still a gap between
the West and the East of Germany in terms of economic prowess, it is
lessening ("Bruttoinlandsprodukt" 2013; "Arbeitslosenquote" 2015).
The basic economic success of unification should not be surprising. It
came with a hefty price tag, much higher than the numbers that have
been discussed more recently during the euro/Greek crisis. The financial transfer is hard to specify, other than being massive and prolonged.
Estimates range between 1.3 and 2 trillion euros, which were (and continue to be) transferred from West Germany to the five new states in the
East (Müller 2009; Greive 2014). The productivity gap between the two
parts of Germany has narrowed. The unemployment rate, however, is still
much higher in the East. In July 2015 the East German Länder had a
combined unemployment rate of 9.0 percent, as compared to the West
German Länder with 5.7 percent ("Arbeitslosenquote" 2015). If both
numbers are taken together, overall unemployment rises only slightly to
6.3 percent—which demonstrates another important point, namely, that
the East German data have only limited influence on Germany's overall
economic situation.

This leads us to one more basic fact to keep in mind when comparing the East and the West of Germany: the five new states (not count-
ing united Berlin) have a combined population of 12.78 million people,
according to the Federal Office of Statistics census data for 2011/12,
while the Western Länder (including Berlin) have a population of 68.99
million. Since political clout in democracies is directly related to the

number of votes any given group can bring to the table, these demographics serve as a reminder of why the electoral and thus political influence of the Eastern Länder has remained limited after unification. Certainly, the federal character of the political system does guarantee different patterns of influence in the Bundesrat, where each state has at least three and at most six votes—not quite the equality of the American Senate, but still a federalist means of shifting influence to the smaller states disproportionately to their demographic strength. Nevertheless, the fact remains that North Rhine-Westphalia alone brings 17.84 million people to the table—more than the entire East combined. Even Bavaria (12.59 million) comes close to the combined demographic weight of the new states, as does Baden-Württemberg (10.78 million).

The demographic decline of East Germany is not just a post-Wende narrative. In fact, it has continuously accompanied the mostly fruitless attempts of East German governments, both GDR and post-Wende, to increase the population or at least slow down the decline. In 1950 there were 18.3 million people on the territory of the GDR; in 1988 only 16.6 million remained. Negative migration numbers had a huge impact on the diminishing population, especially after 1990, when migration was no longer punished by either years of state harassment or mortal danger.

Since 1990 the East has lost roughly 1.5 million people owing to migration toward the Western Länder. Saxony-Anhalt has lost a dramatic 10 percent of its erstwhile population. For many years only Potsdam (close to Berlin) and Jena (home to a growing university and the East German high-tech center) enjoyed any population growth at all among the major East German cities. By now, there are some positive signs in cities like Dresden and Leipzig: Both lost a significant number of citizens right after the Wende but have now turned the tide. Yet the negative trends prevail overall. Gera, for a long time the second largest city in Thuringia, has lost about one-third of its people since the Wende. Chemnitz, formerly Karl-Marx-Stadt, has lost 20 percent of its population, Frankfurt an der Oder more than 30 percent, Neubrandenburg slightly less than 30 percent, and the list could go on and on (Weitz 2016). These numbers denote not just problems with demography and problems in political and social realms but are also indicative of the loss of identity and the general mood in these areas. They tend to exacerbate hurt feelings among the "loser" regions of unification.

There is no doubt that there are still many differences between East and West in Germany more than two decades after unification. One has to bear in mind, however, that many of these differences were already quite prevalent even before East and West set out on their diverging paths. After all, the differences between Schleswig-Holstein and Bavaria are just as pronounced as anything that might culturally divide other regions of Germany. A citizen of Schleswig-Holstein probably has more in common with his next-door neighbor in Mecklenburg (or in Denmark, for that matter) than with the stereotypical Bavarian. And these differences are by no means a uniquely German phenomenon. When embarking on a reconstruction of the discourses of unity in post-Wende Germany, we must keep in mind that the normal state of affairs worldwide is not one of uniform cultural identity within the borders of any nation-state but rather the maintenance of distinct dissimilarities. After all, Sicily and Venice may be part of the same country but are hardly easygoing brothers. And anyone who asks about the degree of unification or difference after the Wende might just as well ask the same question with regard to Massachusetts and Mississippi a century and a half after the end of the Civil War.

Intellectual Discourses and United Germany

In keeping with the challenge of coming up with a united Wende narrative, there is actually not just one intellectual discourse surrounding German unity but at least four different ones, which have very little overlap among them. For the purposes of this overview, we shall characterize them as follows:

1. The "evil empire" discourse; divisive but politically powerful and enduring
2. The "pedestrian signals" discourse; less powerful but even more enduring, mostly in the East
3. The "Who cares?" discourse; mostly neutral, and although common in both parts of Germany, more prevalent in the West
4. The "Rodney King" discourse; where we can all just get along— the politically most desirable discourse, yet perhaps more wishful thinking than reality at the moment

We need to have a closer look at these four discourses and their roles more than two decades after unification to understand thought processes in and reflecting on unified Germany.

Discourse 1

The "evil empire" discourse[4] is closely related to the perception of East Germany as an "Unrechtsstaat," a state in which the rule of law was superseded by political considerations and the police and Stasi permeated the very fabric of everyday life. This discourse is multifaceted and stirs up powerful emotions on both sides. West Germans often take it for granted that East Germany was, in fact, an Unrechtsstaat, while East Germans see this as a sweeping critique that condemns their individual lives as well.

One of this discourse's most symbolic and powerful components is certainly the political and legal debate surrounding the Mauerschützen, the border guards who shot at and killed those attempting to flee East Germany. On August 17, 1962, for example, Peter Fechter became the first victim of the violent determination of the GDR to keep its population within its borders. On February 6, 1989, Chris Gueffroy was the last victim to be shot and killed. During the early 1990s united Germany had to deal with the problem of how to bring the perpetrators to justice under the conditions of the rule of law. Even the number of victims is anything but certain. Estimates are wildly divergent, between 100 and 245 ("Todesopfer" 2017). The exact number is more a problem for historians and not so much for legal recourse, as prosecutions have to deal with individual cases, not with aggregates. The proceedings against the Wall's border guards started in 1992 with the trial of Honecker and other leading members of the political leadership, and they lasted until 2004, when two guards were found guilty in the final trial. This last verdict was rendered on November 9, exactly fifteen years after the fall of the Wall. The trials garnered an enormous amount of publicity. According to the rules laid down in the unification treaty, the border guards had to be tried according to the penal code of East Germany. In East German law as in West German law, it was illegal to shoot to kill someone fleeing the country. The order to do so never had legal status; it was only administrative practice. Between 1992 and 2004 only ninety defendants faced the courts, and of those found guilty, only eleven actually had to serve a sentence in jail.

This was hardly a satisfactory result to the relatives and friends of the victims, and yet, it was the best a unified Germany and its legal system could offer. The words of the former human rights activist Bärbel Bohley resonate here as well as in other contexts: "We wanted justice, and we got the rule of law."[5] But even this sentence, if read carefully, can be interpreted as expressing acceptance more than anger. The rule of law, after all, is the only version of justice that is readily available in modern liberal democracies. Justice, when tempered with safeguards and respect for the rights of the defendants, is nothing if not the rule of law. Everything else would be capricious and arbitrary.

Another important aspect of the evil empire discourse is the recurring Stasi debate. For how long shall the practice continue of checking all aspiring civil servants' Stasi files for any collaboration with the Stasi during the East German regime? How many years of living in a democratic political system are enough to eradicate what may have been a youthful indiscretion with the Stasi? It turns out that nobody knows, and the similarities with the postwar treatment of former Nazis are striking. This, in turn, spikes the evil empire discourse at its divisive best (or, rather, worst) by evoking the old Nazi discourses and the inevitable questions as to whether a comparison between the National Socialist and the SED regimes is intended. Political science and political theory saw a resurgence of the theory of totalitarianism during the 1990s, but this has since subsided. The totalitarian paradigm may be good political science but probably not good politics, at least not now, long after unification (Maier 2003). The 2017 case of the Berlin undersecretary Holm, who had to resign when his former Stasi connection—and his attempts to hide it—came up, demonstrates both the current significance and the divisiveness of debates along these lines.

An additional integral part of the evil empire discourse was the vilification of the PDS/Die Linke, the successor to the SED. Simply equating it with its predecessor proved irresistible to the right-of-center coalition partners CDU and FDP right after unification, but every once in a while, this practice still surfaces today. By and large, these comparisons have helped the PDS conjure up an atmosphere of righteous persecution, which is always good for a party and its followers—especially when it does have a murky past, which is the case here. The vindictiveness of engaging in these discourses from a victor's perspective was not lessened by the fact that both CDU and FDP had nominal predecessors in the East German party system, as well. In fact, these parties were mere lackeys to the rule of the SED. Still, they had their own personnel and property. It did not impress East Germans that the CDU and FDP incorporated these parties and most of their members and property into their Western-dominated party bodies while simultaneously decrying the very existence of the PDS.

For the most part, Western intellectuals were more readily willing to forgive and forget and to accept some form of cooperation with the PDS, while East German former civil rights advocates usually (though not always) adopted a much more unforgiving approach. When Gesine Schwan, the Social Democratic candidate for the office of Bundespräsident in 2004 and 2009, refused to call East Germany an Unrechtsstaat, she faced a lot of criticism, not just from conservative politicians but also from the East German left. And in the East German state of Thuringia in 2008 a bitter dispute erupted among the leading politicians of the opposition Social Democrats. The *Wessi* lawyer Richard Dewes wanted to convince the party to be open to the idea of forming a coalition with the Left (Linke) Party; the *Ossi* pastor Christoph Matschie was strictly opposed. After the election of 2009, the SPD became part of the governing coalition, yet as a junior partner to the CDU and not holding the office of minister-president, which might have been possible in a coalition with the Left. There is some irony in the fact that CDU Minister-President Christine Lieberknecht had been a member of the last authoritarian East German "parliament," while her 2014 challenger, Left Party chairman Bodo Ramelow, had a pedigree as a West German union functionary. Ramelow won the election and now heads a Left/SPD/Green coalition, the first minister-president from the Left. One of the consequences of this development is that members of the state parliament who had Stasi connections in East Germany are no longer regarded as "unworthy" of being legislators. This move met with the expected protests, but it was accepted nevertheless (Sommer 2015).

The evil empire discourse has been declawed at another level as well. A constant stream of criticism had been directed against the East German habit of widespread doping in sports. In this case, over time German sports authorities and federations often sided with the coaches and not with the former athletes who were the victims of these practices. Recent discoveries regarding doping in West Germany during the 1960s and 1970s have dampened these allegations, even though the scope and official involvement were far from being on par in the two German states.

Discourse 2

The "pedestrian signals" or "Ampelmännchen" discourse is a less serious and more symbolic version of the first discourse, but with the geographic direction reversed. In this case, East Germans decry the overpowering and overbearing presence of West German culture and of supposedly arrogant Wessis, who overtake East Germany without any respect for its own cultural heritage. This discourse is a form of low-level "resistance" to cultural domination. Attempts to change the figures—the "Ampelmännchen"—on East German pedestrian signals turned them into a cultural icon that they never had been before.

Holding onto symbols is, of course, a means of manifesting identity, even more so in times of rapid change. The figures seen on pedestrian signals in Germany were slightly different in the East and West. The East German version was designed in 1961 and came into widespread use in the 1970s ("*Ampelmännchen*" 2017). After unification, the routine renovation of pedestrian signals in Berlin was done by West German companies, which used—probably without giving it much thought—the West German version of the figures. The result was an uproar of indignation in the Eastern parts of Berlin, which spread rapidly throughout the new Länder.

The real-life significance of these events was limited, especially when compared with overhauling the entire economic and social system of a country, closing most of its factories, and firing numerous public employees. Yet its symbolic relevance should not be underestimated. It is precisely the real-life insignificance that made the Ampelmännchen the perfect symbol of Western arrogance and of the East German will of self-preservation. It became a question of recognition, of *Anerkennung* of East German lives and worth. Recognition has been a central topic of modern political theory since the days of Fichte and Kant and was further developed in the work of Hegel (Habermas 1968), and this recognition was denied in the crude Ampel maneuver without even thinking about it.

When the protests escalated, West German authorities almost immediately backed off and replaced the outworn pedestrian signals with a new design, which remained faithful to the familiar East German cutouts. By now, this new design is routinely used in the West as well. Western public opinion was taken by surprise, and the reaction was mostly a collective shrug of the shoulders and a willingness to give in to the East German grievance. One could even argue that the immediate "victory" of the East can be understood as a fresh slight. The West simply did not care and thus was willing to grant a meaningless victory to East Germans.

What started as a symbolic political protest has morphed into a veritable industry. After the Ampelmännchen was reinstalled, merchandizing of all sorts arose. Today, there are several shops in Berlin and elsewhere in the East where the unsuspecting tourist, the proud East German, and everyone else can buy towels, mugs, T-shirts, lamps, and everything in between—all adorned with the green or red Ampelmännchen.[6] "Ampelmann" is, in fact, also the name of a chain of stores, restaurants, and cafés, and its webstore. The flagship store is located at number 35 Unter den Linden, the most prestigious street in the East of Berlin, running from the Brandenburg Gate to the Imperial Castle, the latter of which is currently in the process of being rebuilt.[7]

There is a slightly less symbolic and more harmful version of this dialogue. It surfaces at irregular intervals, whenever a perception arises that a new group of Über-*Wessis* needs to be put into their place. This can take regionalism to the level of xenophobia, especially when it acquires political implications. Some campaigns by the East German Left, formerly the PDS and before that the communist state party SED, play with this narrative. But it can be used by other political parties as well. As recently as 2009 the Junge Union, the youth organization of the CDU, waged a sinister campaign in the state elections of Thuringia. They used posters that juxtaposed a Thuringian bratwurst as a "genuine Thuringian" against a portrait of Bodo Ramelow, the top candidate of the Left (Meisner 2009). The caption read "fake Thuringian," and the explanation was "not one of us/not one for us." Ramelow was born in West Germany but had lived in the East since immediately after the Wende, that is, for twenty years by the time of the state election of 2009. The xenophobic poster was condemned outright, including by the governing CDU itself. In 2014 the images no longer played a role during the state elections, and the denunciation did not stick. As noted above, since 2014—i.e., one election cycle after the 2009 campaign—Ramelow has been minister-president of the state.

As long as Ostalgie remains a powerful emotion, and as long as recognition is perceived as lacking, the "pedestrian signal" discourse will stay potent. It might therefore be taken as a good sign that the political implications of this discourse are less and less prevalent. Even the Ampelmann shops in Berlin are by now more or less normal souvenir stores, no longer selling attitude on the side. Sometimes a coffee mug is just a coffee mug, even if it shows an Ampelmännchen.

Discourse 3

In a way, the "Who cares?" discourse is not a discourse at all; it describes a silent effort to deliberately ignore the other side and to forget the past. This lack of interest is common in both parts of Germany, but it is more pronounced in the West, where East Germany plays less of a role in public debates than one might imagine. This disinterest started right after unification. For example, at that time the "hottest" debate on German identity and history was not connected to East Germany at all. Put simply, Hitler trumped Honecker hands down as a public debate topic.

In 1996 the German version of Daniel Goldhagen's doctoral dissertation, *Hitlers willige Vollstrecker*, initiated the most intense debate of the decade. Most historians dismissed Goldhagen's accusations as simplistic and outdated, but the waves of public and academic discourse ran high (Schoeps 1996; Heil and Erb 1998), both in the Western part of the country and in its Eastern part. A year later, another debate dealt with the legacy of World War II. The concentration camp in Buchenwald was not abolished in 1945 but rather used by the Soviet Union as a camp for its own political prisoners. It had been impossible to discuss this camp during East German times, but after 1989 many families who had had relatives in Buchenwald after 1945 hoped for moral restitution. When historians concluded that by and large most inmates of the camp after 1945 were indeed, as the Soviet Union had claimed, old Nazis, public outrage was immense (Quast 2013). This outrage and the ensuing debate, however, were strictly local; they were limited to East Germany. In the Western part of the country some historians took notice, but the general public was not interested in a debate about Buchenwald. And this is the important point for our context. One-sided debates have been a structural problem that goes back to the issue of recognition. The West's lack of interest in anything concerning the East is overwhelming.

Discourse 4

The most desirable discourse would be a "Rodney King" discourse: namely, an earnest debate on how to get along with each other. This discourse would be the opposite of "Who cares?," since it would mean people getting involved in a debate on uniting and dividing factors. Most importantly, it would mean mutual recognition. While a lot of this has occurred on an individual level, in debates between Wessis and Ossis who have moved to the other part of the country or who have married beyond regional confines, there has not been a systematic debate along these lines in society as a whole. The "Who cares?" discourse wins out over the "Rodney King" discourse by leaps and bounds. Trying to actively get along with each other requires an amount of interest in the other that for the most part does not exist in West Germany. What is lacking here is recognition of the other side: the effort to take the "other" life stories seriously enough to engage with them.

It may not even be conscious, but rather a subconscious decision that what really matters are the problems of the West, of the European Union, of the world, but not the parochial misgivings in East Germany. Let us examine two symbolic examples to illustrate this matter.

First, there are the *Kirchentage*, the regular meetings of Protestant laymen and clergy, which are held on a biannual schedule. Between 1991 and 2015 these gatherings have been convened fourteen times, usually attracting over one hundred thousand participants. During these years, the meetings were held in East Germany only twice, in Leipzig in 1997 and in Dresden in 2011. The other twelve meetings were held in various West German cities. In Leipzig in 1997 the topics under discussion included globalization, social problems, Hartz IV debates, G8 summits, ecological concerns, dialogue with other religions—in other words, just about every ailment of the world, but nothing about German unification and the specific problems of East Germany. To be sure, there were East German topics in the program, but they never were a priority.[8]

Second, in 2009 *Magazine Deutschland*, which is regularly published by the German Foreign Office as part of its cultural diplomacy, had an entire issue devoted to the fall of the Wall. The Wall was prominently displayed on the front cover as well as on the back cover, where four pictures were used to promote tourism to Germany. Page 1 of the sixty-six-page magazine featured a Trabi, the iconic East German car. In the history section East Germany appeared exactly four times: in 1953 (uprising on June 17), 1961 (building of the Wall), 1974 (Jürgen Sparwasser defeats the West German soccer team with his winning goal), and 1989 (with plenty of information about the fall of the East German regime). Other than that, there was absolutely nothing about life in East Germany—not one remark on sixty-six pages. No Ulbricht or Honecker, no Katharina Witt, no *Sandmännchen*, no Siegmund Jähn, no Peter Schreier or Theo Adam, no TV police investigator Bruno Ehrlicher (in real life Peter Sodann, an actor and briefly a 2009 Left Party candidate for federal president). To add insult to injury, the only actor with East German roots who was mentioned was Jan Josef Liefers, who was born in Dresden. But his best-known role is "Professor Karl-Friedrich Boerne," the overcultivated, arrogant epitome of a Wessi who is a major character in the wildly popular detective series *Tatort*, set in Münster.

Clearly this is only one example, and its importance should not be overstated. Still, the result is sobering. In an official publication of Germany's Foreign Office dedicated to commemorating the fall of the Wall, East Germany exists only in its great calamities, in one goal scored against West Germany (which went on to become world champion in 1974) and in the revolution of 1989.

What is responsible for this lack of interest by the West? Why is there no significant "Rodney King" discourse, assuming there should be one? This is related to another topic, namely to the question of if and how much life changed for West Germans during the process of unification, or, indeed, since then.

West Germany and the East

There are numerous academic studies that deal with the question of how life changed in the East and what the transformational processes brought about in that part of the country (Brussig 2003; Kollmorgen 2005; Goerz 2014; Apelt and Schneider 2016). There does not appear to be any similar book that examines transformations in West Germany; and even the studies by Brussig and Kollmorgen and others like them focus almost exclusively on East Germany, not on Germany as a whole! A search for "transformation" as a general topic in the German context reveals for the most part books on migration, not on internal processes, some isolated examples to the contrary notwithstanding (Best and Holtmann 2012; Decker 2014).

Intellectuals are conspicuously absent in this transformation discourse. There are, of course, plenty of books, speeches, and papers, but to a large extent intellectuals have excluded themselves from the discourses or debates. Most East German dissidents in 1989/90 wanted a specific East German "third way" instead of unification (Sabrow 2010). The divide between these intellectuals and the people manifested itself in the March 1990 election for the first and last freely elected East German parliament, the Volkskammer. North Carolina-based historian Konrad Jarausch (2001, 288) calls this election "the intellectuals' Waterloo" and goes on to note the "unexpected swing from revolutionary elation to unification depression," which for all practical purposes marginalized intellectuals. The election was a triumph for the CDU and its allies, which set the two German states on track toward an inevitable unification.

How about Jürgen Habermas, Germany's foremost public intellectual? In an essay on unification written in 1990 he talks about the libidinous fixation on the "D-Mark," the West German currency, in the East and continues, "It is difficult not to write a satire on these blossoming flowers of a chubby-faced DM-nationalism."[9] It is difficult to read this statement without feeling quite underwhelmed by it, especially since

Germany's foremost philosopher has had nothing of substance to add to the topic of united Germany since the early 1990s.

Since then, there has been a remarkable lack of interest in the topic among German intellectuals. Günter Grass warned extensively against unification and remained skeptical until the end of his life. In his final years—for example, in his 2010 novel *Grimms Wörter*—he remarked that the essence of being German for him was the use of the beautiful and rich German language. Nothing wrong with that; but if that is one's preoccupation, it is unlikely that the Nobel laureate would have anything pertinent to say regarding East German concerns. And he did not.

Martin Walser, a right-of-center intellectual, debated unification issues with Günter Grass—but even here both sparring partners insisted on debating the issue not so much on its own immediate merits but rather in the context of German history, which in turn always leads back to the Nazi regime and to the Holocaust.

In a sense, this is a continuation of the 1980s. West Germany, by and large, does not care now, and it did not care then. The dominant intellectual debates of the decade were the *geistig-moralische Wende* ("moral turnaround"— it is quite telling that *Wende* is the same term used a few years later for the revolution!) after Helmut Kohl became chancellor and advocated a change in attitude in West Germany: the Bitburg debate, the Historians' Debate, the debate on the historical museums, and the Jenninger affair. None of these discourses, none of these narratives, had any relation to East Germany at all, and there is no need to go into the details of them here.

Today, not much has changed. East Germany plays a part in debates if they are related to the Soli-Zuschlag, a special tax that benefits the East and is about to expire; or when the Länderfinanzausgleich, the financial transfer between the sixteen states, is highlighted in political debates (Woisin 2016). In both cases, East Germany is seen as the ongoing beneficiary of West German largesse: a free rider who diverts resources from West German states and local governments, which by now are poorer in some cases than their East German counterparts. It is a discourse centered on the burden "East Germany" exerts on "Germany," not on its contribution. In fact, it is not even common knowledge in West Germany that the special Soli-Zuschlag tax is withheld from East German salaries in the same way it is taken from West German taxpayers. Once again, debates are about each other, not with one another.

What is lacking in these nondiscourses? The concept of "recognition," which has come up repeatedly here. Recognition is a central topic in German philosophy, from Kant's "Categorical Imperative" through Hegel and on to Habermas. There is one related issue: the problem of silence.

In 1997 Gesine Schwan published a remarkable book with the title *Politik und Schuld: Die zerstörerische Macht des Schweigens.* The American version was published in 2001 as *Politics and Guilt: The Destructive Power of Silence*. In the book she talks about how political issues can become destructive when they are "silenced" (*beschwiegen*)—an active act of non-recognition, of avoiding the issue—indeed, of failing to notice that there might be an issue in the first place. Schwan's short book dealt with the Holocaust and its devastating impact on German identity, but the same concept can be used to describe the lack of a post-Wende dialogue.

One can argue that even today, East Germany (and East Germans) are not "recognized." They are "silenced"; sometimes in a very noisy way, but silenced nevertheless. East German history is to a large extent reduced to the turbulent weeks of 1989. East German life before and after that time period does not exist in West German discourses. To the extent that it exists in East German public discourses (i.e., outside the realm of families and their lore), one must be wary of Ostalgie and the blind longing for a past that never existed. If any major discourse has actually taken place, it is the one we have classified as the "evil empire" discourse. The concentration on an Unrechtsstaat and its crimes has led and continues to lead to a high degree of polarization, even though this discourse was, of course, itself necessary.

Finally, three examples shall serve to illustrate this state of affairs. One example is symbolic, one is taken from politics, and one from the realm of polity. First is the soccer club FC Carl Zeiss from Jena, which during its glory days won the East German championship three times and made it into the finale of the UEFA Cup Winners' Cup in 1981. By almost all accounts, Jena is a poster city for unification as a success story. The university is thriving; Carl Zeiss, Jenoptik, and Jenapharm are internationally competitive companies that have led the way for other firms; and the city is gaining inhabitants and not losing them like most East German cities. And yet, when the soccer team was relegated to third-league status in the German soccer hierarchy (and even to fourth-league in 2012), the city went into mourning. For many years, there was no East German team left in the first league; only during the 2016/17 season did Leipzig join the elite soccer league—and even that club is controversial (Kroemer 2016). This is a topic in the East; it hurts Eastern pride when their teams play no significant role in Germany's national sport. The West could not care less.

Second is the case of Angela Merkel. Even when it comes to the German chancellor, where the enormous success of her political career is indisputable, her East German roots are almost invisible. Angela Merkel is hardly recognizable as an Ossi, even though her success story should be remarkable by any account. Of course, being a regional candidate would get a politician only so far in an electoral contest, but still: Schröder and Kohl, not to mention Stoiber, put their regional roots much more prominently on display. Chancellor Merkel, whose own electoral district is in Mecklenburg-Vorpommern in the far north of the former East Germany, has never used her background in any way in her national campaigns.

Finally, there is Art. 23 of the Grundgesetz—the Basic Law—and the technicalities of unification in 1990. Unification was possible via Art. 23 or Art. 146 of the West German constitution. Using Art. 23 meant that the East German states were to simply join West Germany individually and thus incorporate its constitutional and legal order in one big chunk. Art. 146 would have meant the election of a constitutional assembly and the development of a new constitution. Certainly, there were many good reasons why Art. 23 was the way chosen to achieve unification. Art. 146 would have been long and messy, and it is open to discussion whether the result could conceivably have been any better than the constitution that already existed and had proven its merits time and again. But it would have been possible to achieve unification using Art. 23 and still hold a popular referendum afterward. There is no doubt that this referendum's result would have been something upward of 80 percent in favor of the Grundgesetz; possibly even much more. It is a pity that the legitimacy that such a referendum would have conferred not just on the Basic Law but also on the entire process of unification was expressly not sought by the West German Kohl administration. Holding a referendum, and thus an explicit vote of East and West Germany coming together in recognition of a common constitution, would have been a powerful signal. It would have meant the recognition of East Germany joining the West of its own accord, not just by jumping onto an existing bandwagon. Putting the German polity onto this basis would not have meant that the lack of recognition emphasized above would have completely vanished. Nevertheless, it would have provided a different starting point and served as a symbol, which would have been useful during the past decades.

We still seem far away from a "Rodney King" discourse on Germany, the German question, and German unification—a discourse focusing on getting along, on recognition of the other, and on unity. It is understandable that this discourse did not occur—or even get started—in the whirlwind year of unification, 1989/90. But today, a quarter of a century down the road, this discourse is still not happening. This is not to say that a harmonious discourse of unity should lull the German people into a false sense of contentment, thereby neglecting the problems, differences, and distances of history. Yet the recognition, the *Anerkennung*, of East Germans and their lives cannot be compressed into those few weeks of late 1989. Benign neglect—or indifference—is certainly not the way to deal with the issue of recognition.

Notes

[1] Images, symbols, buildings, or music can be just as powerful political expressions as written texts are. The US Supreme Court has acknowledged this in numerous opinions on the freedom of speech, and the Cambridge School has used it as

a methodological device. This essay follows the methodology of the Cambridge School (cf. Skinner 2002).

[2] On the significance of cartoons for the understanding of German unification see Martens (2016).

[3] For example, in September 2011 the Bundestag decided that former Stasi members had to leave the Birthler Agency—the Stasi Records Agency—after having worked there for two decades. In January 2017 an undersecretary in the Berlin State Government lost his position as well as his job at Humboldt University when it was uncovered that he had lied about his Stasi connection—a connection that had lasted for only a few months when he was seventeen (Opitz and Wöhrle 2017).

[4] The term is obviously borrowed from President Reagan's characterization of the Soviet Union.

[5] "Wir wollten Gerechtigkeit und wir bekamen den Rechtsstaat" (Malzahn 2010).

[6] Markus Heckchausen, managing director of Ampelmann GmbH, reveals in an interview the marketing strategies and future vision of the brand ("Ampelmann" 2008).

[7] Compare the merchandise at http://www.ampelmann.de/—what started as a collective outcry has morphed into a successful commercial and capitalist enterprise.

[8] The Kirchentag 2017 was held in East Germany again. But Wittenberg was chosen not because of its East German location but as the starting point of the 1517 Reformation and Martin Luther's home.

[9] "Es fällt schwer, auf die ersten Blüten eines pausbäckigen DM-Nationalismus keine Satire zu schreiben."

Works Cited

"Ampelmann—Die Entwicklung vom Verkehrszeichen zum Markenartikel." 2008. *Businesson.de*. January 10. http://www.business-on.de/berlin/ampelmann-die-entwicklung-vom-verkehrszeichen-zum-markenartikel_id2560.html.

"*Ampelmännchen*." 2017. *Wikipedia*, July 4. https://de.wikipedia.org/wiki/Ampelmännchen.

Apelt, Andreas H., and Hanns Schneider, eds. *Alte Länder—Neue Länder: Gemeinsame Perspektiven und Herausforderungen*. Halle (Saale): Mitteldeutscher Verlag.

"Arbeitslosenquote in Deutschland nach Bundesländern 2015 | Statistik." n.d. *Statista*. http://de.statista.com/statistik/daten/studie/36651/umfrage/arbeitslosenquote-in-deutschland-nach-bundeslaendern/.

"Arbeitslosigkeit in Deutschland." n.d. *Spiegel on-line*. http://www.spiegel.de/flash/flash-26018.html.

Best, Heinrich, and Everhard Holtmann, eds. 2012. *Aufbruch der entsicherten Gesellschaft: Deutschland nach der Wiedervereinigung*. Frankfurt am Main: Campus.

Brussig, Martin. 2003. *Konflikt und Konsens: Transformationsprozesse in Ostdeutschland.* Opladen: Leske und Budrich.

"Bruttoinlandsprodukt (BIP) je Einwohner nach Bundesländern im Jahr 2013, Statistik." n.d. *Statista.* http://de.statista.com/statistik/daten/studie/73061/umfrage/bundeslaender-im-vergleich---bruttoinland sprodukt/.

Decker, Markus. 2014. *Zweite Heimat: Westdeutsche im Osten.* Berlin: Ch. Links.

Goertz, Anja. 2014. *Der Osten ist ein Gefühl: Über die Mauer im Kopf.* Munich: Deutscher Taschenbuch Verlag.

Goldhagen, Daniel. 1996. *Hitlers willige Vollstrecker: Ganz gewöhnliche Deutsche und der Holocaust.* Rheda-Wiedenbrück: Bertelsmann.

Grass, Günter. 2010. *Grimms Wörter: Eine Liebeserklärung.* Göttingen: Steidl.

Greive, Martin. 2014. "Deutsche Einheit kostet 2.000.000.000.000 Euro." *Die Welt,* May 4.

Habermas, Jürgen. 1968. "Arbeit und Interaktion: Bemerkungen zu Hegels 'Jenenser Philosophie des Geistes.'" In *Technik und Wissenschaft als Ideologie,* 9–47. Frankfurt am Main: Suhrkamp.

———. 1990. "Der DM-Nationalismus." *Die Zeit* (14), March 30.

Heil, Johannes, and Rainer Erb, eds. 1998. *Geschichtswissenschaft und Öffentlichkeit: Der Streit um Daniel J. Goldhagen.* Frankfurt am Main: Fischer.

Jarausch, Konrad. 2001. "The Double Disappointment: Revolution, Unification, and German Intellectuals." In *The Power of Intellectuals in Contemporary Germany,* edited by Michael Geyer, 276–94. Chicago: University of Chicago Press.

Kollmorgen, Raj. 2005. *Ostdeutschland: Beobachtungen einer Übergangs- und Teilgesellschaft.* Wiesbaden: Verlag für Sozialwissenschaften.

Kroemer, Ullrich. 2016. *RB Leipzig—Aufstieg ohne Grenzen.* Göttingen: Verlag Die Werkstatt.

Küntzel, Matthias. 1997. *Goldhagen und die deutsche Linke: Oder die Gegenwart des Holocaust.* Berlin: Elefanten Press.

Magazin Deutschland: Forum für Politik, Kultur und Wirtschaft. 2009. Frankfurt am Main: Societäts-Verlag.

Maier, Hans. 2003. *Totalitarismus und Politische Religionen: Konzepte des Diktaturvergleichs.* Vol. 3: *Deutungsgeschichte und Theory.* Paderborn: Ferdinand Schöningh.

Malzahn, Claus Christian. 2010. "Sie wollte Gerechtigkeit und bekam den Rechtsstaat." *Die Welt,* September 11.

Martens, Ulrike. 2016. *Deutsche Karikaturisten über die Teilung Deutschlands, die Friedliche Revolution und die Wiedervereinigung: Ein Beitrag zur politischen Bildung.* Berlin: Frank & Timme.

Meisner, Matthias. 2009. "JU-Wurst gegen Wessi Ramelow." *Der Tagesspiegel,* August 1.

Müller, Uwe. 2009. "100 Milliarden Euro fließen pro Jahr in den Osten." *Die Welt*, August 21.

North, David. 1997. *Antisemitismus, Faschismus und Holocaust: Eine kritische Besprechung des Buchs "Hitlers willige Vollstrecker" von Daniel Goldhagen*. Essen: Arbeiterpresse.

Opitz, Olaf, and Christoph Wöhrle. 2017. "Der Sturz des Staatssekretärs oder: So sieht Rot-Rot-Grün nach vier Wochen aus." *Focus Magazin* (4), January 28. http://www.focus.de/politik/deutschland/politik-und-gesellschaft-der-sturz-des-staatssekretaers-oder-so-sieht-rot-rot-gruen-nach-vier-wochen-aus_id_6520353.html.

Quast, Christina. 2013. *Die Debatte über die Neugestaltung der Gedenkstätte Buchenwald*. Munich: Grin.

Sabrow, Martin. 2010. "Der vergessene 'Dritte Weg.'" *Aus Politik und Zeitgeschichte* 11 (March 15): 6–13. http://www.bpb.de/apuz/32883/der-vergessene-dritte-weg?p=all.

Schoeps, Julius, ed. 1996. *Ein Volk von Mördern? Die Dokumentation zur Goldhagen-Kontroverse um die Rolle der Deutschen im Holocaust*. Hamburg: Hoffmann & Campe.

Schwan, Gesine. 1997. *Politik und Schuld: Die zerstörerische Macht des Schweigens*. Frankfurt am Main: Fischer. Translated by Thomas Dunlap as *Politics and Guilt: The Destructive Power of Silence*. 2001. Lincoln: University of Nebraska Press.

Skinner, Quentin. 2002. *Visions of Politics*. Vol. 1: *Regarding Method*. Cambridge: Cambridge University Press.

Sommer, Gerline. 2015. "Rot-Rot-Grün will Ex-Stasi-Spitzel nicht mehr 'parlamentsunwürdig' nennen." *Thüringer Landeszeitung*, February 5.

"Thema: Bundesländerranking." 2015. *Wirtschaftswoche*, August 28. http://www.wiwo.de/themen/bundeslaenderranking.

"Todesopfer an der Berliner Mauer." 2017. *Wikipedia*, June 16. http://de.wikipedia.org/wiki/Todesopfer_an_der_Berliner_Mauer.

Weitz, Roswitha. 2016. "Demografische Herausforderung als Chance?" In Apelt and Schneider 2016, 168–72.

Woisin, Matthias. 2016. "Das Ende der Solidarität? Die Zukunft des Länderfinanzausgleichs?" In Apelt and Schneider 2016, 141–54.

Zips, Martin. 2010. "Titanic-Covergirl—Zonen-Gaby packt aus." *Süddeutsche Zeitung*, May 17. http://www.sueddeutsche.de/kultur/titanic-covergirl-zonen-gaby-packt-aus-1.48095.

"Zonen-Gaby (17) im Glück: Meine erste Banane." 1989. *Titanic: Das endgültige Satiremagazin* 11, November 1, cover. http://www.titanic-magazin.de/heft/1989/november/.

Epilogue: The Wende and the End of "the German Problem"

Peter Hayes

WHAT TURNED WITH THE WENDE and how much? And how much remained? The essays in this volume, speaking from the vantage point of an array of disciplines, represent highly varied attempts to answer that question. This chapter is an economic and political historian's response, an argument that the Wende highlighted and completed a profound transformation in Germany's international role during the second half of the twentieth century, with results that are likely to prove both lasting and beneficial.

A "German Problem" No More?

For much of the period between 1848, at the latest, and 1989, something called "the German Problem" constituted a consistently ominous and periodically destructive flashpoint of European politics. What the problem actually was, however, varied over time. In its earliest and final phases, the problem emerged from the country's division and the tensions aroused by desires to either overcome or maintain that condition. In the long middle interval between 1871 and 1945, the problem stemmed from the opposite situation, namely the concentrated power and ambition of a single state that called itself throughout the period, despite three distinct governing systems (monarchy, republic, and dictatorship), simply *das Deutsche Reich*, the German Empire.[1] But whether born of division or unity, the chief consequence of the German Problem always seemed the same: war. That was the upshot in 1864, 1866, 1871, 1914, and 1939. It also was very nearly the result in 1875, 1906, 1911, 1936, 1938, 1958, and 1961. Some highly placed people, notably Prime Minister Margaret Thatcher of Great Britain, thought that war would be the consequence of the Wende, too.[2]

Why were they wrong? Why do contemporary laypeople and scholars have no use for or comprehension of the phrase "the German Problem"? Why did 1989 mark the end of an epoch—though, of course, not "the end of history" that Francis Fukuyama (1992) rather foolishly proclaimed? To answer these questions, one has to begin with a sense of what conditions gave rise to the German Problem. Identifying them has been one of the central preoccupations of historical writing on Germany since the dawn of the twentieth century. As a result, there is no shortage of explanations of what made Germany so explosive and disruptive a country for almost 150 years. Oversimplifying somewhat, I boil these accounts down into four broad groups.

Germany and Historians' Narratives

The first explanatory school fixes on the power of essentialist and racist self-images in Germany, the tradition of the singularity and superiority of the *Volk* that goes back to Herder and the study of the Sanskrit-based tongues of the Aryans by nineteenth-century philologists.[3] Here the stress is on the aggressive impulse built into political romanticism and on the provincial self-congratulation epitomized by the phrase "Und es mag am deutschen Wesen / Einmal noch die Welt genesen."[4] The German Problem, according to this view, resided in the prevalence among Germans of a self-glorifying tribalism, which has been particularly virulent when aimed at the supposedly "decadent" French, "shopkeeping" British, and "slovenly" Slavs.[5]

A second line of argument also highlights an at least quasi-intellectual tradition, one that cultivated a sense of enduring national victimization at the hands of earlier, more unified lands. This strain of self-pity attributed Germany's long-standing divisions to the machinations of outsiders and blamed them for the country's status as "the delayed nation" that after 1871 had a great deal of catching up to do in the realm of politics and international power, though hardly in the realms of intellect and the spirit, and that was entitled, as the previously injured party, to be insistent about its claims. On this showing, the German Problem lay in a mix of grievance and aspiration, each stoked by the remarkable achievements of German culture and science in the late nineteenth century. The nation that gave the world the PhD, aspirin, the internal combustion engine, and germ theory felt disadvantaged and cheated on the international stage and justified in seeking redress.[6]

A third interpretation of German dangerousness stresses the influence of Prussian traditions of authoritarianism and militarism, noting that Germany was most menacing precisely when it was most dominated by Prussians: that is, from 1867 to 1945. A corollary to this argument highlights the social and political influence of Prussian grain producers, many of them aristocrats, whose demands for tariff protection sharpened political divisions in Germany and whose lobbying had fateful consequences, notably in preventing a negotiated peace during World War I and in bringing Hitler to power in 1933. Here the German Problem is located in a particular region and the retrograde nature of its political, economic, and social systems, and the disappearance of the problem is explained by the demise of those systems.[7]

A fourth and final school of analysis stresses the consequences for German statecraft of a particular historical moment somewhat akin to the passing of the frontier in American historiography. This is the end of agricultural self-sufficiency that occurred around 1880, the final year in which German food production more or less covered national food consumption. Thereafter, the nation depended on either commerce or conquest to feed itself, and the widespread perception of an imbalance between population and territory, aggravated by the territorial losses inflicted by the Versailles Treaty, was captured by the title of a runaway bestseller of the 1920s: Hans Grimm's *Volk ohne Raum* (People without Space). I need hardly highlight the importance of this sort of thinking to the expansionism of Adolf Hitler.[8]

There is much truth in these angles of vision. Righteousness, envy and resentment, material and status anxiety, the prestige of military methods, the power of Prussian landowners, and the sense of having deserved better at the hands of history all played a part in making Germany a destabilizing force in European politics for over a century. Conversely, shame at what these things led to under Hitler, the ceding of the Prussian heartland to Poland and the Soviet Union, and the decline of imperialism as a status symbol in the course of decolonization had much to do with the fading of such attitudes after 1945. No one seriously suggested in 1949 that the word *Reich* should appear in the name of either of the two new German states, and that fact is highly significant. As Heinrich-August Winkler (2006–7) has emphasized, the deathblow dealt to the "cult of the Reich" by World War II marks a genuine watershed in the history of Germany, a profound turning point that has gone largely unnoticed.

Post-1989: Goodbye to Centrality, Disproportionality, Scarcity

Nonetheless, at the risk of sounding abstract, I believe that the reasons that Germany after 1989 did not live down to predictions can be understood best by focusing on three keywords: *centrality, disproportionality,* and *scarcity*. In earlier eras, these were the key drivers of the German Problem, and their alteration after 1945 is the core explanation of why Germany has become a pillar of the European political system rather than a menace to it.

First, centrality: Germany has always been the land in the middle of Europe, pulled toward both East and West, constantly maneuvering between and defining itself against each, whether under Bismarck,

Wilhelm, Stresemann, or Hitler, and always considering itself exposed. Some historians, including the venerable Gordon Craig, have found the roots of German militarism and deference to authority in this sense of vulnerability (Craig 1982, 15–26; Winkler 2007, 101). Certainly, it is true that the fault lines of Europe have long and often run through Germany: the limes of the Roman Empire, the contested religious frontier between Catholicism and Protestantism, the dynastic jockeying of Bourbon and Habsburg, and the Iron Curtain. But a key development after 1949 was Konrad Adenauer's insistence on *Westbindung*, by which West Germany explicitly chose the side of Western Europe via NATO and the Common Market (Ninkovich 1988; Hanrieder 1989; Schwarz 1986–91). In addition, because of the wartime retreats and postwar expulsions of Germans from Eastern Europe, virtually no irredenta pulled ethnic sympathies outward. The Ostpolitik of the 1970s amounted to the renunciation of claims to the lands lost at the Potsdam Conference of 1945. And then in 1989, the outer boundary of the West moved east, and Germany's embedding in the West became geographically obvious as well. By then, bipolarity had long since replaced the balance of power in the calculations of German leaders, and forty years of being in military and strategic terms a protectorate of the United States had created the situation captured by the subtitle of one of Hans-Peter Schwarz's books: *Von der Machtbessessenheit zur Machtvergessenheit* (1985; From obsession with power to forgetting power).

Second, disproportionality: from 1871 on, Germany was geographically, demographically, and economically disproportionate to its neighbors and principal rivals (Britain and France), and the gap kept widening. In every twenty-year interval from 1840 to 1940 the German population grew more than the French or the British. Indeed, by most economic indices between 1890 and 1945 and by most military ones except during the Weimar Republic, Germany had a plurality, though not a majority, of the power in Europe. This fact tempted Germans into grander visions (Chancellor Bülow's "Place in the Sun," Adolf Hitler's *Großgermanisches Reich*), and it seemed to legitimize them. This form of seduction or self-delusion constituted the passageway from Bismarck's *Kleindeutschland* (Small Germany) to Hitler's version of *Großdeutschland* (Large Germany). But 1945 brought truncation and partition, so much so that even after 1989, the unified Federal Republic might well be called *Kleinstdeutschland* (Smallest Germany). Having been roughly equal in area to France in 1871, Germany is now only about half as large. Although even the Bonn Republic still had a larger population than either Britain or France, higher GNP (though not per capita), and a greater volume of exports, Germany was literally cut down to size after 1945 and embedded in a web of supranational entanglements, from NATO to the EU, that fostered a sense that the country had more to gain by cooperation than by conflict. Frankly, most Germans, even those descended from the refugees of 1944–45, came to think their nation better off without Silesia, Posen, Pomerania, and East Prussia and grew uninterested in having them back. Relative wealth has fostered recognition of interdependence rather than fantasies of domination (Schissler 2001; Jarausch 2006; Conze 2009).

Third, scarcity: the issue of agricultural self-sufficiency is only a microcosm of Germany's general resource poverty. The country possesses coal, water, wood, earth, and air, and not much else. This is one of the reasons why, for all the nation's burgeoning industrial power in the nineteenth and early twentieth centuries, living standards, as measured by anything from automobile ownership to weekly consumption of meat were lower than in Western Europe and Great Britain right up until the early 1950s.[9] This relative scarcity intensified class warfare at home and a mercantilist view of international relations as a zero-sum game in which the acquisition of land and resources from neighbors was the royal road to national prosperity. The Economic Miracle of the 1950s, which had diverse roots, changed all of this, and West Germany's export-based model of prosperity finally settled the argument between commerce and conquest (Ambrosius 1977; Nicholls 1994; Mierzejewski 2004). Once again, calls to purely national aggrandizement lost their allure.

The common denominator of all three changes is integration and the force that drove it: the collective European cry after 1945 of "Nie wieder Krieg" (Never Again War; Judt 2005, 803–31). Postwar West Germany operated for forty years in an integrated context and in large measure sought to do so as a way of living down its past and winning reacceptance in the family of nations. That post-1989 Germany has refuted the naysayers of 1990 is a consequence of this integration, for the alteration of the three conditions I have highlighted is what gave Germany the breathing room after 1945 for the fundamental transformations in culture, politics, and society that remade the country as an international citizen. The notion of "going it alone" in economic or foreign policy is now inconceivable to Germans in precisely the way that its reverse was unthinkable to Wilhelm II or Adolf Hitler. A mutually reinforcing process of change in the measures of international standing and the principal and feasible aspirations of ordinary people has meant that the political resemblance between pre- and post-1945 Germany has grown very faint indeed.

For all of these reasons, the German Problem, in the sense of Germany being the disturbing force in European affairs, is no more. German society will continue to grapple with the aftereffects of the past and will strain to look away from its worst aspects like other societies with much to be ashamed of, including several of the country's neighbors. Germany will also generate ugly moments of racist recrudescence, especially toward immigrants and refugees, and the nation will not stand alone in Europe or in the world in this regard, either. The peculiarities of the nation's economic history, above all deep-seated and traumatic memories of inflation, depression, and destruction, will entrench policy priorities that diverge from those of other members of the European Union or the Eurozone. But future threats to the peace of Europe are likely, to put the matter mildly, to come from elsewhere.

Notes

[1] Two classic accounts of the German Problem in its many manifestations are Calleo (1978) and Gruner (1993).

[2] See the account in Stern (2006).

[3] The newest study is Arvidsson (2006); the most venerable is Mosse (1981).

[4] Originally a fairly harmless line from an 1861 poem by Emanuel Geibel, this phrase acquired an imperialistic quality in the hands of Emperor William II. It roughly translates as "the world will one day be healed by adopting the German way."

[5] Of many works in this vein, probably the prototypical one is Kohn (1960). Sophisticated modern descendants of this tradition are Berger (2004) and H. W. Smith (2008).

[6] Here, the classic text is Plessner (1974); more recently, see Craig (1982).

[7] Among a host of examples of this school of thought, see Rosenberg (1967) and Dahrendorf (1967). In a related vein, see Citino (2005).

[8] See W. D. Smith (1986) and, for an early insight in this regard, Dehio (1962, 225–26).

[9] One of the few works to call attention to "the myth of Germany's peculiar economic superiority" is Adam Tooze's brilliant *The Wages of Destruction* (2006), especially xxii–xxiii.

Works Cited

Ambrosius, Gerold. 1977. *Die Durchsetzung der Sozialen Marktwirtschaft in Westdeutschland 1945–1949*. Stuttgart: Deutsche Verlags-Anstalt.

Arvidsson, Stefan. 2006. *Aryan Idols: Indo-European Mythology as Ideology and Science*. Chicago: University of Chicago Press.

Berger, Stefan. 2004. *Germany*. London: Hodder Arnold.

Calleo, David. 1978. *The German Problem Reconsidered*. New York: Cambridge University Press.

Citino, Robert M. 2005. *The German Way of War*. Lawrence: University Press of Kansas.

Conze, Eckart. 2009. *Die Suche nach Sicherheit: Eine Geschichte der Bundesrepublik Deutschland von 1949 bis zur Gegenwart*. Munich: Siedler Verlag.

Craig, Gordon A. 1982. *The Germans*. New York: G. P. Putnam's Sons.

Dahrendorf, Ralf. 1967. *Society and Democracy in Germany*. London: Weidenfeld & Nicolson.

Dehio, Ludwig. 1962. *The Precarious Balance*. New York: Vintage Books.

Fukuyama, Francis. 1992. *The End of History and the Last Man*. New York: Free Press.

Gruner, Wolf D. 1993. *Die deutsche Frage in Europa 1800 bis 1990*. Munich: Piper.

Hanrieder, Wolfram F. 1989. *Germany, America, Europe: Forty Years of German Foreign Policy*. New Haven, CT: Yale University Press.

Jarausch, Konrad H. 2006. *After Hitler: Recivilizing Germans, 1945–1995*. New York: Oxford University Press.

Judt, Tony. 2005. *Postwar: A History of Europe since 1945*. New York: Penguin.

Kohn, Hans. 1960. *The Mind of Germany*. New York: Scribner.

Mierzejewski, Alfred C. 2004. *Ludwig Erhard: A Biography*. Chapel Hill: University of North Carolina Press.

Mosse, George L. 1981. *The Crisis of German Ideology: Intellectual Origins of the Third Reich*. New York: Schocken Books.

Nicholls, Anthony J. 1994. *Freedom with Responsibility: The Social Market Economy in Germany 1918–1963*. Oxford: Clarendon Press.

Ninkovich, Frank A. 1988. *Germany and the United States: The Transformation of the German Question since 1945*. Boston: Twayne.

Plessner, Hellmuth. 1974. *Die verspätete Nation*. Frankfurt am Main: Suhrkamp.

Rosenberg, Hans. 1967. *Große Depression und Bismarckzeit*. Berlin: W. de Gruyter.

Schissler, Hanna, ed. 2001. *The Miracle Years: A Cultural History of West Germany, 1949–1968*. Princeton, NJ: Princeton University Press.

Schwarz, Hans-Peter. 1985. *Die gezähmten Deutschen: Von der Machtbesessenheit zur Machtvergessenheit*. Stuttgart: Deutsche Verlags-Anstalt.

———. 1986–91. *Adenauer*. 2 vols. Stuttgart: Deutsche Verlags-Anstalt.

Smith, Helmut W. 2008. *The Continuities of Germany History*. New York: Cambridge University Press.

Smith, Woodruff D. 1986. *The Ideological Origins of Nazi Imperialism*. New York: Oxford University Press.

Stern, Fritz. 2006. *Five Germanys I Have Known*. New York: Farrar, Straus and Giroux.

Tooze, Adam. 2006. *The Wages of Destruction*. New York: Penguin.

Winkler, Heinrich A. 2006–7. *Germany: The Long Road West*. 2 vols. New York: Oxford University Press.

———. 2007. *Auf ewig in Hitlers Schatten?* Munich: C. H. Beck.

Contributors

KERSTIN BARNDT is associate professor of German Studies at the University of Michigan and affiliated faculty member in the Museum Studies Program. Her research and teaching focus on the literary and visual cultures of the twentieth century with a current emphasis on museum history and exhibition culture. She is the author of *Sentiment und Sachlichkeit: Der Roman der Neuen Frau in der Weimarer Republik* (2004) and, with Kathleen Canning and Kristin McGuire, of *Weimar Publics/Weimar Subjects: Rethinking the Political Culture of Germany in the 1920s* (2010). She has also published articles on German modernism, gender theory, museum studies, and the history of reading. Her current book project, *Layers of Time: Exhibiting History in Contemporary Germany*, analyzes post-1989 exhibition culture against the background of migration and deindustrialization.

STEPHEN BROCKMANN is professor of German at Carnegie Mellon University, Pittsburgh, Pennsylvania, and was president of the German Studies Association in 2011–12. Since 2013 he has served as president of the International Brecht Society. He is the author of *Literature and German Reunification* (1999), *German Literary Culture at the Zero Hour* (2004), *Nuremberg: The Imaginary Capital* (2006), *A Critical History of German Film* (2010), and *The Writers' State: Constructing East German Literature 1945–59* (2015). In 1985–86 he spent ten months in Leipzig, German Democratic Republic, where he worked on his doctoral dissertation at the Deutsche Bücherei and at what was then called the Karl-Marx-Universität.

MICHAEL DREYER is a political scientist. He teaches political theory and American politics at the Friedrich-Schiller-University Jena, where he has also served as the chairman of the Political Science Department. Previous positions include a DAAD Visiting Associate Professorship for German and Political Science at Northwestern University. His research interests include nineteenth- and early twentieth-century German and American political thought, minorities and political theory, and US politics and the Supreme Court. His recent publications include *Always on the Defensive? Progressive Bewegung und Progressive Politik in den USA* (2015), edited with M. Enders et al.; *Weimar als Herausforderung* (2016), edited with A.

Braune; and *Weimarer Republik: Nationalversammlung und Verfassung* (2016), with A. Braune, as well as several articles and book chapters.

ANDREAS EIS is a political scientist and professor in the Department of Social Science at the Kassel University in Kassel, Germany. Previous positions included a visiting professorship at the Johann Wolfgang Goethe University in Frankfurt am Main as well as assistant professorships at the Universities of Augsburg and Jena and a teaching position in politics and ethics at the high-school level. Born in East Germany, Eis could not attend a university and thus worked as a carpenter and as a singer/songwriter until he immigrated to West Germany in 1987. After the Wende, he studied at the University of Jena as well as in Rennes, France, and at Michigan State University in East Lansing. Recent publications include *Europäische Bürgerschaftsbildung: Die Neukonstruktion der Bürgerrolle im europäischen Mehrebenensystem* (2010); *Demokratie in der Krise: Krisenpolitik und demokratische Legitimation* (2013), edited with Harald Büsing and Manfred Klöpper; and *Gesellschaftliche Umbrüche gestalten: Transformationen in der Politischen Bildung* (2014), edited with David Salomon, as well as articles in journals, anthologies, and textbooks on political education and the didactics of politics.

APRIL A. EISMAN is associate professor of art history at Iowa State University, where she teaches courses on modern and contemporary art. Her research interests focus on the relationship between art and politics in the twentieth and twenty-first centuries, with a particular emphasis on the German Democratic Republic. Her first book, *Bernhard Heisig and the Fight for Modern Art in East Germany*, is currently under review at Camden House. She has received an NEH award for 2018–19 for her next book project, *Angela Hampel: A Contemporary Artist in East Germany*. Recent publications include "Painting the East German Experience: Neo Rauch in the Late 1990s" (*Oxford Art Journal*, 2012) and "East German Art and the Permeability of the Berlin Wall" (*German Studies Review*, 2015). Cofounder of the Transatlantic Institute of East German Art, Eisman also co-organizes the "GDR and Socialisms" network for the German Studies Association.

PETER HAYES is professor of history and German, a former chair of both departments, and Theodore Zev Weiss Holocaust Educational Foundation Professor of Holocaust Studies Emeritus at Northwestern University. He specializes in the history of Germany in the twentieth century, particularly the Nazi period. He is the author or editor of twelve books, including *Industry and Ideology: I. G. Farben in the Nazi Era* (1987; 2nd ed., 2001); *From Cooperation to Complicity: Degussa in the Third Reich* (2004); *The Oxford Handbook of Holocaust Studies* (2010), edited with John K.

Roth; *Das Amt und die Vergangenheit: Deutsche Diplomaten im Dritten Reich und in der Bundesrepublik* (2010), with Eckhard Conze, Norbert Frei, and Moshe Zimmermann; *How Was It Possible? A Holocaust Reader* (2015); and most recently, *Why? Explaining the Holocaust* (2017), with German and Spanish translations forthcoming. He is currently working on a study of German big business and the persecution of the Jews and a manuscript on German elites and National Socialism. A recipient of the Weinberg College Distinguished Teaching Award and the Northwestern Alumni Association Excellence in Teaching Award, from 2007 to 2010 Hayes also held the Charles Deering McCormick Professorship of Teaching Excellence, the university's highest honor for teaching.

FRANZISKA LYS is professor of German and former chair of the Department of German at Northwestern University. Her research is concerned with the application and evaluation of the effectiveness of media-related and technological innovations to improve the learning and teaching of foreign languages. She is the coproducer and codirector of four documentaries and has published a wide variety of material in such volumes as *Schnittstellen: Lehrwerke zwischen alten und neuen Medien* (2000), edited by by Erwin P. Tschirner, Hermann Funk, and Michael Koenig, and *Task-Based Instruction in Foreign Language Education: Principles and Practices* (2004), edited by Betty Lou Leaver and Jane R. Willis, and in the journals *Fremdsprachen Lehren und Lernen*, *CALICO*, *Die Unterrichtspraxis*, *LL&T*, *IDV-Magazine*, and the *GFL-Journal*. She has received numerous awards for her work, among others the ACTFL/FDP-Houghton Mifflin Award for Excellence in Foreign Language Instruction Using Technology. Most recently, she held the Alumnae of Northwestern Teaching Professorship at Northwestern University from 2006 to 2009. Her interest in the topic of unification started with her first documentary, *Drehort: Neubrandenburg I*, which was shot on location in 1991, followed by *Drehort: Neubrandenburg II*, shot on location in 2002 (both documentaries co-directed with William Anthony). The documentaries chronicle the lives of East Germans and how they experienced unification over a ten-year period.

CHARLES S. MAIER is the Leverett Saltonstall Professor of History at Harvard University. His specialties are comparative twentieth-century European political, economic, and social history; global and international history, including comparative empires; Cold War and European-American relations; and German and Italian national histories. His books include *In Search of Stability: Explorations in Historical Political Economy* (1988), *The Unmasterable Past: History, Holocaust, and German National Identity* (1988), *Dissolution: The Crisis of Communism and the End of East Germany* (1997), *Among Empires: American Ascendancy and*

Its Predecessors (2006), and *Leviathan 2.0: Inventing Modern Statehood* (2014). He is currently collaborating with William Kirby and Sugata Bose on a world history of the twentieth century and writing on the rise and decline of territoriality and on the history of the modern state. He also supervises graduate reading fields in early modern and modern international history, modern social and economic history, and German and Italian history. He has directed dissertations on the comparative history of the welfare state, aspects of the Nazi regime, and the history of the German Democratic Republic, among other topics, and encourages research in the era since 1945.

Andreas Niederberger is a professor in the Department of Philosophy at the University of Duisburg-Essen, Germany. His current research focuses on the ethics of migration, human rights, transnational democratic theory, and the history and the role of law in modern politics and political thought. He has published many scholarly articles. Recent book publications include *Demokratie unter Bedingungen der Weltgesellschaft? Normative Grundlagen legitimer Herrschaft in einer globalen politischen Ordnung* (2009); *Globalisierung: Ein interdisziplinäres Handbuch* (2011), edited with Philipp Schink; *Republican Democracy: Liberty, Law and Politics* (2013), edited with Philipp Schink; and *Internationale Politische Theorie* (2016), edited with Regina Kreide.

Mary-Elizabeth O'Brien is professor of German at Skidmore College and holds the Courtney and Steven Ross Chair in Interdisciplinary Studies. She teaches courses in German language, twentieth-century German literature, German cinema, and international affairs. Her primary research interests are the intersections between art and politics. She is the author of *Nazi Cinema as Enchantment: The Politics of Entertainment in the Third Reich* (2004) and *Post-Wall German Cinema and National History: Utopianism and Dissent* (2012).

Daniel Ortuno-Stühring is a musicologist at Rostock University in Rostock, Germany, and an active organist and choir director. He also teaches musicology at the Weimar Conservatory. Ortuno-Stühring's research focuses on sacred music of the seventeenth to nineteenth centuries, the New German School, Franz Liszt, Georg Philipp Telemann, Johann Mattheson, music and the Age of Enlightenment, and the emergence of the middle-class music culture in the eighteenth and nineteenth centuries. Among his most recent publications are "Franz Liszts Legende von der heiligen Elisabeth und die oratorische Aufgabe" in *Musik und Kirche* 77 (2007) and *Musik als Bekenntnis: Christus-Oratorien im 19. Jahrhundert* (2011).

Index